One Nation Divisible

Also by Richard Polenberg

War and Society:
The United States, 1941–1945

Reorganizing Roosevelt's Government, 1936–1939

The American Century:
A History of the United States since the 1890s
(with Walter LaFeber)

America at War:
The Home Front (editor)

Radicalism and Reform in the New Deal (editor)

One Nation Divisible

Class, Race, and Ethnicity in the United States Since 1938

Richard Polenberg

The Viking Press New York

First published in 1980 by The Viking Press
625 Madison Avenue, New York, N.Y. 10022
Published simultaneously in Canada by
Penguin Books Canada Limited

LIBRARY OF CONGRESS CATALOGING IN PUBLICATION DATA

Polenberg, Richard.
One nation divisible.
Bibliography: p.
Includes index.
1. United States—Social conditions—1933–1945.
2. United States—Social conditions—1945– 3. Social classes—United States. 4. United States—Race relations.
5. Ethnicity. I. Title.
HN64.P75 309.1'73'0917 79-21403
ISBN 0-670-22497-9

Printed in the United States of America

Acknowledgments

June Jordan: From *Cameo No. II.* Copyright © 1971 June Jordan

MCA Music: From *Baby Remember Me,* words and music by Lonnie Johnson. © Copyright 1979 by MCA Music, a division of MCA, Inc., New York, New York, all rights reserved. From *Policy Blues,* words and music by Lester Melrose and Johnny Wilson. © Copyright 1935 by MCA Music, a division of MCA, Inc., all rights reserved. Both used by permission.

William Morrow & Co., Inc.: From *Black Feeling, Black Talk, Black Judgment* by Nikki Giovanni. Copyright © 1968, 1970 by Nikki Giovanni. By permission of William Morrow & Company.

New Directions Publishing Corp.: From *A Coney Island of the Mind* by Lawrence Ferlinghetti. Copyright © 1958 by Lawrence Ferlinghetti. Reprinted by permission of New Directions Publishing Corporation.

For Marcia

Preface

Whether or not written history is, as Charles Beard once said, "an act of faith," it most assuredly is an act of choice. To make sense of American history during the forty years from 1938 to 1978, I have chosen to focus on patterns of class, race, and ethnicity. I have done so partly out of personal interest but primarily out of a conviction that developments in those areas have been of central importance in the lives of the American people. Since I am concerned, moreover, with why and how change has occurred, I begin by evaluating class, racial, and ethnic patterns as they stood in the late 1930s; proceed by examining the impact on them of the Second World War, the anticommunist impulse, suburbanization, social reform, and the war in Vietnam; and conclude by analyzing those patterns as they appeared in the late 1970s. Where I discuss political, economic, constitutional, social, and cultural issues it is through the three-way prism of class, race, and ethnicity.

I do not mean to give the impression that hard-and-fast lines can be drawn between class, racial, and ethnic groups. No such clear distinction is possible, for the relationships among the three are subtle and complex. If all Americans can somehow be ranked according to class, most can also be defined in ethnic or racial terms. Some can be viewed on any or all levels: a Japanese American businessman, for example, simultaneously belongs to a particular social class, racial minority, and ethnic community. Although I treat immigrants primarily as members of ethnic groups and blacks primarily as members of a racial group, there has always been a close connection between ethnicity and race, on the one hand, and class, on the other. I endeavor at appropriate points to make that connection clear.

The problem of definition, particularly as it concerns class, is no less troublesome than that of demarcation. This book relies rather heavily on the work of sociologists, but ever since Max Weber first criticized Marxist theory, sociologists have differed sharply over the meaning of class and its relationship to status and power. There is no evidence to suggest that those differences are about to be reconciled. I use the term "class" simply to refer to distinctions in styles of life arising from differences in wealth, occupation, and education. Although there is no perfect correspondence between class and status (one thinks of a well-heeled gangster and a poorly paid professor), there is usually a reasonable congruence between the two. It remains difficult to improve on the common-sense definition that "class is a matter of how you carry yourself."

With respect to ethnicity the difficulty is primarily one of delineation. It is one thing to say that an ethnic group possesses a common national origin, religion, culture, or language, but quite another to apply those standards consistently. The two most commonly used criteria—national origin and religion—are usually but not always satisfactory. Some nations contain more than one ethnic group, some ethnic groups are dispersed over several nations, and in any case, national boundary lines change over the years. Similarly, while religion is indelibly linked to ethnicity, there are important differences between Catholics from Ireland and Catholics from Italy, between Jews from Germany and Jews from Russia. Anyone who writes about ethnic groups risks blurring these distinctions, but I use the term "ethnicity" to encompass country of origin, language, or religion as the context seems to require.

Race is itself frequently considered as one aspect of ethnicity. I treat it separately for the obvious reason that in the United States racial issues have always had dimensions ethnic issues have not. I focus on the experience of blacks not because they are the only racial minority, but because they are the largest, they have received the most scholarly attention, and they have served as a bellwether group. The American approach to racial problems in general can be measured by the approach to blacks in particular.

In writing this book I have incurred many debts which I am happy to acknowledge. My research was supported, in part, by the Colonel Return Jonathan Meigs First (1740–1823) Fund, which was created with money left by Dorothy Mix Meigs and Fielding Pope Meigs, Jr., of Rosemont, Pennsylvania. Two research assistants, Emily Goldstein and Kathy Andriko, were most helpful. Maureen Rolla and Doren Arden, of Viking Penguin Inc., provided much encouragement. I am especially grateful to Harry Levin, formerly dean of Cornell's College of Arts and Sciences, who saw to it that administrative responsibilities would not interfere with my writing.

I wish to thank Joanne Florino, Kevin O'Brien, Hilmar Jensen, Douglas Slaybaugh, and Ross Clendon, all of whom offered useful criticism. Pearl Hanig, a superb copy editor, gave sound advice. I received many valuable suggestions from Alvin H. Bernstein, Robert Divine, Don Herzog, Walter LaFeber, R. Laurence Moore, and Marcia Polenberg. Above all, I am indebted to my father, Morris Polenberg, whose rigorous intellectual standards, acute historical insight, and extraordinary editorial talents improved the mansucript in places too numerous to mention.

Richard Polenberg
Ithaca, New York

Contents

	Preface	7
1	The Eve of War	15
2	Wartime America	46
3	The Cold War	86
4	The Suburban Nation	127
5	The Age of Reform	164
6	Vietnam	208
7	A Segmented Society	251
	Notes	293
	Essay on Sources	321
	Index	347

One Nation
Divisible

[1]
The Eve of War

Travelers crossing the United States by automobile in the late 1930s were often struck by the sharp regional contrasts they found. Driving along highways the very names of which suggested a regional past—the Robert E. Lee Highway, for example, or the Mormon Trail—they easily recognized what part of the country they were in, not merely by the physical landscape but also by the food served in restaurants, the accents of tourist-home proprietors, the roadside architecture. One traveler remarked: "To cross the Atlantic Ocean does not give one such a sensation of change as to cross from Tennessee to Arkansas."[1] Beyond regional distinctiveness, however, were other kinds of segmentation, less obvious perhaps to casual tourists but even more significant. American society on the eve of World War II was sharply divided along class, racial, and ethnic lines. Those divisions, largely transcending regional boundaries, shaped the most important aspects of the way people lived.

1.

During the late 1930s American sociologists, who had long shown an interest in remote and primitive societies, turned their attention closer to home. They were influenced in this by the work of W. Lloyd Warner of Harvard University, who believed that many of the same techniques social anthropologists had used in studying Australian aborigines could throw light on American society. Armed with questionnaires, note pads, and theories of "prestige stratification," scholars took up residence in towns in New England, the Midwest, and the South, befriended the inhabitants, and set to work. Occasionally they identified the places they studied, but more often, following the precedent set by "Middletown," the Lynds' classic study of Muncie, Indiana, they invented mythical names: "Yankee City" for Newburyport, Massachusetts; "Cottonville" or "Southerntown" for Indianola, Mississippi; "Jonesville" or "Elmtown" for Morris, Illinois; "Old City" for Natchez, Mississippi; and "Plainville" for a community in Missouri. Intended to preserve informants' anonymity and make possible an unbiased appraisal, this device lent the studies a scientific aura conveying the impression that the findings were broadly applicable.

What these scholars found was, to be sure, what they had expected to find: the existence of a rather rigid system of social stratification. "The social system of Yankee City," Warner explained, "was dominated by a class order."[2] The criteria for membership in the three classes—upper, middle, and lower (each of which was then subdivided into upper and lower strata)—varied little from place to place: the neighborhoods people lived in, the kinds of homes they owned, the ways they derived their income, their family backgrounds, and their community reputations. The majority of people, some 60 to 70 percent, fell in the lower-middle and upper-lower categories; about 15 percent belonged to the upper-middle classes; the remaining 15 to 25 percent constituted the lower-lower class. Class membership determined virtually every aspect of an individual's life: the subjects one studied in high school, the church one attended, the person one married, the clubs one joined, the magazines one read, the doctor one visited, the way one was treated by the law, and even the choice of an undertaker. Movement across class lines, if not impossible, was markedly infrequent.

Equally interesting was the language people used to discuss these matters. With the lines between residential neighborhoods etched so sharply, geographical terms often served as euphemisms for social class. Thus, one moved down the social scale in Newburyport from "Hill Streeter" to "Side-Streeter" to "Riverbrooker." Americans did not speak of capitalists, bourgeoisie, and proletarians, but rather of "society," or "good, honest, self-respecting, average, everyday working people . . . who are *all right,"* or "the don't-give-a-hoots." Southern blacks turned the very word "class" into a verb: "Joe can't class with the big folks" meant that he could not travel in certain social circles. A fine etiquette governed class relations. Since everyone knew just about where everyone else stood, no one had to be overly explicit about it. Instead, class deference was ordinarily exhibited by "inflections of speech [rather] than outspoken admittance of superiority or inferiority."[3] As if by osmosis, most children had absorbed an understanding of the entire system with all its subtleties and complexities by the time they were ten or eleven years old.

If sociologists erred, it was not in identifying these patterns of class behavior but in assuming that similarly well-defined patterns characterized large cities as well as small towns. This was not necessarily the case, for the anonymity and impersonality of urban life blurred certain distinctions. Yet the United States was, in 1940, still predominantly a rural and small-town nation. Of the 131.7 million Americans listed in the census, 74.4 million—or 56.5 percent—were designated as "urban" dwellers. This, however, reflected the Census Bureau's quaint definition of "urban" as "places having 2,500 inhabitants or more." If a more sensible definition is adopted, a different picture emerges. Fewer than 50 percent of all Americans lived in cities with more than 10,000 inhabitants, fewer than 40 percent lived in cities with more than 25,000, and only 30 percent lived in cities with more than 100,000. As late as 1940 some 70 million people lived in places with fewer than 10,000 inhabitants, precisely the kinds of places that figured so prominently in the sociological literature.

Spectacular differences in class position, and in accompanying styles of life, resulted from rather modest differences in actual income. In 1939 factory workers earned about $1,250 a year; a highly skilled, experienced tool inspector in an automobile plant might make as much as $1,600. One advertisement had a man speak glowingly of retiring on $150 a month, enjoying "lifelong security and freedom to do as I please." A salary of $2,500 marked one as well-to-do. Only 4.2 percent of all those in the labor force earned that much in 1939. Even among the most highly paid group—urban males who worked full time—only 11.8 percent earned $2,500. When public opinion polls asked people what they would consider a totally satisfactory income, more than half named a figure below $2,500. Annual earnings of $5,000 were beyond what most could imagine. On such an income the head of a department store in Burlington, Vermont, maintained a fifteen-room house with a solid cherry staircase, stained glass windows, and crystal chandeliers; he also owned a summer home on Lake Champlain; his family wanted for nothing.

At the opposite end of the pyramid were the unemployed, the underemployed, and the seasonally employed. A severe recession in 1938 drove joblessness from 7.5 million to more than 11 million, and in 1940, even after an expanded program of government spending on relief and national defense had produced an upturn, unemployment still hovered around 9 million. Of those who did hold jobs nearly one-quarter worked fewer than nine months. Partial employment and joblessness account, in part, for one of the more revealing statistics in the census returns. In 1939, excluding the 2.5 million people on public relief projects, 58.5 percent of the men and 78.3 percent of the women who were working or seeking work earned less than $1,000. For a glimpse behind the statistics one can turn to a family of sharecroppers in Mississippi whose 1939 income came to $26. Sixteen people lived in a three-room shack, slept under gunnysack blankets, used a privy with a crumbling roof, and relied on a stove that was ready for the scrap heap. Children were being nursed long past an age when they were old enough to have been weaned because it was the cheapest way to feed them.

The contrast between the Vermont businessman's home and the Mississippi sharecropper's hovel is instructive, for nothing better illustrated class distinctions than housing conditions. The census returns again provide a wealth of information, particularly if one makes the reasonable assumption that a family's social standing was directly related to the rent it paid and the amenities it enjoyed. The 1940 census included information on 35 million dwelling units: 31 percent lacked running water, 32 percent used an outside toilet or privy, 39 percent did not have a bathtub or shower (even one shared with other tenants), 27 percent lacked any refrigeration equipment (either mechanical or ice), and 58 percent had no central heating of any kind. A large discrepancy existed between rural and urban dwellings in each case, but the number of "urban" residents wanting these necessities was not inconsiderable: 12 percent lacked refrigeration, 23 percent a private bath, and 42 percent central heating. Social status in America before World War II determined not only whether one could enjoy luxuries, but whether one could take a bath, preserve food, or stay warm.

Social class also dictated the quality of medical care people received and, to some extent, the diseases they were likely to contract. The "National Health Survey," a house-to-house canvass of 740,000 families conducted by the U.S. Public Health Service, demonstrated that low-income families were sick longer and more frequently than better-financed families but called doctors less often. In 1936 American families spent an average of $59 a year on medical care. Poor families spent less than half that amount, and wealthy families nearly twice as much. As one writer observed, "illness is greatest in the population group least able to bear the economic burden involved." Serious illness often impoverished its victims, for while 1 in 250 heads of families earning $2,000 a year was chronically disabled, 1 in 20 heads of families on relief was physically unable to work. Conversely, dismal living conditions contributed to the spread of sickness. A study of Cincinnati noted that the high death rate from intestinal disorders "involved mainly the underprivileged class" and centered geographically in congested areas where most houses lacked adequate sanitation.[4]

Education, no less than income, housing, and health, provided an accurate gauge of social position. Just as rather small differences in income could mean substantial variations in living standards, so rather small gradations in schooling took on considerable significance. In 1940, of the 74.8 million Americans twenty-five years of age or older, only 2 of 5 had gone beyond the eighth grade, 1 of 4 had been graduated from high school, 1 of 10 had attended college, and 1 of 20 had been graduated from college. Nearly 875,000 full-time students were enrolled in colleges at the end of the decade, for increasingly a college degree was becoming recognized as the passport to a middle-class career. Fully half the graduates in the Wesleyan class of 1939, for example, looked forward to careers in business, medicine, the law, or education. Yet the cost of attending college remained prohibitive for most people. Tuition, fees, room, and board ranged from $453 at state colleges to $979 at private universities.

During these years the federal government took a few tentative steps toward alleviating the distress resulting from the maldistribution of income. Under prodding from Senator Robert F. Wagner of New York, Congress passed a housing act in 1937. Wagner had originally proposed a $1 billion program extending over sixty years, but his plan was first whittled down by Secretary of the Treasury Henry Morgenthau, who believed it would "just shoot the government credit to hell," and then carved into little pieces by southern Democrats, who represented rural constituencies and had little interest in the urban poor.[5] The bill finally adopted created a U.S. Housing Authority which could spend $500 million to finance the construction of low-income homes. Within three years nearly 120,000 units were being built for families with incomes ranging from $400 to $1,100. In 1938 Congress established a minimum wage, set at 25 cents an hour but scheduled to rise to 40 cents within three years, and also provided for a forty-hour week. To gain needed support from southern Democrats, however, the sponsors agreed to exclude farm laborers and domestic workers and to permit regional wage differentials.

Even such well-intentioned legislation could, under certain circumstances, have unfortunate consequences. In 1938 some 8,000 Mexican Americans worked as pecan shellers in San Antonio, Texas. Employed on a seasonal basis, they earned perhaps 5 or 6 cents an hour; the median income, for a fifty-one-hour week, was $2.73. But employers could not pay the new 25-cent minimum wage without completely mechanizing their plants. Rather than do this, many temporarily shut down. When the plants later reopened on a mechanized basis, they employed 3,000 workers, leaving 5,000 others the victims of technological unemployment. Similarly, public housing projects could leave slum dwellers without roofs over their heads. The San Antonio housing authority, for example, received federal funds to build a project in the Mexican slum district, an area in which 75 percent of the families did without electricity and 90 percent without indoor plumbing. Plans called for the construction of 1,260 units, but the new three-room apartments would rent for $6.75 a month, three times what most Mexican American families were paying. One study revealed that seven of every ten families of pecan shellers earned too little to afford these rentals.[6] Although the minimum wage and housing laws undoubtedly helped most workers, some were hurt, especially in the short run.

These were the last substantive reform measures enacted during Franklin Roosevelt's second administration. By the fall of 1938 the New Deal, which had been chugging along with difficulty for some time, finally ran out of steam. At least four developments were responsible. A strong Republican comeback in the 1938 elections guaranteed that Congress would be increasingly inhospitable to social reform. At the same time the President's growing concern with national defense and foreign policy made him reluctant to sponsor measures that would alienate congressmen, especially southern Democrats, whose support he needed. Then, too, by the late 1930s some New Deal officials were busy jockeying for influence within the federal bureaucracy and were even prepared to sabotage proposals that seemed to threaten their position. Finally, entrenched interest groups, exerting a cobralike charm over many congressmen, injected their deadly venom into proposed reforms.

The failure of the Wagner national health bill in 1939 demonstrated the combined force of congressional conservatism, presidential detachment, bureaucratic squabbling, and interest-group opposition. The measure authorized federal aid for child and maternity care, public health services, and hospital construction. More important, it permitted federal supervision of state efforts to implement such wide-ranging health programs as compulsory insurance. Designed to assist the medically indigent, those most in need of care and least able to afford it, the bill nevertheless met with a cold reception in Congress and failed to gain Roosevelt's endorsement. It also encountered criticism from the Surgeon General and the Public Health Service. "If the Wagner bill died completely," wrote one official, worried about losing jurisdiction over certain programs, "it might be all to the good."[7] The American Medical Association detected in the program a threat to the doctor-patient relationship. Given all this, Roosevelt ultimately endorsed a very limited proposal to construct (but not support the maintenance of) "forty little hospitals," at a cost of $50 million, in poor, largely rural areas. The Senate approved in 1940, but the House never even considered the measure.

By then a note of irritation had begun to creep into the President's statements, at least those made in private. "I am sick and tired of having a lot of long-haired people around here who want a billion dollars for schools, a billion dollars for public health," he said in exasperation in July 1939. "Just because a boy wants to go to college is no reason we should finance it."[8] Roosevelt's outburst may have reflected, at least in part, a recognition that his favoring such programs was not of much use since enacting them was impossible and that worrying about them only distracted him from more urgent concerns. But if on the eve of World War II large numbers of Americans were ill-clothed, ill-housed, and ill-fed, and, one might add, ill-educated and ill-cared-for, that was only partially the fault of the Roosevelt administration. These conditions derived from a class system so deeply rooted and so widely accepted that it stubbornly resisted most efforts at change.

2.

No less pervasive than social class was what sociologists usually termed caste but what might more accurately be called the color line. Drawn with meticulous care around most black Americans, it also limited the opportunities available to people of Mexican, Indian, and Asian descent. Racial lines, unlike class lines, could not ordinarily be crossed. One's position was fixed forever at birth. Essentially endogamous communities resulted, for no fewer than thirty states outlawed intermarriage between Negroes and whites, and social sanctions elsewhere were nearly as powerful as legal ones. Despite important regional variations, the color line invariably implied economic subordination, political disfranchisement, legal insecurity, and social inferiority.

The 1940 census documented some of the consequences for the nation's 12,866,000 Negroes. Blacks almost always worked at menial, unskilled, low-paying jobs. Although nearly one of three white males held a professional, proprietary, managerial, clerical, or sales position, only one of twenty black males was employed in a white-collar occupation. Among white women who worked, one of ten was employed as a maid; among black women, six of ten were so employed. Twice as many blacks as whites farmed, but a much smaller proportion worked their own land. Data on housing, health, and education revealed a similar pattern. Four times as many nonwhites as whites lived in houses with more than two persons per room, but only half as many lived in houses with two rooms per person. The Negro mortality rate was nearly twice that for whites. In Washington, D.C., for which statistics were typical, the infant mortality rate among whites was thirty-seven, among blacks seventy-one. Negroes could expect to live an average of twelve years less than whites. Among blacks over the age of twenty-five, 1 in 10 had not completed a single year of school while 1 in 100 was a college graduate.

More than three-fourths of all Negroes lived in the South, where segregation was rigidly enforced. Jim Crow meant more than physical separation. Separate waiting rooms at bus stations, separate railroad cars, separate sections in movie theaters, separate schools and churches, separate restaurants and drinking fountains—these were the system's most visible manifestations, but there were more subtle ones as well. Social conventions that implied mutual respect, such as shaking hands or tipping one's hat, were taboo. White merchants frequently refused to permit blacks to try clothing on for size before making a purchase or to return merchandise that did not fit. So strong was the presumption that blacks would never enter the front door of a white person's home that, one observer noted, "many white people, when they go out for a short time, will lock the back door against thieves and leave the front door open. They assume that no colored person would go in the front way and, apparently, that no white person would steal."[9] When two automobiles approached an intersection, the white driver assumed he had the right-of-way, and the black driver knew he would be blamed for any collision.

Not only did such rituals reinforce the line between the races dozens of times a day, but language itself served constantly to remind Negroes of their inferior place. Southern whites ordinarily called Negroes, no matter what their ages, by their first names or "boy," "girl," "aunty," or "uncle," while blacks always addressed whites formally. Even when whites used a title, such as "professor," they did so condescendingly, to refer, perhaps, to a black high school teacher who had never gone to college. Local radio stations broadcast police court trials in which a female defendant might be referred to as the "nigger wench." In small towns in the Deep South, telephone operators, asked to place a long-distance call to a "Mr. Jones," might inquire, "Is he colored?" and, if the answer was yes, reply, "He ain't 'mister' to me." To avoid such derogation, "middle- and upper-class Negro women never permit their first names to be known. They use either initials or their husband's names."[10]

Segregation rested on a theory of racial supremacy that southerners proclaimed without a trace of defensiveness. Whites asserted that Negroes were, by nature, mentally and morally inferior, lazy and shiftless, congenital liars incapable of controlling their passions. (There was, though, a certain envy in the stereotype, for blacks supposedly lived life to the fullest, laughed easily, enjoyed freedom from social restraints, and seldom felt remorse.) Savage racial characterizations were the very stuff of public discourse in the Deep South. In August 1938 a Jackson, Mississippi, newspaper evaluated the appeal a certain pension plan would have for Negroes in these words: "Golly, wouldn't that be water on the wheel for Sambo, and likewise Aunt Mandy! It would mean plenty o'possum, sweet potatoes, and watermelon throughout all the days of their lives."[11] The following year a city judge in Atlanta, Georgia, after sentencing a Negro woman to twenty days in the stockade, was handed a "poem" from a probation officer informing him that the woman had a small son. The judge read it aloud from the bench: "This poor li'l pickaninny's pappy is dead/ And you sent his mommy to the big stockade;/ Please send her back to the probation shelf,/ Or I'll have to adopt this coon myself." Having discovered an acceptable basis for leniency, the judge changed the sentence to probation.[12]

Political disfranchisement went along with social discrimination. Several devices kept Negroes from voting in the South. The white primary, which the Supreme Court upheld in 1935, permitted the Democratic party to exclude blacks, thereby preventing them from voting in the only contests which, in a one-party region, had any meaning. The official emblem of Alabama Democrats—a lusty game cock under a scroll reading "White Supremacy"—conveyed the message unmistakably. In eight states the poll tax barred poor whites and blacks, but especially the latter, since political machines would sometimes pay the taxes of whites in an effort to buy their votes. Although the tax ranged from $1 to $2, it had to be paid months before election day and accumulated, if unpaid, from year to year. Even where a Negro was willing to vote only in the general elections and was able to pay the poll tax, registering to vote required running a gauntlet of registrars who asked impossible questions and "leering hangers-on who habitually loaf about the courthouse offices."[13] The vast majority of southern blacks, therefore, did not vote.

They were, in addition, legally defenseless, subject often to the caprice or malice of whites. As Gunnar Myrdal put it, "a white man can steal from or maltreat a Negro in almost any way without fear of reprisal, because the Negro cannot claim the protection of the police or courts."[14] Excluded from the legal process or given at best a token role, blacks were not hired as policemen in the Deep South. In 1940 Mississippi, South Carolina, Louisiana, Georgia, and Alabama—states in which blacks constituted more than one-third of the population—had not a single black policeman. Nor did Arkansas and Virginia, where Negroes made up one-quarter of the population. Judges, and lesser court officials, were exclusively white. Blacks seldom served on juries, although after a 1935 Supreme Court decision declaring such exclusion unconstitutional they might, every once in a while, be placed on federal jury rolls. Black lawyers in the South were hard to find—4 in Alabama compared with 1,600 whites, and 6 in Mississippi compared with 1,200 whites. In any event, black attorneys normally did not represent black clients in courtroom cases. Courts exhibited great leniency toward Negroes accused of committing crimes against other Negroes and even greater harshness toward Negroes on trial for crimes against whites.

Given a situation in which a black might find himself in trouble with the law merely for contradicting a white, in which the judicial system was stacked against him, and in which brutal sentences, including the death penalty, might be imposed as a means of reaffirming racial superiority or appeasing white opinion, it was only natural that blacks would often identify with someone charged with committing a crime against whites. To quote Myrdal again: "The arrested Negro often acquires the prestige of a victim, a martyr, or a hero, even when he is simply a criminal. It becomes part of race pride in the protective Negro community not to give up a fellow Negro who is hunted by the police."[15] In one Mississippi town in the late 1930s two blacks, accused of murder, were sentenced to be hanged. One confessed and gave evidence of contrition; the other, named Roy, remained obdurate, a "hard sinner." At their funeral one black onlooker expressed a conviction based more on the arbitrary nature of southern justice than on the facts in the case: "Dis man wuz chicken-hearted and scary. But dat Roy wuz de man."[16]

Northern blacks confronted a color line, too, but of a different and rather less onerous sort. Negroes living in Chicago, New York, or Detroit could reasonably expect to have fair trials and experienced no difficulty in registering to vote. Indeed, a larger proportion of Chicago's blacks than of its whites went to the polls. Public facilities were not segregrated, although restaurant proprietors would sometimes try to discourage black patrons by treating them discourteously, overcharging them, or oversalting the food. In two vital areas, however, housing and jobs, skin color placed blacks at an overwhelming disadvantage. Huge residential tracts—some eleven square miles in Chicago alone—were closed to them as a result of either restrictive covenants (under which homeowners agreed not to sell or lease to non-Caucasians) or informal exclusionary agreements between landlords and real estate agents. Confined to the dirtiest, least desirable jobs because of inadequate training opportunities, the prejudice of employers, the hostility of unions, or some combination of the three, blacks were also the last to be hired. In 1940, making up 8 percent of the Chicago labor force, they constituted 22 percent of the city's unemployed.

That nearly all Negroes suffered from certain forms of discrimination did not imply an absence of class divisions within the black community. If anything, they acquired additional importance for blacks because whites tended to overlook such divisions. Yet class lines did not run parallel to those among whites. The black upper and middle classes were much smaller than the white, and the lower class was much larger. The criteria governing class membership differed accordingly. The black upper class consisted largely of professionals and businessmen, people whose life-styles would have been considered middle-class in white society. Similarly, the black middle class included many semiskilled workers and clerks. With occupational choice and place of residence restricted, class distinctions came to rest heavily on such matters as family stability, educational achievement, church membership, and adherence to a strict code of morality.

The black underworld, especially in northern cities, cut vertically across class lines, offering opportunity and social prestige to a few and providing some sort of livelihood for many. In Chicago there were as many blacks employed in the "numbers" or "policy" racket—writers, runners, clerks, and checkers—as there were Negro doctors, dentists, teachers, social workers, and lawyers. As the sociologists St. Clair Drake and Horace Cayton observed, policy was big business. Policy kings became recognized race leaders who exerted political influence and supported worthy philanthropic causes. For many, policy acquired the status of a cult, with each combination of numbers having a mystical power and special meaning. Although policy was usually regarded as a harmless, if illicit, activity, since bettors lost more than they won, there nevertheless existed a feeling that policy writers were parasites who preyed on the poor. Yet if "Louisiana Johnny" 's 1938 blues recording is any indication, that resentment was directed at the small-time writer rather than at the big-time operator: "If I don't catch policy, kill every writer I see/ I'm gettin' tired of you policy writers 3-6-9in' for me." The 3-6-9 combination, as everyone who heard the song knew, signified animal and human excreta.[17]

There were, in 1940, nearly 1 million Americans who belonged to other racial minority groups or, to be more exact, to groups commonly considered racially different whether or not any biological distinctions existed. They also worked at the hardest jobs, earned the least money, lived in the most wretched homes, and died most frequently of preventable disease. The census counted 377,000 Mexican-born persons in the United States, although the true number, including those who had entered illegally, was undoubtedly greater. Barred as aliens from public works projects, they worked, when work was to be had in the lettuce fields of California, the sugar-beet fields of Michigan, and the cotton fields of Texas. American Indians, who numbered 361,000, scratched out meager existences on arid reservation lands. Their infant mortality rate was nearly twice the national average, and their death rate from tuberculosis three or four times as great. The 127,000 people of Japanese descent enjoyed somewhat better living standards but could find employment predominantly in agriculture, gardening, household service, or businesses, such as hotels and restaurants, catering to other Japanese.

The federal government in the late 1930s largely ignored the issue of racial inequality. There was little pressure to do otherwise, for minority groups were politically impotent. First-generation Japanese Americans, those who had emigrated before the 1924 exclusion act, were ineligible by law for citizenship; their children, although they were citizens if born in the United States, were in most instances still too young to vote. Mexicans who crossed the border illegally were, so far as politics went, invisible, and even those who entered legally often did not apply for citizenship or, if they did, migrated in search of work so frequently that political activity was out of the question. American Indians had benefited in many ways from a 1934 act that provided for tribal autonomy and self-government on the reservations. But Indians remained outside the broader political culture. Disfranchisement in fact, if not in law, was a common experience of racial minorities.

New Deal officials seemed insensitive to racial injustice largely because they, like Roosevelt himself, were gradualists and pragmatists. As such they saw no reason to risk alienating southern voters and congressmen by championing civil rights for Negroes. The President's behavior in the case of the Scottsboro boys illustrated the caution with which he approached racial controversies. In 1938 five of the nine black youths charged with raping two white women on a train in Alabama in 1931 were still in prison, serving seventy-five-year terms. Roosevelt, having been reliably informed that the prosecution's case was built on "a mass of contradictions and improbabilities," undoubtedly knew, as did almost everyone else, that the convictions were unjust. He privately urged Governor Bibb Graves of Alabama to commute the sentences, on the grounds that Graves had led people to expect he would do so and on condition that the youths leave Alabama "with a guarantee on their part that they would not turn up again." Couched in the gentlest terms, the request was nevertheless refused, and Roosevelt then decided to remain silent.[18]

The President's silence on the antilynching bill was no less deafening. From 1933 to 1935 lynch mobs murdered sixty-three Negroes while southern sheriffs and deputies often looked the other way. Civil rights groups proceeded to draft a bill making lynching a federal crime and prescribing punishment for members of lynch mobs. In 1937 such a mob in Duck Hill, Mississippi, took two Negroes from a jail, set them on fire with blowtorches, then ghoulishly hanged them. The House then passed the measure, despite a warning from Speaker William Bankhead of Alabama that "what Fort Sumter started will be only a picnic" compared to what approval of the bill would mean.[19] But a threatened filibuster killed its chances in the Senate, and in 1938 an actual filibuster ensured its defeat. A cloture motion failed to receive a simple majority, much less the two-thirds vote it required. The issue split the Democratic party along sectional lines, with southern Democrats in the House, with two exceptions, voting against the measure and southern Democrats in the Senate without exception, opposing cloture. The House again passed the measure in January 1940, only to have it expire again in the Senate. Roosevelt, recognizing the bill's divisive potential and resigning himself to its defeat, never took a stand.

The New Deal aided Negroes chiefly by providing relief for the unemployed. By 1940, as more jobs in the private sector became available to whites, blacks constituted an increasing proportion of those on federal work projects. Yet as the record of the Farm Security Administration indicated, the color line was drawn even in some areas of economic assistance. Created in 1937 to help combat chronic rural poverty, the FSA made loans to tenant farmers for the purchase of land and tools, promoted the formation of agricultural cooperatives, and endeavored to scale down farm indebtedness. But powerful congressmen contrived to prevent the agency from tampering with established racial patterns. Plans to appoint a Negro to a state FSA committee were scotched, for example, when Senator James F. Byrnes of South Carolina warned that even such a seemingly small step would "disturb the friendly relations now existing between the races."[20] The FSA aided black farmers, but not in proportion to their need. In eight southern states, where five of every ten tenants were black, two of every ten loans were awarded to Negroes. FSA administrators, concerned about their agency's reputation for fiscal prudence, sought always to stay on the good side of the chairmen of congressional appropriations committees.

In June 1941 the Roosevelt administration made its boldest move in behalf of civil rights as a result of union leader A. Philip Randolph's threat to lead 100,000 Negroes in a march on Washington. Demanding an end to discrimination by defense contractors and the armed services, Randolph placed the issue squarely at Roosevelt's doorstep by calling on him to issue an executive order to accomplish those goals. Alarmed by the specter of angry blacks parading down Pennsylvania Avenue, the President leaked word that he "can imagine nothing that will stir up race hatred and slow up progress more than a march of that kind."[21] When it became apparent that Randolph would not retreat, however, the administration offered a compromise. On June 25, 1941, Roosevelt issued Executive Order 8802 calling for an end to discrimination in hiring by government agencies and by manufacturers holding defense contracts and creating a Committee on Fair Employment Practices (FEPC) to investigate complaints. Nothing was said about integrating the armed forces or equipping the FEPC with power to enforce its orders. That the executive order was regarded as a genuine breakthrough showed only how accustomed most Americans were to observing the color line and how unaccustomed they were to federal efforts to erase it.

3.

A third source of social differentiation in prewar America, along with class and race, was ethnicity. In 1940 foreign-born whites, numbering 11,419,000, constituted 8.5 percent of the population. They included 1,624,000 people from Italy; 1,323,000 from Russia, Lithuania, and Rumania; 1,238,000 from Germany; 993,000 from Poland; 845,000 from Denmark, Norway, and Sweden; 678,000 from Ireland; and 163,000 from Greece. More than 23 million native-born whites, one or both of whose parents were immigrants, constituted an additional 17.5 percent of the population. Put somewhat differently, more than one in four Americans was a first- or second-generation immigrant. Statistics are not available for the third generation, the grandchildren of immigrants, but they, too, despite the process of assimilation, frequently retained strong ethnic group affiliations.

Immigrants and their children still formed the greatest part of the population in many cities, accounting for two-thirds of the people in Cleveland, Ohio, three-fourths of those in New York City, and three-fifths of those in Newark, New Jersey. In all, they constituted better than half the total population in twenty large cities. The foreign-born, although tending to cluster in large industrialized areas, could be found everywhere. Large numbers of Finns lived in Montana, Norwegians in North Dakota, Germans in Wisconsin, and Czechs in Iowa. People of foreign birth or parentage, many of them French Canadians, constituted 40 percent of the population of Burlington, Vermont. The Deep South, the region with the fewest immigrants, nevertheless had sizable ethnic colonies in the larger cities.

It was by no means unusual for a person's entire life to be encompassed by the ethnic community, for his social world to be defined by it. The parochial school one's children attended, the church at which one worshiped, the stores in which one shopped for groceries, the clubs to which one belonged, the circle of friends one saw—all might be ethnically exclusive, or largely so. Similarly, the holidays people observed reflected their national origins. Italians celebrated the defeat of Austria at the Battle of Vittorio Veneto, Swedes commemorated the death of Gustavus Adolphus at the Battle of Lützen, and Armenians honored St. Sahak and St. Mesrop, inventors of the Armenian alphabet. In ethnic enclaves religious festivals gave a distinctly European texture to life. Every July, for example, New Yorkers in Italian Harlem celebrated the fiesta of Our Lady of Mount Carmel. A procession of clergy and barefoot pilgrims, led by a brass band and carrying a statue of the Virgin, would wind through the streets, while people standing at tenement windows tossed donations, which were then pinned to banners. "Occasionally the procession halts under the window of a particularly generous donor and the priest recites the *Dispensorio* while . . . the throng stands with bowed heads."[22]

Foreign languages, which were still used extensively, bolstered the sense of ethnic identification. One Boston guidebook noted that "five minutes' walk from the State House will take the visitor to any one of several sections of the city where English is a foreign language."[23] In 1940 no fewer than 237 foreign-language periodicals were being published in New York City, 96 in Chicago, 38 in Pittsburgh, 25 in Los Angeles, and 22 in Detroit. In all, more than 1,000 newspapers and periodicals were printed wholly or in part in a foreign language with a combined circulation of nearly 7 million. At a time when nearly 22 million people could inform census takers that English was not their mother tongue—not the language, that is, used in the homes in which they were reared—foreign-language movie houses, theaters, and bookstores flourished. San Francisco, for example, saw regular amateur theatrical performances in Russian, German, Yiddish, Italian, Spanish, Greek, Arabic, Czech, Finnish, Polish, and Japanese.

Foreign-language radio programs served a vital integrative function within the immigrant community. On the eve of World War II more than 200 radio stations carried such broadcasts, so that in large cities there was virtually no time of day when a Polish, Jewish, Spanish, German, or Italian "hour" could not be heard. These shows usually offered the listener an opportunity to return, however briefly, to a world of familiar music, language, and jokes. They appealed especially to elderly people by offering a highly sentimentalized picture of the old country. In Boston's North End, 85 percent of the Italian Americans listened regularly to such broadcasts (a larger proportion than listened to English-language programs). Popular shows became subjects of community discussion. One enterprising company sponsored an amateur hour that drew on local talent, and people "followed the radio to listen to their children or their neighbor's children." Local stores displayed placards announcing certain programs, while the announcer, who might work in the store, discussed shows with his customers. To cement their audiences' loyalty still more securely, stars of ethnic radio programs made frequent personal appearances. As one observer pointed out: "There is none of the distance between these people and their radio idols that there is between those who hear the Lux Hour and, say, Marlene Dietrich."[24]

Ethnic background often determined where people lived. In cities like New York older homogeneous immigrant areas were in the process of disintegrating, but the process was far from complete. In many parts of the city immigrant groups had staked their claims with nearly as much care as prospectors during a gold rush: Italians in the South Bronx; Jews in Brownsville; Germans in Yorkville; the Irish in Manhattanville. In smaller cities like Manchester, New Hampshire, it was still possible to speak of "Little Canada," "Irish Acre," "German town," and "Norwegian Village." Sometimes people who wanted to leave ethnic enclaves were thwarted by real estate agents who would not show them certain homes or by landlords who would not rent to them. Yet, for many, ethnic neighborhoods were undoubtedly the neighborhoods of choice. A woman in Burlington, Vermont, explained why she and her husband had passed up a chance to move into an Old Yankee area: "It looked so lonely. There wasn't a person in the streets. They were even too classy to sit out on their porches. Here folks are always passing by and coming in to visit with me."[25]

Ethnicity was as closely related to occupation as to place of residence. People at the time often associated particular nationality groups with certain kinds of work: Greek restaurant owners; Jewish tailors; Polish foundry workers; Italian shoe repairmen; Irish mill hands; Swedish lumberjacks; Portuguese fishermen. Like most stereotypes, these exaggerated the connection between nationality and work. But the connection was real enough. For example, a survey of men with distinctively Jewish names in the New York telephone book found that 10.7 percent worked in the needle trades; this compared with 1.7 percent of the people named Smith.[26] Three-fourths of the shoe repair and shoeshine shops in New York were owned by Italian Americans. Immigrants sometimes moved to an area precisely because they found certain kinds of work appealing. Scandinavians settled in Astoria, Oregon, because it was a fishing, shipbuilding, and lumbering town. In 1940 half of the city's 10,000 people were of Scandinavian extraction.

Nationality communities within each city might center on the church, the gymnastic society, and the coffeehouse or, perhaps most commonly, on the "hall." Originally conceived as a mutual aid society, the hall also became a hub of social life and, as such, helped transmit a sense of cultural uniqueness. Halls usually contained small libraries, where one could read the latest foreign-language newspaper; game rooms, where one could shoot pool; and bars, where one could drink in congenial surroundings. They were, in short, places where members could "feel free from the inhibiting presence of superior-feeling and authoritative Americans." The ambivalence immigrants often felt about the virtues of assimilation was illustrated, literally, in two murals painted on the walls of a Czechoslovakian hall in Tarentum, Pennsylvania. On one side "a towering feudal castle, a peasant boy and girl on a village street, and a legendary meeting of a knight and the virgin" recalled an idealized version of the Old World; on the other side "a river scene with a 'No hunting, no fishing' sign suggests that the locale is American."[27] Fraternal organizations alone, representing twenty-five different national groups, counted nearly 3 million members in 32,000 branches.

Ethnic loyalties had much to do with the way people responded to events abroad, particularly to the outbreak of World War II in September 1939 and to the conduct of American diplomacy until the attack on Pearl Harbor. Isolationist sentiment was strong among German and Italian Americans not, it seems, because those groups were enamored of fascist ideology but rather because they had an emotional attachment to their homelands, an aversion to fighting against their compatriots, and a fear of being treated harshly or, worse yet, being stigmatized as disloyal, should the United States become involved. Americans of Irish descent were not inclined to extend aid in any form to Great Britain. Conversely, Jews often favored measures to help the Allies, as did Poles, Danes, and Norwegians, people whose countries the Nazis had overrun. The most ardent interventionists of all were old-stock Anglo-Saxon Protestants with strong cultural and ancestral ties to England.

The political repercussions of these ethnic attachments influenced the 1940 presidential election. Although social class remained the most important determinant of political behavior, with the poor tending to vote Democratic and the rich Republican, ethnicity also played a part in the outcome. Republican candidate Wendell Willkie, although hardly less interventionist in his outlook than Roosevelt, nevertheless attracted isolationist votes, partly because of his German ancestry and partly because he was not above appealing to Anglophobia (promising a

Boston audience that "we shall not undertake to fight anybody else's war").[28] Willkie made a remarkably strong showing among normally Democratic German and Irish American voters, and he even did well among Italian Americans. Of the twenty counties in which Roosevelt's share of the vote dropped the most sharply since 1936, no fewer than nineteen were predominantly German American in composition. The only three districts in Brooklyn to vote Republican were mainly Irish. But the Democrats also benefited from ethnic partisanship. Roosevelt did better than expected among French Canadians, Scandinavians, Poles, and Jews. In the ethnic realignment Roosevelt lost slightly more than he gained, but he still received 55 percent of the popular vote.

The war also produced a sharpened sense of ethnic self-awareness. It could hardly have done otherwise given the close ties that existed between immigrants in the United States and their friends or relatives in the warring nations. Sometimes the result was a feeling of mutual accord between national groups who shared antifascist or, for that matter, profascist sentiments. But a different reaction appears to have been more common. As the debate over American intervention in the war grew more acrimonious, bad feelings between certain ethnic groups, never very far below the surface in the best of times, erupted in an ugly fashion. Like cactus in a desert, those feelings thrived in the parched and arid atmosphere of war.

One symptom was the spread of anti-Semitism among a substantial number of Irish and German Americans. Father Charles E. Coughlin did his share to whip up hatred of Jews among the Irish when, in 1938, he began serializing the *Protocols of the Elders of Zion* in his weekly magazine. A well-known and discredited forgery, the *Protocols* depicted an alleged worldwide Jewish plot to undermine Christian civilization. While hesitating to vouch for their authenticity, Coughlinites nevertheless insisted that the factualness of the documents was "as well established as the factuality of the noonday sun." Coughlin also supported an organization called the Christian Front which drew up a "Christian Index" listing merchants who promised neither to patronize nor to employ Jews. The German-American Bund, which attracted 25,000 members, voiced a yet more blatant brand of anti-Semitism. "We do not consider the Jew as a man," said Bund leader Fritz Kuhn, and one of his lieutenants spoke of the eventual need "to wipe out the Jew pigs."[29] The Bund and the Christian Front differed in that Kuhn's group wore Nazi uniforms and marched under the emblem of the swastika while Coughlin's claimed to be superpatriotic. But both sought to link Jews with international communism and accused them of pulling invisible strings to lead the United States into war.

The fate of the Wagner-Rogers bill in the spring of 1939 demonstrated that the members of these groups had no monopoly on anti-Semitism. The bill was drafted as a result of events in November 1938, when Hitler, ostensibly reacting to the assassination of a Nazi official by a Jewish youth, unleashed a ferocious assault on German Jews. Synagogues were burned to the ground, cemeteries desecrated, businesses demolished, huge fines levied, and many Jews shipped to concentration camps. Afterward more Jews sought to enter the United States than the combined annual immigration quotas for Germany and Austria of 27,000 could accommodate. A measure was therefore introduced in February 1939 that would have allowed 20,000 additional children under the age of fourteen to enter the United States over a two-year period. The bill ran at once into a stone wall of opposition. Critics maintained that the 20,000 children would form an opening wedge for thousands more. Polls indicated that two-thirds of the American people opposed the measure. In fact, Jewish spokesmen themselves were divided, with some fearful that a sudden influx of immigrants would inflame anti-Semitic sentiment. Under these circumstances President Roosevelt remained aloof, penciling "File, no action" on a letter from a congressman requesting his opinion. The bill was so emasculated in committee that its sponsors decided against bringing it to a vote. The wife of the U.S. Commissioner of Immigration captured the prevailing mood. The trouble with the measure, she remarked casually at a cocktail party, was "that 20,000 children would all too soon grow up into 20,000 ugly adults."[30]

Hostility toward Jewish refugees was part of a more general suspicion of aliens. Fostered by the signing of the Russo-German pact in August 1939 which appeared to link the twin menaces of communism and fascism, that suspicion was further heightened by the lightning-like success of German forces in the spring of 1940, a success widely attributed to Nazi "fifth column" activities in Holland, Norway, and other conquered nations. Fear that such a fifth column existed in America approached near-panic proportions by mid-1940. It was reinforced by magazine articles describing industrial sabotage and "treachery in the air"—shortwave radio stations flashing secret signals across the ocean, minuscule transmitters easily concealed in coat pockets, "the ether around us . . . crackling" with subversive messages.[31] The alarm was sounded not only by FBI Director J. Edgar Hoover, who by temperament and profession was inclined to exaggerate such things, but also by liberals, who usually viewed such claims skeptically. *The Nation,* asserting that "treasonable elements are feverishly at work," called for a group libel law to permit a crackdown on fascist sympathizers.[32] In the same way, Lewis Mumford favored "keeping every fascist group or profascist speaker off the air, denying the use of the United States mails to every fascist publication . . . and finally putting into jail—or sending into exile—the active ringleaders of fascism, under a law which would make the espousal of fascism itself an act of treason against democracy."[33]

The Roosevelt administration exhibited a good deal of uneasiness over its belief that fascist and communist agents might be plotting to disrupt defense production, the former by sabotaging factories and the latter by instigating strikes. In May 1940, as Hitler's armies swept toward the English Channel, Roosevelt told a group of Cabinet members and congressional leaders: "Of course we have got this fifth column thing, which is altogether too widespread through the country." Warning that "we have got to be pretty darned careful" in recruiting federal employees, he recalled a story, almost certainly apocryphal, about Secretary of Labor Frances Perkins. She had been on the verge of appointing a man to handle employment problems when she discovered him to be "100% affiliated and associated with the Communist movement. . . . You have to be careful on that." Then the President added: "Also be careful not to get pro-Germans. There are a good many Americans who love efficiency and are pro-Germans for that reason."[34]

These anxieties, whether founded on fact or fancy, produced stringent measures aimed at curbing the entry of aliens, controlling the activities of those in the United States, and facilitating their deportation. As a first step, Roosevelt, in March 1940, approved Secretary of State Cordell Hull's recommendation that all aliens applying for temporary visitors' visas be fingerprinted. In 1941 the Bloom–Van Nuys bills provided for a painstaking review of all entry applications and for the rejection of all candidates who "because of their mental philosophy" might serve as enemy agents. The Smith Act, passed in June 1940, imposed additional restrictions. It required the 4.9 million aliens in the country to register, be fingerprinted, and list any organizations to which they belonged. The act also provided for the deportation of those who had belonged to a communist or fascist group "at any time, of no matter how short duration or how far in the past." In September 1940 Attorney General Frank Murphy, considered by all a staunch friend of civil liberties, offered some insight into the mood gripping the nation. "Unless we are pudding headed," he said, "we will drive from the land the hirelings here to undo the labors of our Fathers."[35]

Having taken these steps against aliens, the government moved against citizens it suspected of disloyal behavior. In May 1940 the President approved the placing of wiretaps on telephones used by those whom the Attorney General "suspected of subversive activities." The Smith Act itself, although concerned primarily with aliens, also made it illegal for anyone to conspire to teach or advocate the violent overthrow of the government. In October 1940 Congress passed a measure requiring the registration of any organization that was "subject to foreign control" or that favored violent revolution. California and several other states barred communist-affiliated parties from the ballot. The Justice Department used whatever pretext it could find to put those it considered dangerous behind bars. Bund leader Fritz Kuhn, accused of misappropriating $500 of his organization's funds, was sentenced to several years in Sing Sing. The head of the Communist party, Earl Browder, was charged with a technical infraction involving the fraudulent use of a passport. Found guilty, he was sent to jail for two to four years, a sentence that one Supreme Court justice privately conceded was "outrageous."[36]

The fear of fifth-column activities in 1940 and 1941

has been termed a "little red scare," an accurate enough designation, although one requiring a dual qualification. First, the Roosevelt administration, unlike the Wilson administration after World War I, did a good deal to reassure the public and check the hysteria. Although Roosevelt supported tighter controls over individuals he regarded as subversive or potentially so, he either vetoed or succeeded in sidetracking legislation that would have further eroded free speech, curbed political dissidents, and deprived aliens of their civil liberties. Second, public fears eventually centered more on the threat of fascism than on that of communism. Anticommunist sentiment probably reached a peak after Russia invaded Finland in November 1939 and American communists escalated their attack on Roosevelt's policies. That sentiment ebbed swiftly after Germany invaded the Soviet Union in June 1941 and American communists, reversing their position, gave their support to a policy of intervention.

Fear of fifth-column activities derived, for the most part, from the troubled course of events in Europe. But the fear had another source as well: the persistence of ethnic loyalties among many Americans and the recognition that those loyalties, reinforced as they often were by the war, might well produce disunity and fragmentation. It was ironic, if understandable, that public attention, to the degree it focused on social divisions at all, focused on those deriving from ethnicity. For after the United States entered the war, those divisions would be the easiest to reconcile. Tensions arising from the existence of a class structure and from the practice of racial segregation, on the other hand, would prove more difficult to resolve. All three would be deeply affected by the experience of war.

[2]

Wartime America

In the spring of 1942, as part of an attempt to stimulate a "community sense of patriotic participation at home in the war effort," the Office of Civilian Defense staged a number of "town meetings for war." Widely reported in the news media, the ceremonies included speeches honoring local war heroes, celebrities selling war bonds, and bands playing patriotic songs. The agency's director, James M. Landis, informed the President that the participants included "whites and negroes," "old Americans and new Americans with traces of their homeland accents," "chambers of commerce . . . and the workers in the war plants."[1] Landis expressed the widely shared hope that patriotic sentiment would serve as a unifying agent among races, ethnic groups, and classes. To some extent it did, but the hope was never fully realized. The war, while healing certain divisions within American society, never effected as complete a cure as Landis and others contemplated.

1.

The attack on Pearl Harbor clearly demonstrated war's potential as a unifying force in society. It was perhaps predictable that those who had favored intervention all along would express relief that Japan's action, by posing the issue in such stark and decisive terms, had left the United States no alternative to war. But the speed with which former isolationists recanted was surprising. Within days one had declared that his earlier disagreement with the Roosevelt administration "lies buried somewhere in the waters of Pearl Harbor," and another had asserted that had he been a congressman he "certainly would have voted for a declaration of war." Yet a third, playing King Henry IV to Roosevelt's Pope Gregory VII, appeared at the White House as if at Canossa to say "that he had been wrong in his isolationist policy—that he wanted to confess his error."[2] In the early months of the war Americans talked about how they had been "electrified into unity in a single Sunday afternoon."[3] Rhetorical exaggeration aside, the talk was not wholly without foundation.

The government publicized an interpretation of American war aims designed to foster national unity, and most citizens accepted that interpretation in good faith. After December 7, 1941, two propositions commanded general agreement: Japan and Germany had, without provocation of any sort, attacked the United States as part of their master plan to enslave the world; in responding to that challenge, the United States had no selfish ambitions but wished only to ensure freedom and security for people everywhere. As officials concerned with the condition of public morale put it: "The ideas are simple to state: slavery and freedom." Historians would later challenge both propositions, and even during the war many government officials realized that matters were considerably more complex than they wanted to admit or than the popular viewpoint suggested. Yet they also recognized that presenting the war in a certain way could itself contribute to social cohesion: "By making this a 'people's' war for freedom, we can help clear up the alien problem, the negro problem, the anti-Semitic problem."[4]

Millions of people achieved a vicarious sense of participation in the trials of combat by volunteering to become air-raid wardens, fire fighters, auxiliary policemen, and nurses' aides. Even those who did not enlist directly in civilian defense activities were, in many cases, made to feel that the war was closer to home than it actually was. In 1942 and 1943 state civilian defense agencies staged mock air raids. Ostensibly designed to test warning systems, they imparted a feeling of common peril and dramatized people's dependency on one another. In Wyoming, for example, the Civil Air Patrol bombarded communities with leaflets cut in the shape of bombs, each bearing a pledge to buy a war bond. To add a dimension of realism to a blackout in Charlottesville, Virginia, airplanes dropped sand bombs on the city. In 1943 more than 200 pilots took to the skies over Chicago and released 250,000 paper bombs constructed by schoolchildren. "Sirens screamed," reported the newspapers. "At various spots traffic was abruptly halted."[5]

Two other devices, although less sensational than simulated raids, instilled a similar sense of mutual cooperation: bond drives and scrap drives. Secretary of the Treasury Henry Morgenthau knew that selling war bonds did not constitute the most effective means of raising revenue and that an overly flamboyant sales campaign "might easily lead to the talk of 'slacker' and other excesses." But he also believed that bond drives could "make the country war-minded." In April 1942 Morgenthau reported: "Right now, other than going in the Army and Navy or working in a munitions plant, there isn't anything to do." The opportunity to purchase bonds would provide everyone with a direct means of participation. By emphasizing the sale of low-denomination bonds through payroll savings plans, Morgenthau explicitly sought to avoid class bias in the drives. He indicated as much by disapproving a billboard display that featured an actress wearing a mink coat and requesting instead, only half-facetiously, "a girl from

Amalgamated Clothiers Union swathed in a pair of overalls."[6] Bond drives ultimately raised $135 billion, and if purchases declined toward the end of the war, Morgenthau nevertheless partially realized his original goal of fostering feelings of national solidarity.

Drives to salvage scarce materials evoked similar feelings. Well-publicized efforts to collect rubber, metals, paper, kitchen fats, and used clothing encouraged a high level of community integration. Localities boasted of surpassing their quotas and took great pride in the exploits of children, who relished the chance to ransack basements, attics, and garages. Iron fences around schools, churches, and old mansions were ripped up for the scrap heap, and this removal of physical barriers sometimes assumed psychological importance. In Chicago "one woman, who had lived apart, celebrated the 'de-fencing' of her lawn by a neighborhood party."[7] Those who directed scrap drives developed strong feelings of camaraderie and, when the drives ended, experienced an emotional letdown. "No more parades. No more street parties. No more Nazi leaflets over Memphis. No more rubber piles at stations, or rubber days at movie houses," lamented a representative of the petroleum industry at the close of a nationwide rubber drive. "Nothing to do now but stagger back to the prosaic business of selling gasoline and motor oil."[8]

Advertisements in newspapers and magazines played on the guilt of those who had not done their part and on the pride of those who had. "Are you comfortable, brother?" asked a typical advertisement. "That's good, brother. Just sleep right through this war. Let some other guy do your share! What's it to you that a kid just got bumped off in the Solomons . . . because *you* couldn't be bothered with scrap collection? . . . You're exhausted thinking up reasons why *not* to buy War Bonds . . . while thousands of American boys are going without food and sleep to protect your hide. . . . Come on, get up off that fat can of yours," the advertisement concluded, employing the gruff idiom legitimized by the war, "stop riding and start pushing." By contrasting the comforts of civilian existence with the deprivations of military life, advertisers sought to create a sense of emotional involvement and, in so doing, sell their products. Advertising, in the words of one scholar, "self-consciously came to promote a coherent view of what the war was all about, why the United States was involved in it, and what the significance of an American victory would be."[9]

The image of the American soldier that civilians received from war correspondents and novelists powerfully reinforced the idea of national unity. In *Here Is Your War* and *Brave Men,* to take the most popular books of their kind, correspondent Ernie Pyle depicted GI Joes who embodied all the traits that Americans believed distinguished them as a people. Pyle's soldiers were individualistic, democratic, optimistic and, above all, united with their comrades. Although infantrymen hailed from every corner of the country, the caldron of war had dissolved all ethnic, class, and racial enmities. "The battlefield does produce a brotherhood," Pyle wrote. "The common bond of death draws human beings toward each other over the artificial barriers of rank." Having overcome internal discord, the GIs had contempt for civilians who placed group interest ahead of the common good. "Just mention a strike at home to either soldier or officer," Pyle reported, "and you had a raving maniac on your hands."[10]

Two novels published in 1944 conveyed a similar message. John Hersey's *A Bell for Adano* was the story of Major Victor Joppolo, an Italian American from the Bronx, whose decency and humaneness won over the villagers in a town in occupied Sicily. "America is the international country," Hersey explained in a foreword. "Our Army has Yugoslavs and Frenchmen and Austrians and Czechs and Norwegians in it, and everywhere our Army goes in Europe, a man can turn to the private beside him and say: 'Hey, Mac, what's this furriner saying?' . . . And Mac will be able to translate." In *A Walk in the Sun,* Harry Brown depicted an American platoon whose mission was to capture a farmhouse in Italy. The very names of the soldiers—McWilliams, Friedman, Tranella, Archimbeau, Rand, Rivera—suggested that men of diverse backgrounds could work together congenially. At one point Jake Friedman asked his buddy, "What nationality are you, Rivera?" "I'm a god-damned Irishman. What did you think I was?" Rivera replied, indicating that since, whatever his background, it assuredly was not Irish, nationality made no difference. The question was irrelevant; all that mattered was his ability to handle a machine gun.[11]

Neither of these books portrayed the Italian people in an unfavorable light, but the same could not be said for wartime treatment of the Germans and, to an even greater degree, the Japanese. In fact, psychologists pointed out that hatred of a common enemy served a unifying function during the war by draining "internal antagonisms . . . out of the group." Germans, especially Nazi leaders, were described as militaristic, cold-blooded, and arrogant, as men who carried discipline to inhuman lengths. "They despise the world of civilians," *Life* said of the German General Staff. "They wear monocles to train themselves to control their face muscles. They live and die for war."[12] Images of the Japanese revolved around the stereotypical themes of treachery, fanaticism, and cruelty. Worship of the emperor and the use of suicide, or kamikaze, raids, both wholly in keeping with well-established cultural traditions in Japan, seemed inexplicable to Americans and therefore terrifying. The commonly accepted explanation was that the Japanese lacked normal human emotions. "The Japs don't understand the love we have for our women," said Cary Grant, in the role of a submarine commander in the film *Destination: Tokyo.* "They don't even have a word for it in their language."

Hatred of a dehumanized enemy had an obverse side: affirmation of a common nationality. The war years saw a heightened interest in American history, tradition, and culture, a search for common roots that would provide a means of collective identification. This accounted, in part, for the popularity of musical shows like *Bloomer Girl* and *Oklahoma!* In the Broadway production of the former, Evelina Bloomer was a northern abolitionist and dress reformer who was engaged to be married to a southern slaveholder. When the Civil War broke out, he left her to enlist, but a funny thing happened to him on his way to the Confederacy: He heard a speech by Abraham Lincoln, turned around, and rode home to Evelina. One historian has commented: "The stated American ideals of liberty for all and unity of moral principles despite diversity of regions and ways of life are evoked and symbolized by their personal union."[13] Rodgers and Hammerstein's *Oklahoma!,* which opened in March 1943 and played to more than 2 million people in its first two years, not only reassured audiences that the land they belonged to was grand but suggested, in the romance of Curly McLain and Laurey Williams, that the marriage of individual members of a community gave the community new life. In their vision of a pastoral and innocent past, their portrayal of life as a simple conflict between good and evil, their evocation of a common land and common ideals, and their conviction that the destiny of the individual was linked to that of the broader community, these plays accurately reflected wartime assumptions.

Echoes of national unity reverberated through American cultural life. Popular songs, such as Earl Robinson's "The House I Live In," celebrated the contributions made by diverse groups. In modern dance, Martha Graham's *Appalachian Spring* affirmed the bedrock strength of American character by portraying the life of a young couple in a rural community in nineteenth-century Pennsylvania. Aaron Copland's score used an old Shaker hymn whose words seemed entirely appropriate: " 'Tis a gift to be simple/ 'Tis a gift to be free/ 'Tis a gift to come down/ Where we ought to be." A week after the attack on Pearl Harbor, Norman Corwin's radio drama *We Hold These Truths* was broadcast to commemorate the 150th anniversary of the Bill of Rights. Spokesmen for different social classes explained how they continued to benefit from the ideals of "Tom Jefferson, George Mason, Pat Henry, Jimmy Madison." (Worker: "We got the right to bargain collectively." Manufacturer: "There is nothing in any law which forbids us to forget class differences.") Corwin's version of the rights guaranteed in 1791 may have stretched historical truth, but it accorded perfectly with the prevailing mood: "Yes! United proudly in a solemn day. Knit more strongly than we were a hundred and fifty years ago!"[14]

The appeal to cultural and historical traditions had much in common with official interpretations of how the war began and what the United States was fighting for, with the emphasis on civilian involvement in war-related tasks and willingness to make sacrifices, and with the images of American soldiers and the enemies against whom they fought. All reinforced the idea that what united Americans was a great deal more important than what divided them. All implied that the differences between classes, races, and ethnic groups would be submerged in fighting the war. Distinctions of long-standing duration were, in fact, not so easily forgotten. But it would be unfair to belittle the extent to which World War II stimulated a sense of national solidarity.

2.

During the war, festivals celebrating the contributions made to America by different immigrant groups became something of a ritual. For example, a mammoth Festival of Nations was held in St. Paul, Minnesota, in May 1942; it lasted three days and involved some 2,000 people representing thirty-two nationalities. The sponsors of these affairs, however, sometimes exhibited a certain nervousness, suspecting that the very act of preparing for the festivals—sewing native costumes, cooking ethnic foods, learning the old folk dances—might magnify the differences between people. But while it is unlikely that these pageants contributed much to improved understanding, neither did they justify such fears. The festivals, one writer noted, did not encourage immigrants to reject American nationality. "Daily life in America is so entirely removed from the costumed peasant dancing a hora or a jig" that participation was more likely to "serve as a medium for emotional release of tension and conflict."[15] Indeed, in no other area of American life were the unifying effects of war felt more strongly. The war set in motion forces that went far toward eroding the bases of ethnic exclusivity.

One such force was unprecedented migration. During the war 12 million men and women left home in order to enter the armed forces, and more than 15 million civilians moved across county lines, most of them to seek jobs in national defense. Not only did extraordinarily large numbers of people move in a relatively short time, but they moved at more frequent intervals and over longer distances. The rate of migration was highest for those between the ages of twenty and twenty-four, and young people were the most likely to sink roots in new communities, a pattern that would also hold true for returning servicemen. Whatever the proportion of ethnic minorities, especially second- and third-generation immigrants, among the migrants—a statistic the government did not compile—it surely was substantial. The sense of ethnic attachment, which drew support from the fixed social structure of the immigrant community, waned as wartime mobility disrupted old neighborhoods.

At the same time institutions that bound immigrants to their native cultures, particularly foreign-language radio programs and newspapers, fell on hard times. The government, recognizing the potential value of foreign-language broadcasts as a way of reaching immigrants, wanted to be certain that the right message came across. The Federal Communications Commission therefore required stations carrying such broadcasts to approve scripts in advance, to monitor programs to ensure they did not deviate from the scripts, and to investigate the backgrounds of (and fingerprint) everyone connected with the shows. If not always observed in every situation, these rules by their restrictive nature inevitably proved burdensome. The war years witnessed the beginning of a sharp decline in the number of stations broadcasting in foreign languages, from 205 in 1942 to 126 in 1948.

The foreign-language press found itself in deep financial difficulty. Revenue dropped suddenly, for the war cut into the sources upon which those newspapers relied: advertisements by steamship lines and foreign exchange branches of banks, and subsidies from foreign governments. Moreover, foreign-language newspapers and magazines depended on being able to obtain articles, news items, and stories from European publications, which they often clipped and reprinted verbatim.

The war interrupted the flow of that material. Forced to devote more space to domestic issues, foreign-language publications competed with English-language publications more directly and lost some of their unique appeal. From 1940 to 1945, 165 foreign-language publications, about 15 percent of the total, folded.

The chaotic situation in Europe deepened the existing political divisions within each ethnic group in the United States. Among immigrants from Axis nations, for instance, a minority apparently sympathized with the fascist regimes, thereby infuriating the majority, which did not. Immigrants from Finland, Denmark, and other nations that collaborated in some measure with Hitler were sharply divided over the propriety of such action. Among the many Finnish Americans in Duluth, Minnesota, "there existed a sharp cleavage between those who bitterly resented the sending of help to Russia and those who were against the policy of the Nazified regime in Finland." Even power struggles involving the fate of European monarchies produced dissension. To cite two examples: Rumanians in America "began taking sides on the issue of supporting King Carol if and when he is ever returned to the Rumanian throne," and Greek Americans, like the people of Greece themselves, sided with either royalists or parliamentarians.[16]

Similarly, the Polish community in America mirrored the political divisions within Poland. Most of the 2.9 million first- and second-generation Polish Americans were Roman Catholics, and most of them distrusted the Soviet Union. But opinion during the war was hardly unanimous. An observer reported the Poles "divided among themselves on how far the government-in-exile ought to allow Russia to dominate or acquire the portions of Poland lost to Russia after Hitler's invasion." One group, the most politically conservative, considered the London-based government-in-exile too soft in its response to Russian territorial demands, while another group, far to the left, thought the London government too rigid in its response. When a spokesman for the first group condemned the Yalta agreements on Eastern Europe, a spokesman for the second urged Roosevelt to "reject the divisive and vicious utterances of certain Polish misleaders."[17] From 1939 to 1941 the war had reinforced ethnic cohesiveness, but after Pearl Harbor, in the case of Poles and other immigrants, it did the reverse.

Statistics on naturalization provide perhaps the best index of wartime assimilation. From 1934 to 1939 an average of 148,291 aliens were naturalized annually, but from 1940 to 1945 the average jumped to 295,872. More than 1,750,000 aliens became citizens in that six-year period, nearly 442,000 of them in 1944 alone. Since an immigrant could seek naturalization within two to seven years after filing a declaration of intent, the 1944 figure undoubtedly includes many people of German and Italian descent who decided to become citizens in the early months of the war. The government also provided a simplified naturalization procedure for aliens who were serving in the armed forces, one that waived most requirements (including residency) for men who had entered the country legally, were serving honorably, and were recommended by their superior officers. Nearly 150,000 soldiers exercised this option. With few immigrants able to enter the country during the war, the proportion of noncitizens in the population fell sharply.

In two wartime cases the Supreme Court extended broad protection to naturalized citizens whose loyalty was questioned. In 1943 the Court, by a 5–3 vote, found in favor of William Schneiderman, who had been denaturalized in 1939 on the grounds that he was a communist when he acquired citizenship in 1927 and as such could not have honestly supported the principles of the Constitution. However they voted, the justices understood the implications of the decision for an ethnically pluralist society. Felix Frankfurter, who supported the minority view, reminded his brethren in conference that he alone, among them all, was the son of a naturalized citizen: "I was at college when my father became naturalized and I can assure you that for months preceding it was a matter of moment in our family life, and when the great day came it partook for me of great solemnity."[18] Frankfurter believed that restoring Schneiderman's citizenship amounted to a denial that the *Communist Manifesto* and the U.S. Constitution were incompatible. Frank Murphy, who wrote the majority opinion, disagreed. He disliked "having a person's citizenship cancelled ten years after it was conferred" without "clear, unequivocal and convincing" evidence of a lack of attachment to constitutional principles. "We are a heterogeneous people," Murphy said. "In some of our larger cities a majority of the school children are the offspring of parents only one generation, if that far, removed from the steerage of the immigrant ship." Naturalized citizens, he concluded, must not be afraid to think and speak freely or must not fear "further exile" if they did.[19]

Furious at what he considered the intrusion of political considerations—in this instance the desire to accommodate the Soviet Union as a wartime ally—into the judicial process, Frankfurter predicted that "when we get the case of the Bundists next year there will be some fine somersaulting."[20] Contrary to that expectation, the justices who had defended a communist's right to citizenship also defended a fascist's. The case involved Carl Wilhelm Baumgartner, a member of the German-American Bund, whose citizenship had been revoked in 1942 on the grounds that he had taken the oath of allegiance ten years earlier with mental reservations. In 1944 the Court unanimously overturned his denaturalization. Frankfurter's opinion noted that the evidence concerning Baumgartner's fascist leanings derived from his activities after, rather than before, he had become a citizen. In that sense, the situation was not analogous to Schneiderman's, and the difference allowed Frankfurter to claim that his position in the two cases was consistent. In a concurring opinion, however, Murphy contended the cases were alike. The same rule was "equally applicable" whether the naturalized citizen stood on the right or the left of the political spectrum.[21]

Government policy toward aliens of enemy nationality reflected the benign atmosphere in which ethnic issues were resolved. There were, at the time, approximately 264,000 German and 599,000 Italian aliens. Required to register, to notify the government if they changed jobs or addresses, and to obtain permission to travel outside their home communities, enemy aliens were also subjected to other restrictions that were, on the whole, related to military security. They were barred from entering strategic areas, from traveling in airplanes, and from possessing cameras, shortwave receivers, signal devices, maps of installations, and "papers, documents or books in which there may be invisible writing."[22] In October 1942 Attorney General Francis Biddle, with Roosevelt's blessing, ruled that Italian aliens would no longer be classified as aliens of "enemy nationality" and would therefore be exempt from these regulations. Biddle made the announcement at a Carnegie Hall rally on Columbus Day. He later learned that Arturo Toscanini, after hearing the broadcast, "threw his arms round the machine . . . held it close while he took in the roar of applause . . . kissed it, turned it off and burst into tears." For Italian Americans, as one scholar has commented, "war was the fuel of the melting pot."[23]

Having exempted Italians, the Roosevelt administration came under some pressure to extend similar leniency to German aliens. Biddle hinted broadly in 1942 that such a step was under consideration, but it was never taken. For one thing, the political payoff seemed less certain. Democrats generally considered the Italian vote more vital than the German vote and more likely to be won by such a gesture. For another, Italians in the United States lived in more closely knit communities than did Germans and maintained stronger ties with relatives in their homeland. News of the reclassification might therefore encourage the Italian people, who Roosevelt once said were "ordered against their will" to support the Axis, to desert Mussolini. No such argument was raised in behalf of the Germans. Finally, Roosevelt may have suspected that Italians were more trustworthy, although he managed to express that suspicion in condescending terms. According to Biddle, the President said: "I don't care so much about the Italians. They are a lot of opera singers, but the Germans are different, they may be dangerous."[24]

In statements meant for public consumption, however, Roosevelt took pains to praise German Americans, pointing out in 1944 "how many good men and women of German ancestry have proved loyal, freedom-loving, and peace-loving citizens." In doing so, he was, no doubt, following the advice of vote-conscious politicians who begged that "a pat on the back be given to German-Americans" and who assured the President that "as it did with Italians it will do with Germans."[25] Yet there was more to Roosevelt's statement than sheer political calculation, for in suggesting that ethnic loyalties were losing their force, he was not wide of the mark. The war, while not erasing all sense of ethnic distinctiveness, surely softened it, as older immigrant communities and the institutions that served them lost strength, as echoes of European political battles resounded in America, as increasing numbers of aliens acquired citizenship and the Supreme Court defended their status, and as the government pursued a tolerant policy toward the foreign-born.

3.

The *Wall Street Journal,* in the fall of 1942, published several articles about "the new poor." Inspired by a recently imposed limitation of $25,000 (after taxes) on salaries, the series described the tribulations about to be experienced by business executives earning $100,000 a year. These men were planning to hitch up their belts by cutting back on golf club memberships, boarding up summer homes, and doing without vacations. Despite these economies, one of them expected to go "practically broke," and another to find himself "deep in trouble." The articles warned that the salary limitation would work a yet more severe hardship on poor people, such as caddies on deserted golf links, gardeners at vacated estates, and elderly servants whose employers could no longer afford to keep them on the payroll. In every respect the articles seemed to corroborate the editors' view that the salary limitation was the last word in demagoguery, a plan calculated to subvert the liberties of the most humble citizen, for "if one is made the victim of tyranny, all may be."[26]

The history of the ill-fated $25,000 salary limitation provides a useful point of departure for considering the impact of the war on social class. Imposed by Economic Stabilization Director James F. Byrnes in November 1942 as a means of assuring equality of sacrifice, the plan always contemplated a good deal less than its enemies feared. Given the prevailing tax structure, the limitation applied only to a few thousand people whose gross incomes exceeded $67,200. Even they were not put under an absolute ceiling, since special allowances would be made for meeting life insurance premiums, mortgage payments, and other "fixed obligations heretofore incurred." The limitation applied only to salaries, not to income derived from investments or interest. Despite its fundamentally symbolic character, or perhaps because of it, the plan inspired nearly as much horror in Congress as it did in the editorial offices of the *Wall Street Journal.* In March 1943, five months after it was announced but before it was ever enforced, the salary limitation was repealed. To avoid the possibility of a veto, Congress attached its repeal to a bill authorizing a vitally needed increase in the public debt. The most explicit attempt to use the war emergency as a justification for narrowing class differences was thereby aborted, and the attempt itself was widely construed, in the words of one congressman, as having been "born out of class hatred."[27]

Conceived less out of any such sentiment than out of a desire to appease workers whose wages were already subject to control and who were asking, with some logic, "If we have our salaries frozen, why shouldn't they?" the salary limitation had three strikes against it from the start.[28] The plan appeared unnecessarily flagrant, did violence to a deeply ingrained success ethos, and approached the problem from the wrong direction. In a variety of ways that were less obvious, and therefore easier to reconcile with traditional values, the government reduced the gap between social classes. It did so, however, not by placing a maximum limit on earnings. Instead, it permitted the rich to get richer at a somewhat slower rate than it allowed the poor to get richer. There is every reason to believe that government officials understood what they were doing. Confronted with the alternative of freezing the positions of social classes as they stood at the outset of war or of granting selective increases that would aid some more than others, the administration chose the latter. As Leon Henderson, an influential figure in the stabilization program, put it, what was at stake was a "change in the distribution of the pie."[29]

Government action in three related areas—taxes, prices, and wages—affected the size of everybody's slice. Wartime taxation, even allowing for unplugged loopholes, assumed a generally redistributive character. In 1939 a married man without dependents who earned $2,000 paid no tax; in 1945 he was liable for $202. In the same period, however, the tax on an income of $5,000 rose from $80 to $844, on $10,000 from $415 to $2,370, and on $25,000 from $2,489 to $9,955. Then, too, the government instituted a system of price controls which, after early difficulties were ironed out, proved largely effective. Although consumer prices rose by about 30 percent from 1941 to 1945, most of the increase occurred early in the war. Finally, the administration imposed wage controls but so gradually and flexibly that income kept ahead of the cost of living. With overtime plentiful and with job classifications constantly being upgraded, these controls affected hourly wage rates far more than real earnings. Weekly earnings in manufacturing actually climbed by 70 percent.

Not only did paychecks keep getting fatter and fatter, but more people than ever before started bringing them home. There was work for nearly everyone who wanted it and for some who did not know they wanted it until they were magnetically attracted by high wartime wages. Large numbers of retired people reentered the labor force, and even larger numbers of teenagers entered it for the first time. In all, 4.5 million women took jobs during the war, until women came to constitute 36 percent of the civilian labor force. Employers welcomed handicapped workers as never in the past. At some Ford plants, workers who were blind, deaf, or otherwise disabled constituted 10 percent of the work force. As more members of the family went to work, family income, the most reliable gauge of real living standards, shot up like a rocket. Millions of people managed to clear up old debts and, perhaps for the first time in many years, put aside savings.

Full employment and favorable government policies led predictably to a more equitable distribution of a much greater national income. One way of measuring this is to compare the changes in income of each stratum of American families from 1941 to 1945. Beginning with the poorest fifth, and moving to the wealthiest, the percentages of income increase were 68, 59, 36, 30, and 20. The share of national income held by the richest 5 percent of the people declined from 23.7 to 16.8 percent. The number of families with incomes under 2,000 fell by more than half, while the number with incomes over $5,000 rose more than fourfold. Put somewhat differently, the same figures tell a more striking tale: before the war, for every family earning over $5,000 there were twelve families with incomes under $2,000; afterward the ratio was nearly even.

Rationing programs narrowed some of the remaining discrepancies between social classes. Such everyday necessities as gasoline, sugar, coffee, meat, butter, fats, and canned goods were rationed, both to ensure that scarce commodities were available for military use and to guarantee that remaining supplies were impartially distributed to civilians. In effect, rationing demonetized currency for the purchase of certain items. The allocation of ration books depended on a family's size rather than on its social position. The egalitarian implications thrilled one reformer who thought that "Rockefeller and I can now get the same amount of sugar, gasoline, tires etc., etc., etc., and the etc's will soon fill many pages."[30] Since the et ceteras could also be bought on the black market, money still talked even after dollar bills were theoretically rendered mute by ration stamps. But trafficking on the black market always carried a stigma and was not widespread enough to offset the most important effects of rationing.

In a variety of temporary, although significant, ways the war undermined certain arrangements that had characterized the system of class privilege. To curb inflation, the government clamped down on installment buying, thereby removing one prerogative of those with good credit ratings. As the demand for labor drew women, teenagers, and members of racial minorities to war industries, the well-to-do found it increasingly difficult to obtain such personal services as having their homes cleaned or their groceries delivered. Ostentatious displays were frowned on, at least officially, and frugality in every form was encouraged. This made for a vivid contrast with the 1930s. Then children had sometimes stayed home from school out of embarrassment at having had to wear threadbare clothing or hand-me-downs that did not fit; now a school in Rockford, Illinois, organized a "patriotic patches" club, membership in which required that children wear patched clothes or those inherited from older brothers or sisters. By equating the avoidance of waste with patriotism, the war suppressed some of the more explicit evidence of class differentiation.

If the pyramid of social stratification was flattened, it nevertheless continued to rest firmly on a base. Since most people improved their positions during the war, those who did not were more acutely aware of their ill fortune, and their numbers, if decreased, were still considerable. In 1944 some 10 million workers, one-fourth of those engaged in manufacturing, earned less than 60 cents an hour, or $24 for a forty-hour week. Fearing that any increase in minimum wages would send inflationary tremors through the economy, the Roosevelt administration opposed permitting employers to offer increases to 65 cents an hour (rather than the 50 cents then allowed). Other groups besides those earning substandard wages also found the going rough: retired people living on Social Security pensions, white-collar workers who had no opportunity to earn overtime pay, and craftsmen whose special skills were expendable when factories converted to war production. Even in flush times many people, in the words of one senator, were "not able to live the way Americans ought to live."[31]

Yet as the election of 1944 demonstrated, the new prosperity had the more important political repercussions. Franklin Roosevelt had built the Democratic coalition around bread-and-butter issues. His pluralities had been based largely on the votes of the poor and the unemployed; his speeches had made a frank appeal to their class interest. But by 1944, as poverty was reduced and unemployment dwindled, the old appeal lost much of its urgency. A public opinion specialist employed by the White House began to observe rising dissatisfaction with the Democrats among the working classes, who "now feel more secure economically [and] are disturbed by the taxes they are paying for the first time."[32] Despite wartime developments that worked to Roosevelt's advantage, including the prestige he gained as Commander in Chief and the vigorous campaign launched in his behalf by the CIO's recently formed Political Action Committee, his share of the popular vote fell from 54.7 to 53.4 percent. Demonstrating his greatest strength in the big cities, Roosevelt defeated Republican Thomas E. Dewey by 3.6 million votes, the smallest margin of any victor since 1916. Far fewer votes were cast in 1944 than in 1940, but the Republican vote dipped by 300,000 and the Democratic vote by 1,640,000.

The Political Action Committee did yeoman work in getting out the labor vote, and while that vote still went heavily Democratic, it should not be assumed that war workers, especially those who had migrated long distances, developed a sense of class solidarity. The persistent force of "self-sufficiency and competitive individualism" together with the heterogeneous character of the workers led in just the opposite direction. At least that is the conclusion drawn by the sociologists who studied conditions in shipyards, airplane factories, and boom towns. At a shipyard in Oakland, California, for example, acute antagonisms developed between the jumble of groups that composed the work force: between older workers with seniority and younger ones who were leapfrogging over them, between men and women, between blacks and whites, between Jews and Gentiles, and between different nationalities. The conflict between older residents of California and "Okies," the generic label for migrants from Oklahoma, Texas, or any southwestern state, assumed a particularly bitter form. Above an obvious passageway someone wrote in chalk, "Okie, this is a door"; and above a urinal, "Okie drinking fountain."[33]

So prevalent was the distrust between older residents and newcomers that an observer across the country, in Portland, Maine, referred to it as a "new class struggle." As hordes of workers poured into boom towns, existing patterns of class relationships became further convoluted. Old-timers and newcomers often resented each other, established residents blaming migrants for disrupting their peace and quiet and for straining sanitary, educational, and recreational facilities, and migrants, in turn, blaming those who were there first for treating them like lepers and for refusing to provide needed community services. In Seneca, Illinois, a shipbuilding center whose population jumped from 1,235 to 6,600, the mutual resentment resulted in the emergence of parallel social structures. Both old-timers and newcomers could be divided into four classes: "upper crust," "better class," "working class," and "bottom of the heap." But except occasionally among the very rich, the members of each group had nothing to do with one another. "Relations between the working-class people of Old Seneca and the newcomers were practically non-existent." Community institutions that might have linked older residents and migrants failed to do so. A shipyard worker's wife, who once attended an older church, recalled bitterly: "They didn't seem to want us either—didn't ask us back."[34]

Faced with what they regarded as a threat to a valued way of life, older residents, among whom class lines were in any case well established, "tended to forget their own social differences and to feel as though they all belonged together." But newcomers, among whom class lines were in the process of being sorted out, responded differently. They devised ingenious ways to clarify social distinctions that wartime exigencies had blurred. The town of Seneca again provides a useful example. Most shipyard employees, executives and workers alike, lived of necessity in government-built housing. All the homes were similar, all the rents were the same, and since space was assigned by the Federal Public Housing Administration on a first-come, first-served basis, rich and poor lived next door to each other. They did, that is, until executives, recognizing there was no way to have their peers for neighbors "except by informally allocating certain space to themselves and keeping others out," persuaded the housing authorities to reserve one block of homes for their use. It became known as Gold Coast Row.[35]

Wartime developments, therefore, did not confirm the prediction of one sociologist that "today's millionaires will suddenly become beggars; and today's beggars, millionaires."[36] Such dramatic reversals seldom occurred. Millionaires were more likely to remain millionaires, especially if they had access to good tax attorneys; beggars, figuratively speaking, were more likely to find jobs in shipyards, although not to live on Gold Coast Row. Partly as a result of government policies respecting taxation, wage and price control, and rationing, the war witnessed a more equitable distribution of national income and a greater opportunity for advancement. Yet the "bottom of the heap" still existed, if sharply reduced in size, and class distinctions did not disappear so much as undergo a change in form. In fact, Americans demonstrated great ingenuity in finding ways to preserve those distinctions in the midst of total war.

4.

Early in 1942, worried about the state of morale in the black community, the government polled Harlem residents: did they think they would be treated better, worse, or the same under "German rule" or "Japanese rule" in the event the United States was defeated? The answers revealed a much keener antagonism toward Germany than toward Japan. Only 1 percent of the respondents expected to be treated better, and 22 percent the same, under the Germans; by contrast, 63 percent expected to be treated worse. But 18 percent believed they would be treated better, and 31 percent the same, under the Japanese; just 28 percent replied they would be worse off, and many more expressed no opinion. The color of the interviewer's skin affected the frankness of the respondents, who admitted more readily to holding favorable attitudes toward Japan when questioned by blacks. However limited in scope, the poll pointed up two aspects of the war that deeply influenced race relations in America: it was being fought against one nation that preached a doctrine of racial supremacy and against another composed of colored people.

The central position racial doctrines occupied in Nazi ideology went far toward discrediting those doctrines in America. For decades anthropologists such as Franz Boas and Otto Klineberg had been challenging the idea that some races were superior to others, but it was only during the war that a popular consensus began to form around their views. A great many books, including Ruth Benedict's *Race: Science and Politics* (1940), Gunnar Dahlberg's *Race, Reason and Rubbish* (1942), and Ashley Montagu's *Man's Most Dangerous Myth: The Fallacy of Race* (1942), addressed primarily to a mass audience, taught similar lessons: all human beings had an enormous amount in common; "the important differences are not differences between 'racial' averages, but between individuals"; migration and intermarriage had rendered the notion of racial purity a fiction; supposedly racial traits were, in fact, subject to environmental influences. All emphasized the plasticity, not the permanence, of human nature. Americans, these scholars reasoned, could no longer afford the luxury of wrongheadedness on these matters. The rise of fascism "shows us today where we end up if we think that the shape of the nose or the color of the skin has anything to do with human values and culture."[37]

As racism lost its remaining shreds of intellectual respectability, blacks found it possible to strengthen their argument for equality by asserting that Jim Crow practices resembled Hitler's racial policies. It became commonplace to refer, as the *Amsterdam News* did, to "race discrimination and segregation, mob brutality—the entire Nazi pattern of U.S. racial conditions." By linking segregation with fascism, the black press found a rationale for its Double V campaign which called for a victory at home as well as abroad. One implication was clear enough: without the first, the second would be worthless. Another implication was less obvious but no less significant: whites would have to pay a price for black support of the war. A 1942 recording by blues singer Lonnie Johnson expressed this view with exceptional candor: "And you can tell the world that I'm fightin'/ For what really belongs to me."[38]

Under these circumstances whites who believed in segregation felt increasingly uncomfortable with the old justifications, although they rarely said so out loud. "The popular beliefs rationalizing caste in America," Gunnar Myrdal noted, "live a surreptitious life in thoughts and private remarks." As if to prove Myrdal right, though nothing could have been further from his mind, Frank Dixon, a former governor of Alabama, told a friend in 1944: "We are behind the times I admit. The Huns have wrecked the theories of the master race with which we were so contented so long." Dixon then attempted to parody the views of those who advocated racial equality: "Blood lines are out. The progeny of a cornfield ape blackened with the successive suns of Africa and Alabama, mated with a swamp gorilla from the Louisiana rice fields has development promise as great as the sons of the great American families. . . . Anthropology so teaches." Dixon declared he would remain unreconstructed so long as he knew that "the sons of Man-O'-War are going to win races against all comers."[39]

If Germany posed as the defender of Aryan supremacy, then Japan claimed to champion the colored peoples of Asia in their struggle against white imperialism. That claim did not lead American Negroes to sympathize with Japan, as the government feared, but it did cause many to respond to certain wartime developments less enthusiastically than whites. Blacks often condemned the discrimination practiced against Japanese Americans and their internment on the West Coast, always resented American propaganda which stressed Japanese racial traits, and sometimes derived vicarious satisfaction from Japanese triumphs in the Pacific insofar as they shattered the myth of white supremacy. Moreover, many blacks appear to have admired Japan's willingness to fight against overwhelming odds, a view expressed by one youth who "said he was going to get his eyes slanted so that the next time a white man shoved him around he could fight back." Negroes were less easily horrified by the atrocities attributed to Japanese soldiers. "I see where the papers are complaining 'cause some Jap slapped a white woman. Well, they been slappin' colored women all these years. Now, they gettin' it back."[40] To a considerable extent, race consciousness shaped perceptions of the war and was, in turn, reinforced by it.

The war not only led to heightened awareness and militancy on the part of blacks but also disrupted certain features of the American caste system. That system, in general, had provided for spatial separation, for finely calibrated distinctions in rank, and for substantial differentials in economic reward. By introducing two powerful solvents—migration and manpower shortages—the war upset the delicate patterns of behavior governing race relations. "I just don't know what to 'spect of white folks, or what they'se 'spectin' of me," a black man told an interviewer, "but I has to do something and so I just decides for myself. They can take it or leave it."[41] As his remark suggested, uncertainty fostered challenges to the existing system. Four focal points of conflict emerged: housing, transportation, jobs, and military service. Tensions in each area erupted at times in violent racial clashes.

Some 700,000 black people joined the wartime stream

of civilian migrants, but patterns of Negro and white migration differed substantially. Blacks began migrating later in the war, as resistance to their employment in national defense lessened; white migration reached a peak in 1943, black migration not until 1945. Once blacks began moving, however, they did so in proportionately greater numbers than whites and more often decided to settle permanently in their new locations. Those locations were almost always centers of war production—Chicago and Detroit in the North; Norfolk, Charleston, and Mobile in the South; and Los Angeles, San Francisco, and San Diego in the West. From 1940 to 1944, while the total population of the ten largest wartime production areas grew by 19 percent, the black population of those areas increased by 49 percent.

The influx of so many people into so few places aggravated interracial tensions. As the conflict over access to housing illustrated, those conflicts were most pronounced where settled lines of demarcation were being disturbed. In many northern cities, as Negro ghettos filled to the bursting point, intense pressures built up toward outward expansion. Frightened by the prospect of being engulfed by blacks, white homeowners in adjacent communities took matters into their own hands. Frequently their action went unrecorded, but efforts to prevent Negroes from living in federal housing projects received considerable publicity. In Buffalo, where many blacks were employed in Bethlehem Steel and Bell Aircraft plants, threats of violence induced the government to cancel plans for just such a project. In February 1942 a mob of whites armed with rocks and clubs prevented black families from moving into the federally built Sojourner Truth Homes in Detroit. Not until April did the Negro families move in, and then only under police escort.

In the South, too, migration and boom conditions

often subjected segregated facilities to severe strains. This was particularly true of city bus lines. Blacks were expected to allow whites to enter a bus ahead of them, were expected to seat themselves from the rear to the front, and were expected to give up their seats as additional white passengers boarded. This caused the least commotion when there were enough seats to go around and when several empty rows separated the races. But buses traveling to and from shipyards, factories, and defense plants were often packed to capacity. Under these circumstances Negroes were less willing, indeed physically less able, to observe the customs prescribed by Jim Crow. With passengers crammed together like sardines, the innocuous act of jockeying for a seat could acquire overtones of racial insubordination. Charleston finally resorted to posting signs on its buses: "If the peoples of the country's races do not pull together, Victory is lost. We, therefore, respectfully direct your attention to the laws and customs of the state in regard to segregation. . . . Avoid friction. Be patriotic. White passengers will be seated from front to rear; colored passengers from rear to front."[42]

Wartime labor shortages worked as profound a change in patterns of racial adjustment as did migration and created a similar potential for conflict. With defense plants eyeing manpower the way a starving person eyes food, much antiblack discrimination simply melted away. When there were no whites to be hired, employers gave up their long-standing reluctance to hire blacks. Unions which excluded Negroes found it more difficult to do so after the government, in 1943, announced that it would refuse to certify them as collective bargaining agents unless they accepted minorities. The War Labor Board provided further support that same year by outlawing wage differentials based exclusively on race. During the war 900,000 Negroes entered the labor force. Constituting only 3 percent of all defense workers in mid-1942, they made up more than 8 percent three years later. As they moved out of domestic service, away from farms, and off the relief rolls, blacks shifted primarily into unskilled, semiskilled, and, to a lesser extent, skilled blue-collar jobs. Whites continued to enjoy a virtual monopoly of managerial and white-collar positions.

The upgrading of Negro workers, their acquisition of union cards, and their opportunity to earn good wages created an angry backlash. White workers who feared the possible loss of their own seniority frequently protested against the upgrading of blacks. In a few instances such fears led workers simply to walk off the job for a few hours in anger. More vicious reactions occurred in Mobile, where white shipyard workers beat up black employees, and in Philadelphia, where a strike of trolley car workers crippled the city. Racial mingling inside crowded plants also served to aggravate sore spots. White employees at a munitions plant in Baltimore, for example, engaged in a work stoppage rather than share washrooms and cafeterias with blacks. The railroad brotherhoods attempted to protect their privileged position by adhering to a union contract that sharply restricted the jobs available to Negroes and their opportunities for promotion.

The government's response to the situation in Philadelphia, Mobile, and Baltimore and to the policies of the railroad brotherhoods illustrates how gingerly it approached sensitive racial problems. In Philadelphia, to be sure, the government acted firmly, dispatching federal troops which manned the trolleys and brought the strike to an end. This proved the exception rather than the rule, however, for more often a compromise was sought. In Mobile the Committee on Fair Employment Practices accepted an arrangement establishing segregated shipways on which Negroes might work as welders, riggers, and riveters (but not as electricians, machine operators, or pipe fitters). In Baltimore an obvious formula suggested itself. Anxious to allocate facilities "in a manner directed toward harmonious relationships of those involved," the FEPC allowed the company to build a larger cafeteria and washroom and assign blacks and whites space at opposite ends.[43] Where the government feared that action to promote equal opportunity might jeopardize war production it took no action. The railroad brotherhoods cavalierly defied an FEPC directive against discrimination, retaining their restrictive contract until the Supreme Court finally declared it unconstitutional in December 1944.

The armed forces were by no means immune to the pressures generating interracial conflict among civilians, even though generals and admirals preferred to think they were. In 1941 the military enforced an ironclad code of segregation calculated to please even the worst of bigots. Blacks could not enlist in the Marine or Air Corps. The Navy accepted them only in a menial capacity. The Army admitted Negroes but maintained segregated training facilities and units, used black troops primarily in a support rather than in a combat role, and assigned black officers to Negro units, where they served under white superior officers. No black officer could ever outrank a white officer in the same unit. This policy was rationalized on the grounds that blacks made poor fighting men, that the Army should not serve as a laboratory for social experimentation, and that integration would destroy the morale of white soldiers. The War Department asserted that it "cannot ignore the social relationships between Negroes and whites which have been established by the American people through custom and habit."[44]

Those customs and habits, however, eventually caused

more trouble than they were worth. As the number of black soldiers spiraled from 100,000 in 1941 to 700,000 in 1944 so did dissatisfaction with military segregation. Negro recruits came in disproportionately large numbers from the North because southern blacks, less well educated and in poorer health, were more likely to fail induction tests. As one black leader informed the President, "many of these young people have lived all of their lives in New York, Detroit, Philadelphia, Chicago and other metropolitan areas where their civil rights have never before been abridged."[45] Even the top brass came to recognize that existing policies led to duplication of effort, meant a shameful waste of manpower, exposed the military to criticism, and depressed the morale of what was now a sizable segment of the Army's forces. As the war progressed, therefore, the Army provided blacks with a greater role in combat, and the Navy instituted a program of gradual integration. But the Army remained segregated, and the resulting agitation disturbed many people, including General George C. Marshall. 'My God! My God! . . . I don't know what to do about this race question in the army," the Army Chief of Staff told one reporter. "I tell you frankly, it is the worst thing we have to deal with. . . . We are getting a situation on our hands that may explode right in our faces."[46]

The explosions when they came were brief but terrible. The race riots that pockmarked the war years involved both soldiers and civilians. Clashes occurred at army bases in eight states, sometimes ending in fistfights and sometimes leading to pitched battles between men armed with guns. Rioting also flared up in cities, most seriously in Detroit, where, in June 1943, 34 people were killed, and more than 1,000 injured. Whether at military camps or in cities, these were race riots in the most literal sense. Bands of blacks and whites set out to kill or injure one another and frequently succeeded. The riots, moreover, exhibited a common pattern. Sparked usually by rumors of an interracial assault (rumors that often proved groundless), the riots, once having been ignited, were further fueled by black resentment at unjust treatment and white resistance to the loss of traditional prerogatives. In this they tragically reflected the abrasive impact of ideological, demographic, and economic change in wartime.

In the wake of the Detroit riot Attorney General Francis Biddle, pondering ways to prevent further bloodshed, proposed that the government prohibit black migration to certain cities. "No more Negroes should move to Detroit," he advised.[47] Almost before the words had left his mouth, Biddle, like everyone else, realized that such a solution was no solution at all. Yet Biddle had correctly identified one of the chief sources of conflict. The very forces that brought about an improvement in the Negro's position—particularly geographical and occupational mobility—also led to an escalation of racial tension. From the black perspective the lowering of some barriers made those remaining seem more intolerable. To many whites, however, the remaining barriers seemed even more desirable than before. The war, consequently, affected race differently from ethnicity and class. Where ethnic distinctions were muted and class lines blurred, racial differences were exacerbated.

5.

The contrasting implications of the war for race and ethnicity were nowhere more clearly revealed than in the case of a group that fitted both categories: the Japanese Americans. Of the 127,000 people of Japanese ancestry in the United States, better than 9 in 10 lived on the West Coast, 93,717 in California alone. Their status was uniquely precarious among immigrant groups. The Issei, foreign-born Japanese who had migrated before the exclusion act of 1924, numbered 47,000. Ineligible for American citizenship, they were automatically classified as enemy aliens when the war broke out. Their children, the Nisei, numbering 80,000, were citizens by virtue of their birth in the United States; their median age, however, was only nineteen. In the spring of 1942 all Japanese Americans on the West Coast, aliens and citizens alike, were herded into relocation centers, where most of them remained for the duration of the war. Before that could happen, the government had to be prepared to identify them not primarily as aliens of enemy nationality but rather as members of an enemy race.

In January and February 1942 pressures mounted on the Roosevelt administration to evacuate all Japanese Americans from the coast. That pressure had many sources: labor unions, small businessmen's groups, and agricultural interests, all of which stood to benefit from the elimination of competitors; racists who thought the Japanese had constituted a "yellow peril" long before the attack on Pearl Harbor; sincere but misinformed people who believed that Japanese Americans were potential saboteurs; and politicians who knew they had everything to gain and nothing to lose by taking a popular position against an unpopular group. The commander on the West Coast, General John DeWitt, his aides, and his superiors in the War Department not only responded to those pressures but ultimately provided a military rationale for evacuation. For several weeks, however, the government treated the Japanese as it did Germans and Italians. All enemy aliens were subjected to certain travel and work restrictions, those few whom the government believed potentially disloyal because of their political activities were arrested, and citizens were left alone. Defending this approach, DeWitt said he opposed "any preferential treatment to any alien irrespective of race."[48]

This policy, emphasizing ethnicity instead of race, provided two effective obstacles to evacuation. First, it prevented the taking of any action against Japanese aliens not also taken against German and Italian aliens. Yet evacuation of the latter groups was unthinkable in view of their size, high measure of assimilation, and political clout. Second, it prevented the taking of any action against the Nisei not also taken against other citizens. Yet the Nisei, it was commonly thought, represented a greater menace than the more elderly Issei, and in any event parents could not very well be moved out while their children stayed behind. These problems and their solution, not to mention the far-ranging implications of that solution, were recognized with frightening clarity by Secretary of War Henry L. Stimson. On February 3 he wrote in his diary that "we cannot discriminate among our citizens on the ground of racial origin." By February 10, however, Stimson concluded that it would be necessary to state publicly what everyone was thinking privately: that the "racial characteristics" of the Nisei rendered them suspect. That "is the fact but I am afraid it will make a tremendous hole in our constitutional system to apply it."[49]

Digging the hole took only a few weeks. By the end of February 1942 the government had resolved to treat Japanese American aliens differently from others and to treat Japanese American citizens as if the Bill of Rights had been repealed. To justify these decisions, the War Department asserted that racial ties predisposed the Japanese to behave disloyally and that the absence of overt acts of sabotage proved only that an "invisible deadline" was approaching. Major Karl R. Bendetsen, head of the Aliens Division of the Provost Marshal

General's office, put the matter this way. What would happen, he asked a San Francisco audience in May 1942, if white people like themselves were to settle in Japan and suddenly find their adopted land at war with the United States? Perhaps they would not actually commit espionage, but the acid test would come when fair-skinned American soldiers launched an invasion against Japan. Bendetsen thought it "extremely doubtful whether we could withstand the ties of race and affinity for the land of our forbears, and stand with the Japanese against United States forces." Why assume that Japanese Americans could any more successfully resist atavistic racial impulses? General DeWitt himself did a sharp about-face, claiming that even second- and third-generation Japanese, those who to all outward appearances seemed fully Americanized, posed a threat because "the racial strains are undiluted" and "racial affinities are not severed by migration."[50]

In emphasizing so-called racial traits, Americans found it expedient to differentiate between people of Japanese and Chinese descent. China, as a wartime ally, rose in public estimation, and sympathy for that nation reached a peak early in 1943, when Madame Chiang Kai-shek visited the United States. Invited to speak to Congress, she received a thunderous ovation, and according to *Time,* "tough guys melted." A newly formed Citizens Committee to Repeal Chinese Exclusion launched a highly successful public relations drive. In the fall of 1943, responding to President Roosevelt's argument that repeal would "silence the distorted Japanese propaganda" and speed victory, Congress ditched the sixty-one-year old Chinese Exclusion Act and granted Chinese immigrants the right to become naturalized citizens. Even so, Congress did not wholly repudiate the racist assumptions upon which the old policy rested. It established an annual quota of 105 for all "persons of the Chinese race" no matter where they were born, so that Chinese born, for example, in Hong Kong, would not fall within the British quota. Nor were the Chinese wives and children of American citizens permitted to enter the United States, although relatives of other immigrants could do so on a nonquota basis. In extending new rights to Chinese Americans, as in denying old rights to Japanese Americans, racial formulas were applied.[51]

Although rationalized on racial grounds, the policy of evacuation had critical implications for Japanese Americans as an ethnic group. The people whom the War Relocation Authority hastily transported to relocation centers were themselves torn by generational conflicts. Those conflicts, common to most immigrant groups, had taken a particularly bitter form among Japanese Americans. Because many had waited until rather late in life before rearing families, the age differential between parents and children was unusually large, and the middle-aged group abnormally small. The older Issei, many of whom adhered to traditional Japanese patterns of culture, stressed filial piety, respect for authority, and the importance of group values. Their children, the Nisei, were for the most part in the process of adopting the values of individualism and self-assertion they associated with America. One Nisei described her friends who, even while being interned against their will, "speak English, sling American slang, jitterbug according to the most streamlined 1942 tradition" and "prefer to sing 'Deep in the Heart of Texas' to some minor-keyed Japanese folk song."[52] The more they were treated as pariahs, the more avidly some Nisei proclaimed their American identity.

Conditions in the relocation centers could hardly have been better calculated to worsen these tensions. Housed in sparsely furnished one-room barracks, fed in central mess halls, and offered menial work no matter how highly skilled or educated they were, older people found their status and authority smashed. The camps had a limited system of self-government, more to give the appearance of democratic rule than to provide its substance, but it further upset generational equilibrium. Only Japanese American citizens were at first permitted to hold elective office, with the result that young men, primarily those in their early twenties, occupied the few positions of official authority. Older people, deprived of their traditional roles in the household and the community, were, according to one Japanese American observer, overwhelmed by a "sense of futility." Worst of all, the internees were divided in their response to what the government had done to them. A substantial number of Nisei, many of them members of the Japanese-American Citizens League, believed that by cooperating with the authorities, by "not questioning the legality or sagacity of the steps which have been taken," they would at last be able to prove their loyalty and ensure their eventual acceptance.[53] The resulting clashes with those who despised the relocation policy and all it meant sometimes led to violence.

Unlike other immigrants, many of whom became naturalized citizens during the war, Japanese Americans sometimes renounced their American citizenship. This happened largely as a result of the government's mishandling of a loyalty questionnaire in 1943. Conceived originally as a test that would enable Nisei men of draft age to qualify for enlistment in the armed forces, the questionnaire was distributed to all adults in the relocation centers. Men and women, Nisei and Issei, were asked to swear "unqualified allegiance" to the United States and forswear any obedience to the Japanese emperor. Of some 75,000 adults responding, more than 65,000 answered yes to the crucial questions. The others, who either said no or somehow qualified their answers, were by no means disloyal. Some feared the government might move them from the relative security of the centers if they answered affirmatively; others responded negatively in protest against the relocation policy itself. The government, ignoring the range of motivation, used "no" answers as a basis for segregating "disloyal" evacuees in certain camps. In 1944 Congress passed a Denationalization Act which made it easier for the Nisei to renounce American citizenship. Ultimately 5,766 of them did so.

The Supreme Court, in passing on the constitutionality of government policy toward the Japanese Americans, viewed the cases through an ethnic rather than a racial lens with a consequent blurring of vision. In June 1943, in *Hirabayashi* v. *United States,* a unanimous Court decided that a curfew order affecting only Japanese Americans did not violate their constitutional rights. Chief Justice Harlan Fiske Stone, who in conference admitted that "it is jarring to me that U.S. citizens were subjected to this treatment," declared: "In time of war residents having ethnic affiliations with an invading enemy may be a greater source of danger than those of a different ancestry." In December 1944, in *Korematsu* v. *United States,* a divided Court sanctioned the order providing for the exclusion of Japanese Americans from the West Coast, although not their continued detention in the absence of evidence of disloyalty. Justice Hugo Black justified the decision by asserting that "Korematsu was not excluded from the Military Area because of hostility to him or his race."[54]

Never was Justice Black more clearly in error. The Court's pronouncement, as Justice Frank Murphy's dissent noted, amounted to a "legalization of racism."[55] Even as early as 1942 one government official had argued against making a film about relocation on the grounds that Axis propagandists would exploit it for their own purposes. "Doesn't it give a sort of justification to the German claim that the Jews are an alien race and therefore should be kept in concentration camps?" he asked.[56] But those who realized that the treatment of Japanese Americans was compatible with fascist doctrine were, like those who realized that Jim Crow laws were consistent with Hitler's Nuremberg Decrees, neither numerous nor influential enough to reverse government policy. In years that saw an extraordinary emphasis on the value of national unity and, to a remarkable degree, the achievement of that unity, race remained the source of deepest division in American life.

[3]

The Cold War

World War II and the Cold War present a study in contrasts. The conflict with the Axis began and ended on dates fixed forever in people's minds; the total mobilization affected people in highly visible ways; everyone knew why the war was being fought and that victory would occur only when the enemy surrendered. The conflict with the Soviet Union lacked this stark simplicity. No one could say for sure exactly when it began, although eventually no one could doubt that it had; partial mobilization affected most people in rather undramatic ways; few understood why the Cold War was being fought, and even fewer knew how victory was supposed to be gauged. If World War II produced national self-confidence, the Cold War led to profound insecurity. That insecurity, expressed in the related fears of communism and conspiracy, swept like a tidal wave over the nation in the late 1940s and early 1950s. It shaped perceptions of social class, influenced approaches to civil rights, and determined government policies toward those who had emigrated to the United States as well as toward those who wanted to do so.

1.

The ambiguity of the Cold War may have contributed to an overly simplified interpretation of its origins. It was perhaps logical that having just concluded a successful war against fascism, Americans would perceive the struggle with communism in similar terms. This helps explain the popularity of the image of "red fascism," an image that, while it obscured as much as it explained, was plausible enough to command widespread acceptance. The Soviet Union, in this view, was a replica of Nazi Germany, and Joseph Stalin was, by analogy, the "Russian Hitler." Russia, like Germany, employed secret police, slave labor camps, purges, and insidious techniques of thought control to regiment its citizens. Communism, like fascism, sought to subvert the liberties of free peoples. The internal dynamics of a totalitarian state drove Russia, no less than they had Germany, to seek worldwide domination through military aggression. Consequently, the American and the Soviet systems were set on a collision course, for, in the words of one group of high-ranking government advisers, "there is a basic conflict between the idea of freedom under a government of laws, and the idea of slavery under the grim oligarchy of the Kremlin."[1]

The fear of communism, while often carried to irrational lengths, did not entirely lack a rational foundation. There were, in fact, well-documented instances of attempted Soviet espionage, as a Canadian investigation made abundantly clear in June 1946, even if a great many more poorly documented cases received widespread publicity. Similarly, there were undoubted examples of Soviet aggression, such as the coup d'état engineered by the communists in Czechoslovakia in March 1948, although other Russian moves which Americans construed as equally threatening were taken in response to Western actions. Politicians of both parties contributed substantially to the spread of anticommunist sentiment. In this, as in so many things, motives ranged across a broad spectrum. Some politicians genuinely considered communism a grave menace, while others, recognizing a good thing when they saw it, cynically manipulated public hysteria for their own political purposes.

By 1947 and 1948 officials in the Truman administration found themselves in an ambivalent position. They were, on the one hand, quite prepared to exploit the fear of communism as a means of gaining support for their policies. Yet they were, on the other, anxious to allay that fear as a means of proving to the public that they had matters well in hand. Perhaps nothing better demonstrated the strength of the anticommunist impulse than the consequences of this dual approach: the policies designed to reassure the public did as much to frighten it as the policies expressly fashioned for that purpose. Five steps taken by the administration in these years illustrate the point: the formulation of the Truman Doctrine, the publication of documents relating to the Nazi-Soviet Pact, the attack on Henry Wallace's third-party candidacy, the institution of a federal loyalty program, and the indictment of Communist party leaders. All contributed in some measure to refining the popular image of red fascism.

In March 1947 President Truman, asserting that Greece and Turkey were in imminent danger of falling to communism, called on Congress to provide $400 million in military and economic assistance. The President believed the crisis to be real enough, but he also believed it necessary to magnify its dimensions—or, in Senator Arthur Vandenberg's phrase, to "scare the hell out of the country"—in order to win public and legislative backing for the aid program. The Truman Doctrine, as the policy came to be called, defined the conflict between the United States and the Soviet Union as one between a political system based on majority will and "free institutions, representative government, free elections, guarantees of individual liberty, freedom of speech and religion, and freedom from political oppression" and a rival system founded on minority will and "terror and oppression, a controlled press and radio, fixed elections, and the suppression of personal freedom."[2] Congress responded within two months by granting Truman's request. More important, the President's rhetoric, by posing the conflict with Russia in the starkest possible terms, went far toward sharpening that conflict.

The Nazi-Soviet alliance of 1939 to 1941 offered the most persuasive historical evidence for those who wished to demonstrate the connection between modern forms of totalitarianism, whether of the left or the right. At the end of World War II the United States, Britain, and France had agreed to publish documents from captured German archives describing Hitler's foreign policy. Each nation reserved the right to publish any portion of those documents separately, and in January 1948 the State Department released a 357-page volume relating to the Nazi-Soviet Pact, its implementation, and its eventual dissolution. Presenting matters solely from the German perspective, the letters, telegrams, and memoranda painted Stalin as the most cold-blooded of rulers. One document reported Stalin's toast when the pact was signed: "I know how much the German nation loves its Führer; I should therefore like to drink to his health." Another had Stalin objecting to the German wording of a joint communiqué justifying the coordinated invasion of Poland on the damning grounds that "it presented the facts all too frankly." If seeking to discredit Stalin in this fashion constituted Cold War propaganda, *Time* explained, it was nevertheless "propaganda with the virtue of sober truth."[3]

Henry Wallace's Progressive party candidacy in 1948 provided yet a third instance in which the Truman administration exploited anticommunist sentiment. Wallace had left the Cabinet in September 1946 and agreed to head a third party in December 1947 largely because he disagreed with the underlying assumptions of American foreign policy. Wallace saw in Russia's domination of Eastern Europe evidence of a desire for security rather than proof of aggressive intent. He told Truman that "the Russian attitude in the Balkan States was not so greatly different from our attitude with regard to Mexico and Cuba."[4] Nor did Wallace expect Stalin to endorse America's plan for international control of atomic energy, since it required Russia to stop scientific exploration before the United States would destroy its nuclear stockpile. The Marshall Plan, widely viewed as a means of providing economic assistance to war-torn nations, was, to Wallace's mind, a device of the "militarists and bankers" to convert Western Europe into a "vast military camp." At a time when Americans were moving closer every day to an interpretation of world affairs in which their nation represented all that was good and Russia all that was bad, Wallace accused Truman of "whipping up another holy war against Russia."[5]

Given the nature of his dissent from the emerging Cold War orthodoxy, it is not surprising that the Truman administration considered Wallace a communist stooge and that it believed voters should be warned that he was. One of Truman's aides outlined the administration's strategy late in 1947. "The men around Wallace are motivated by the Communist Party line," noted Clark Clifford. Democrats should attempt "to identify him and isolate him in the public mind with the Communists." Truman on several occasions during the campaign did just that, referring to "Henry Wallace and his Communists" and affirming that "Communists are using and guiding the third party."[6] Dwight Macdonald's biography of Wallace, written from a left-liberal perspective, utilized the construct of red fascism scathingly: if communism was analogous to fascism, and Stalin to Hitler, then Wallace, as an apologist for Russia, was the equivalent of "the old pro-Nazi isolationists" and, like them, unmoved by "the Nazi (or Soviet) horrors." "It is not true that Henry Wallace is an agent of Moscow," Macdonald concluded, "but it is true that he behaves like one."[7]

Opening the valve of anticommunist hysteria was a good deal simpler than closing it. When the Truman administration attempted to soothe public fears by taking action against suspected subversives, it succeeded only in worsening those fears. To justify a harsh domestic policy, the administration had to claim that a subversive threat existed and, more often than not, to exaggerate its seriousness. This is precisely what happened in the case of the federal loyalty program. Introduced in March 1947 with the purpose of refuting Republican allegations that the federal government, after more than a decade of Democratic control, had become a beehive of subversion, the program required every employee and applicant for a federal job, regardless of the sensitivity of the position, to undergo a check to determine whether "reasonable grounds exist for belief that the person involved is disloyal." The program, however, proved anything but reassuring. That it was even necessary seemed to corroborate charges that disloyal behavior had taken place. The administration found itself in the paradoxical position of denying that government employees had behaved disloyally, yet promising they would not be permitted to do so again.

This dilemma was to worsen over the next few years. As is the case with any government program, the loyalty program was judged by results, and they were meager indeed. Nearly 5 million investigations led to the dismissal of a few hundred employees, not for treason, espionage, or even advocacy of violent revolution but rather for "membership in, affiliation with, or sympathetic association with" organizations branded subversive by the Attorney General, memberships and associations, one should add, that often went back many years. Partly because of bureaucratic momentum and partly because of the administration's desire to outflank its Republican critics, the loyalty program underwent a steady process of escalation. The Loyalty Review Board, designed at first to hear appeals from employees who believed themselves wrongly treated, eventually asserted a right to review any case, even one in which an employee had been cleared. The program was amended so that it was no longer necessary to discover reasonable grounds for believing a person disloyal but only to find "whether there is a reasonable doubt as to the loyalty of the person involved," a crucial shift that placed the burden for establishing innocence on the employee. But the harsher the program and the more narrowly it construed the employee's rights, the more it seemed that so much smoke must surely suggest the presence of some sort of fire.

In the case of the Communist party, the Truman administration behaved as if it were responding to a three-alarm blaze. In July 1948, after harassing the party for more than a year in small ways, the Department of Justice persuaded a grand jury to indict the twelve members of its Central Committee. They were charged with violating the Smith Act of 1940, which made it a crime to conspire to teach or advocate the overthrow of the government by force. At the trial, which began in January 1949, the government introduced as evidence books by Marx, Engels, Lenin, and Stalin which called for revolution. The prosecution claimed that the defendants had conspired in 1945 to reorganize the Communist party (which had temporarily been restructured during World War II as the

Communist Political Association) in order to teach those doctrines. What of the many assertions by American communists to the effect that a peaceful and gradual transition to communism would be possible in the United States? Those assertions, answered government witnesses, merely demonstrated the party's use of "Aesopian" language. Words which seemed perfectly innocent to the average person had, in this interpretation, an utterly different and quite sinister meaning for party members.

The government's claim that the communist leaders were revolutionaries who only pretended to be reformers placed the defendants in what, for followers of Marx and Lenin, was the unenviable position of contending that they were reformers who only seemed to be revolutionaries. "We did *not* advocate the violent overthrow of the United States Government as a solution to the present critical problems," General Secretary Eugene Dennis asserted.[8] The party made a desultory attempt to extract some political advantage from the situation, asserting that the trial was being conducted in a kangaroo court, denouncing Judge Harold R. Medina as an inquisitor, and claiming that the jury system excluded poor people and blacks as a matter of policy. With the dice so heavily loaded against them, they concluded, their only chance for acquittal lay in winning over the American people, a task which, in the prevailing atmosphere, would undoubtedly have defeated Hercules. In October 1949 the jury found the defendants guilty. Most received five-year prison sentences and heavy fines. The Supreme Court affirmed the convictions and the constitutionality of the Smith Act in 1951.

During the course of the trial the government produced as witnesses several FBI agents who had infiltrated the party and who testified that communist leaders had indeed taught revolutionary doctrines.

Angela Calomiris and Herbert Philbrick, both of whom had joined the party at the FBI's request in the early 1940s, had remained members until they shed their covers at the trial. Louis Budenz, a former editor of the *Daily Worker* who had broken with the party in 1945 after ten years, also turned state's evidence. At the same time the House Committee on Un-American Activities, which was conducting its own investigations, brought forth two witnesses who told even more spectacular stories. In July 1948 Elizabeth Bentley reported she had committed espionage during the war by transmitting government documents to Soviet couriers. Then, in August 1948, Whittaker Chambers appeared before the House committee. Claiming to have been a communist until 1938, he went on to name Alger Hiss, a former State Department official and then president of the Carnegie Endowment for International Peace, as a fellow communist during the 1930s. After Hiss sued for defamation of character, Chambers accused him of having handed over classified State Department documents, copies of which Chambers claimed to have saved. When he denied these allegations, Hiss was tried for perjury and, after the first trial resulted in a hung jury, was convicted in January 1950.

The public's perception of the Communist party was shaped, in large measure, by the testimony of these ex-communists and federal agents. All of them published memoirs—Budenz, *This Is My Story* (1947), Calomiris, *Red Masquerade* (1950), Bentley, *Out of Bondage* (1951), Chambers, *Witness* (1952), and Philbrick, *I Led 3 Lives* (1952)—several of which were serialized in popular magazines or made into films and television shows. All presented a roughly similar picture. Communists either committed, or were prepared to commit, espionage. They preached the violent overthrow of the government so vehemently that Philbrick, busily jotting things down for his regular FBI report, said, "I almost dropped my pencil and forgot to take my notes." Communists submitted to a discipline so severe that, according to Budenz, "it cannot be conveyed to a normal American mind."[9] Deceit, dishonesty, and intrigue characterized relations between party members. In a world of aliases, identities were constantly in doubt. "Who is John?" Calomiris asked a comrade. "Martha looked up briefly from the list. 'Don't you know? John is Peter.' " Communists fostered immorality when it suited their purposes. According to Bentley, women "often had to perform unpleasant tasks and had to do a lot of drinking and sleep with many men."[10] Fear was the emotion that held party members in line. It often prevented them from leaving, and Chambers, for a year after he did, "lived in hiding, sleeping by day and watching through the night with gun or revolver within easy reach."[11]

Before long, Hollywood films began to reinforce this image of a communist conspiracy. Cold War films were produced partly as a response to a 1947 investigation of the motion-picture industry by the House Committee on Un-American Activities. That investigation led the studios to state that they would "not knowingly employ a Communist" and to blacklist actors, writers, and producers who refused to cooperate with congressional investigations. In trying to convince skeptical congressmen that Beverly Hills was not a hotbed of radicalism, studio executives found that their most effective defense was not to deny that procommunist propaganda had turned up in films—how, after all, could such denials be convincing when a line such as "share and share alike—that's democracy" was taken by some as unadulterated Marxism?—but rather to talk up earlier films, such as *Ninotchka,* which satirized the Soviet Union.[12] After 1947, satire gave way to humorless condemnation in dozens of anticommunist films, including *The Iron Curtain* (1948), *The Red Menace* (1949), *I Was a Communist for the FBI* (1951), and *My Son John* (1952). Given Hollywood's litmuslike ability to register the popular mood even while helping to define it, such films would undoubtedly have appeared, if not so quickly and in such profusion, even without HUAC to help them along.

"The Cold War movies," one scholar has written, "generally depicted the Communists as faceless intruders seeking to undermine American society."[13] But films further elaborated what was becoming a familiar image. Movies often suggested that communism was most likely to attract intellectuals. In *My Son John*—the story of one of three sons who went astray, joined the Communist party, mocked conventional moral standards, and eventually repented, only to be murdered by his former comrades—a doting mother, unable at first to recognize what her son has become, says proudly, "He has more degrees than a thermometer." Any doubts that John has indeed embraced a pernicious doctrine are removed when, encountering the parish priest collecting for charity, he sneers, "We take care of you in this world, father, and you *promise* to take care of us in the next." An interesting role exchange also occurs: The FBI agent performs the functions usually associated with a priest, advising troubled souls, hearing confession, and granting absolution to the truly contrite. In the Hollywood version, moreover, the communist underground merges with the criminal underworld. The two become indistinguishable as communists, like gangsters, speed about in shiny, black limousines and rub out stool pigeons with tommy guns.

The response to George Orwell's *1984*, published in 1949, demonstrated how receptive the public had become to the image of red fascism. In Orwell's antiutopia the state exterminates honest instincts and emotions, tortures people physically and assaults them psychologically and rewrites history to suit its own purposes. One spokesman boasts: "In our world there will be no emotions except fear, rage, triumph, and self-abasement. Everything else we shall destroy—everything." As language is corrupted by "Newspeak," words lose their meaning. "The word *free* still existed in Newspeak, but it could only be used in such statements as 'This dog is free from lice.' . . . It could not be used in its old sense of 'politically free' or 'intellectually free' since political and intellectual freedom no longer existed even as concepts, and were therefore of necessity nameless." Although Orwell set his story in London and intended to satirize the totalitarian tendencies in all modern, technological societies, most readers assumed that *1984* accurately depicted many aspects of life in communist Russia. *Life* believed that the dictatorial ruler Big Brother, whom Orwell described as "black-haired, black-mustachio'd, full of power and mysterious calm," represented a "mating" of Hitler and Stalin. According to the *Saturday Review of Literature,* the work was "the most convincing indictment of the Russian Government that any novelist has given us to date."[14]

In the face of two climactic events in the fall of 1949—the Russian acquisition of the atomic bomb and the communist victory in China—the Truman administration once again followed a dual policy of trying to reassure the public even while responding to developments in a manner that could not fail to frighten it. In the case of the Soviet test, the administration calmly noted that the ability of Russian scientists to duplicate the Americans' feat had always been taken for granted, that American strategy had been planned accordingly, and, therefore, that not all that much had changed. Yet within a matter of months Truman, explaining that it was his responsibility to "see to it that our country is able to defend itself against any possible aggressor," announced his decision to proceed with the construction of a "hydrogen or super-bomb."[15] Recognizing that at least one type of fallout from the Soviet explosion might be political, Republicans charged that "laxity in safeguarding against Communist espionage has permitted what was once the secret of the atomic bomb to fall into the hands of America's only potential enemy."[16]

Much the same pattern emerged in the American response to the fall of Chiang Kai-shek's Nationalist government in China. More than a month before Mao Tse-tung proclaimed the People's Republic of China on October 1, 1949, the State Department had issued a White Paper defending American policy. A document of more than 1,000 pages, it argued that the United States had done more than could reasonably have been expected to prevent a communist victory, had done nothing to assist it, and could no longer do anything to stop it. Yet in releasing the report, Secretary of State Dean Acheson asserted that the outcome in China was, in truth, a victory for Stalin rather than for Mao because the Chinese communists had "publicly announced their subservience to a foreign power, Russia." Conceding that China had historically resisted outside control, Acheson concluded that in this instance "the foreign domination has been masked behind the facade of a vast crusading movement which apparently has seemed to many Chinese to be wholly indigenous and national."[17] The administration was nevertheless subjected to a fusillade of criticism for "losing" China. Attributing the outcome to "a handful of Communists, fellow-travellers and misguided liberals" in the State Department, Republicans claimed that the White Paper as an alibi was anything but airtight.[18]

In March 1950, even as his policies came under sharp partisan attack, Truman converted the images associated with red fascism into something approaching an actual doctrine. "There isn't any difference between the totalitarian Russian government and the Hitler government," he declared. "They're all alike. They are police governments—police state governments."[19] A month later a report of the National Security Council placed that doctrine squarely at the heart of American policy making. Writing as if they had just put down Orwell's *1984,* the authors of NSC-68 claimed that the Soviet Union sought the "total subjective submission" of those it ruled. "The concentration camp is the prototype of the society which these policies are designed to achieve, a society in which the personality of the individual is so broken and perverted that he participates affirmatively in his own degradation." Utterly unscrupulous and immoral, driven by a fanatical faith, Russia aimed "to impose its absolute authority over the rest of the world." This it could do only by eliminating the United States, "the principal enemy whose integrity and vitality must be subverted or destroyed . . . if the Kremlin is to achieve its fundamental design."[20]

This outlook conditioned the American response to the outbreak of the war in Korea on June 25, 1950. Informed that North Korean troops had crossed the thirty-eighth parallel and invaded South Korea, the administration automatically assumed that the attack was unprovoked, that the North Koreans were acting as Soviet puppets, and that the Russians, in turn, were embarking on their march to world conquest. Only the first of those assumptions appears to have been justified, for North Korea may have acted on its own, and Stalin, if indeed he was responsible, may have wanted to demonstrate to Mao Tse-tung that Russia would continue to have a dominant voice in Asian affairs. But on June 26

Truman told one aide that "there's no telling what they'll do, if we don't put up a fight now," and on the following day he informed congressional leaders that "this act was very obviously inspired by the Soviet Union." The President privately justified American intervention by saying, "If we let Korea down, the Soviets will keep right on going and swallow up one piece of Asia after another. We had to make a stand some time, or else let all of Asia go by the board. If we were to let Asia go, the Near East would collapse and no telling what would happen in Europe."[21]

The Korean War aggravated all the anxieties associated with the Cold War, not so much because Truman intervened, a decision that met with wide acclaim, but rather because he conducted the war on a limited basis even while seeking—in North Korea's capitulation—an unlimited victory. In September 1950, having driven the North Korean troops back across the thirty-eighth parallel, the goal it had originally set, the administration decided to allow General Douglas MacArthur to push northward, hoping thereby to defeat North Korea and make possible the reunification of Korea under pro-American auspices. As MacArthur's forces moved toward North Korea's Yalu River boundary with China, evidence that Chinese troops were preparing to counterattack reached Washington. But no one in the administration had the gumption to order a retreat, and when the counterattack came in November, American troops suffered a terrible defeat. Predictably, MacArthur demanded that Truman fight an all-out war by bombing industrial and military targets in China and blockading that nation. Truman, just as predictably, relieved MacArthur of his command in April 1951. The war dragged on for two more years, with casualties mounting on both sides and with Americans, taught to regard war as a contest between good and evil, wondering why the United States was holding back. As the Cold War escalated into a limited hot war in Korea, the anticommunist impulse escalated along with it.

2.

The anticommunist consensus had wide-ranging implications for the way Americans approached problems associated with class distinctions and racial inequality. Those were just the kinds of problems, it was widely believed, that communists sought to exploit, not in order to right genuine social wrongs but to excite hatred and suspicion. "We will set labor against management," said a fictional communist leader in a radio drama of 1946. "We will join in the battles of minorities against injustice, social and economic. But these minorities need not win their battles; they should *remain* embittered. In that way they will serve us."[22] Yet it was only a short step from insisting that communists did not want to improve conditions to denying that conditions needed much betterment. The Cold War produced a constant tension between a desire to affirm the fundamental soundness of American institutions and a recognition that those institutions, particularly as they affected blacks, were in many respects defective. More often than not, the tension was resolved to the deteriment of reform.

Sociological studies in the 1930s had seemed to confirm the existence of well-defined classes in America, but during the Cold War era scholars began increasingly to challenge the findings of earlier studies and to question their continued applicability. Some writers found a tendency for classes to converge in the middle and for the extremes to drop away. A study conducted in New England in 1946 suggested that only three classes—upper-middle, white-collar, and working—included nearly everyone in the community. Moreover, sociologists noted, Americans demonstrated little, if any, sense of class consciousness. At every level, an article in the *American Sociological Review* in 1952 reported, people "appear to be behaving non-militantly and non-violently within a framework of capitalism."[23] Other writers doubted that classes even existed, pointing out that knowledgeable residents of small towns, if not coached by interviewers set on proving a point, could not agree on how many classes existed, what set them apart, or who belonged to them. Distinctions in status and prestige, these critics said, surely did exist, but these distinctions did not imply that the exercise of political and economic power was related to class position. By the 1950s many had concluded that in the United States "there are no clearly marked social classes."[24]

The views expressed by W. Lloyd Warner, whose own work, along with that of his students, had done much to document the reality of an American class structure, are particularly instructive. In *Social Class in America* (1949) Warner and several associates recapitulated the evidence they had uncovered over more than a decade of research, but their emphasis now was considerably changed. To Warner, the existence of classes was as significant for what it did not mean as for what it did. It did "not necessarily mean class conflict," for relations between the rich and the poor "can be and often are amiable and peaceful." It did not mean that any alternative was possible, for all modern, technologically complex societies, the Russian no less than the American, required some system of rank orders to get essential tasks done. Above all, it did not mean that people were indelibly fixed at a certain level, for the American class system permitted everyone to move up the social scale. Who did Warner expect would benefit from reading his book? Not a radical intent on discovering the inequities of American capitalism, but rather advertisers who had to sell products which were themselves "powerful symbols of status and social class" or executives who, in hiring other executives, needed to know what a person's "experiences in our status order have done to his individuality and character structure."[25]

In September 1949 *Life* devoted a lengthy article to Warner's book which further clarified the way sensitive issues of social class were treated in the Cold War period. The article emphasized the likelihood of upward mobility. Warner was quoted as saying, "The saving grace of the American social system is that our social positions are not fixed artificially, as they are in the so-called 'classless' society of Russia." *Life* was even less guarded in its enthusiasm: "The phenomenon of social 'mobility'—the opportunity to move rapidly upward through the levels of society—is the distinguishing characteristic of U.S. democracy and the thing for which it is famous and envied throughout the world." To drive the point home, the magazine chose as its lower-lower-class representative Sam, a semiskilled worker, whose family lived in a trailer, shared a communal shower, and cooked on a hot plate. "But he has dreams. He is excited about an air-conditioning training program in Chicago which he may join." Should things work out, "Sam will have begun the slow but feasible climb upward." American society, in truth, was "like a ladder," but a wonderful ladder on which those who went up seldom came down.[26]

This interpretation of social class fitted in nicely with the pluralist model of American society, a model that, if not entirely new, surely achieved its widest acceptance in these years. Pluralist theory held that the United States, marked by fluidity, diversity, and freedom, stood at opposite poles from the Marxist description of a capitalist society. That description seemed a horrendous caricature to the economist Peter Drucker, who believed "this country knows no distinct upper-class or lower-class 'way of life.' It knows only different ways of making a living."[27] Lacking clear class divisions, the nation naturally lacked a ruling class with the power to have its own way. In an influential book entitled *The Lonely Crowd* (1950) David Riesman described power in America as "situational," "mercurial," "amorphous," and "indeterminate." When exercised at all, it was exercised by veto groups representing widely assorted and evenly balanced interests which more often than not neutralized each other. "In the amorphous power structure created by veto groups," Riesman said, "it is hard to distinguish rulers from the ruled, those to be aided from those to be opposed, those on your side from those on the other side."[28]

Reinhold Niebuhr's *The Irony of American History* (1952), based on lectures given in May 1949, embroidered these and other aspects of pluralist theory. Starting with the conviction that in the "international contest between Marxism and the democratic world" the United States was "defending freedom against tyranny," Niebuhr praised what he termed the triumph of experience over dogma. He adopted what for the nation's most prominent theologian must have seemed an unscriptural posture: the virtue of America was that it did not practice what it preached. It practiced welfare-state pragmatism even while it preached a free-market dogma. By developing this nonideological approach to social questions, the United States, in Niebuhr's view, had achieved a substantial measure of justice. Businessmen and labor leaders reached sensible, live-and-let-live solutions to their differences. The nation as a whole maintained a fluid class structure and preserved a balance between different groups. Everyone knew the name of the game and played by the rules. Blissfully unencumbered by the "ideological baggage" which weighed down other peoples, Americans had "equilibrated power" in a fashion that only a James Madison might truly have appreciated.[29]

If the Madisonian theory of balancing a "multiplicity of interests" was applauded by Niebuhr and Riesman, it received a standing ovation from the editors of *Fortune*. Before the cheers had died down, they had published *USA: The Permanent Revolution* (1951), a national self-portrait faithfully done in the pluralist style. "Americans live in fundamental agreement concerning certain long-range aims and principles," the editors affirmed. When it came to specific disagreements over public policy, interest groups succeeded in working out tolerable compromises. Businessmen no longer exploited workers but felt responsible for their well-being, while workers, in turn, were "not 'proletarian' and [did] not believe in class war." Did trade unions instill class consciousness? Only in that they had "made the worker to an amazing degree a middle-class member of a middle-class society."[30] The single cloud on this horizon was an atavistic feeling on the part of some workers that business was the enemy.

Concentrating on the sunny side, however, *Fortune* concluded that "never have left-wing ideologies had so little influence on the American labor movement as they have today."[31] That conclusion, indeed the entire pluralist interpretation of social class and ideology, seemed amply validated by the CIO's decision in 1949 and 1950 to expel communist-led unions. That decision reflected the bitter feelings which had existed between pro- and anticommunist unions in the CIO since the late 1930s. Muted somewhat by the spirit of cooperation during World War II, the bitterness intensified along with the Cold War. Of the points at issue between the contending factions, three related directly to Cold War concerns. The first involved the CIO's willingness to comply with the Taft-Hartley Act of 1947, which required union officials to sign noncommunist affidavits if their membership was to enjoy collective bargaining rights before the National Labor Relations Board. To the dismay of its left-wing leaders, the CIO went along this provision, even while lobbying for its repeal, so as not to jeopardize its members' gains. Another issue arose in 1948, when the CIO threw its support to Harry Truman while the left-wing faction backed Henry Wallace. A third controversy arose over the Marshall Plan, which the CIO endorsed even though procommunist union officials did not.

Anticommunist CIO officials, such as Walter Reuther and Philip Murray, believed that communists were unreliable and ineffective union leaders, but they also believed that the CIO's reputation at a time of growing hysteria depended on its willingness to take an anticommunist stand. As early as July 1947 Murray told the CIO executive board, "If communism is an issue in your unions, throw it to hell out, and throw its advocates out along with it." That was more easily said than done, not only because the eleven left-wing unions contained more than 1 million members but also because the so-called communist union officials, some of whom were party members but others of whom were not, had been elected democratically. Expulsion of the entire union seemed the only available option if radical leaders could not be dislodged in elections, and the CIO conventions of 1949 and 1950 did not flinch from the task. Ejection was necessary, Murray explained, "to fight Stalin, to fight Moscow, to fight imperialism, to fight aggression here at home," and to remove "the dirty, filthy traitors."[32]

If the CIO's action was a consequence of Cold War

fears, then Truman's Fair Deal was in certain respects a casualty of those same fears. In 1949, after considerable skirmishing with Congress, the administration did obtain approval for legislation that extended social reforms first introduced under Franklin Roosevelt. Congress broadened the provisions of the Social Security Act, raised the minimum wage, and created a new public housing program. Not only were more people eligible for benefits, but the benefits were increased modestly. Yet when the administration attempted to move in directions not previously charted, it stumbled to defeat. Congress refused to provide federal aid to education, to reform the system of agricultural price supports, or to create a plan of national health insurance. Powerful pressure groups aligned themselves against these proposals, with Catholics opposing aid to education that would exclude parochial schools, organized farm groups opposing any plan that would curtail federal subsidies to large producers, and the medical profession opposing any plan, no matter how cautiously worded, that would involve compulsory health insurance.

The last of these, in fact, was attacked on the grounds that it was communist-inspired or, in the language of an American Medical Association leaflet, that it would create a "monstrosity of Bolshevik bureaucracy."[33] A Cold War atmosphere in which a thoroughgoing critique of social institutions was fast going out of style and in which the administration always put foreign policy considerations first was not an atmosphere in which social reform could prosper. One of Truman's aides, Stephen Spingarn, put his finger on the problem in April 1949, when he noted that "the consuming fear of communism has led many sincere persons into the belief that . . . change (be it civil rights or a compulsory national health program) is subversive and those who urge it are either communists or fellow travellers."[34] Of all the reforms associated with the Fair Deal, nothing exemplified this more vividly than the civil rights issue.

By 1948 Truman had come out in favor of legislation to promote racial equality, and the pivotal role black voters played in the presidential election that year further solidified the President's commitment. Strategically located in large states in the North and West as a result of wartime migration, black voters in effect held the balance of power because white voters tended to divide more or less evenly. Truman won about two-thirds of the black vote and received an even higher percentage in the largest cities. Although he defeated Republican Thomas E. Dewey by what looked like a comfortable margin, with 24.2 million votes to Dewey's 22 million and with a 303–189 edge in the electoral college, the election might easily have gone the other way. In the key states of California, Illinois, and Ohio, Truman obtained razor-thin majorities; pluralities in the black wards of Los Angeles, Chicago, and Cleveland spelled the difference between victory and defeat. Responding then to political realities as well as to his own convictions, Truman in 1949 again urged Congress to eliminate poll taxes in federal elections, establish severe penalties for members of lynch mobs, create a Fair Employment Practices Committee with real authority, protect the right to vote, and eliminate segregation in interstate transportation.

Advocates of this program did all they could to turn the Cold War to their advantage. By ending Jim Crow, they insisted, the United States would improve its image in the world, especially in Asia and Africa. They rarely tired of quoting a remark made in 1946 by Dean Acheson, then Undersecretary of State: "The existence of discrimination against minority groups in this country has an adverse effect on our relations with other countries." Similar justifications were advanced by the

President's Commission on Civil Rights in 1947, when it urged a broad-gauged assault on segregation, and by the Department of Justice in 1948, when it filed briefs supporting the position of the National Association for the Advancement of Colored People (NAACP) in civil rights suits. The theme that implementing racial equality was the most expedient way to conduct the Cold War had an important variation. Depriving people of basic rights, Truman said, was "an invitation to communism," an invitation that could be withdrawn simply by ending the deprivation.[35]

The argument from expediency, however, resembled nothing so much as a boomerang, and those who used it soon found themselves busily dodging their own device. Opponents of civil rights recognized that they could discredit the cause simply by pointing out that communists supported it. Agitation for racial equality, the argument proceeded, played into the hands of the communists by sowing dissension among the American people. So, to Congressman Joseph R. Bryson of South Carolina, the proposed FEPC formed part of "a communist inspired conspiracy to undermine American unity."[36] In 1948, on the day after the Supreme Court ruled in *Shelley* v. *Kraemer* that it was unconstitutional for states to enforce restrictive housing covenants which prohibited the sale, rental, or leasing of property to non-Caucasians, John Rankin of Mississippi rose in the House of Representatives to say: "Mr. Speaker, there must have been a celebration in Moscow last night." Communists had "won their greatest victory" when the Court had voted to "destroy the value of property owned by tens of thousands of loyal Americans.[37]

The States Rights Democratic party offered the clearest example of how the ideology of segregation could merge with that of anticommunism. Formed by southerners in the summer of 1948 after the Democratic party adopted a civil rights platform they found unacceptable, the Dixiecrats, as they were called, nominated J. Strom Thurmond, governor of South Carolina, for the presidency. The more romantically inclined thought the new party stood for "the deepest emotions of the human fabric—racial pride, respect for white womanhood, and superiority of Caucasian blood."[38] Translated into practical political terms, this amounted to an attempt to equate racial integration with communist subversion. In campaign speeches Thurmond declared that "the radicals, the subversives, and the reds" had captured the Democratic party, that the civil rights program had "its origin in communist ideology," that its purpose was "to excite race and class hatred" and thereby "create the chaos and confusion which leads to communism."[39] Thurmond did not receive enough votes to deprive Truman of an electoral college victory and throw the election into the House, as the Dixiecrats had hoped, but his candidacy suggested the way in which civil rights could be linked with subversion.

It was one of the subtler, if not more surprising, ironies of the period that civil rights organizations, even as they were being charged with radical designs, were engaging in a quest for respectability that led them to adopt ever more conservative postures. The NAACP, for example, undertook an internal purge, empowering its national officials to expel branches judged to have fallen under communist control. The NAACP even cooperated with other civil rights and labor groups in creating what one admirer described as "informal intelligence systems through which dossiers were compiled on party activists and information on Communist maneuvers was exchanged."[40] Organizations like the Congress of Racial Equality sometimes backed away from militant direct-action campaigns so as to avoid the taint of radicalism. Civil rights spokesmen were also inclined to curb their criticism of European colonialism. Since the nations that held colonies in Africa—Britain, France, Belgium, and Portugal—were America's allies in the Cold War, the United States said little about European imperialism in Africa even while making much of Soviet imperialism in Eastern Europe. Where many blacks had once argued that this reflected an obvious double standard, after 1947 that argument dwindled to a whisper.[41]

With supporters of racial equality thrown increasingly on the defensive, with southern Democrats in possession of key places on pivotal congressional committees, and with the President anxious insofar as possible to avoid a showdown that might jeopardize action on his foreign policy proposals, it did not take much political savvy to predict the outcome. Civil rights measures were either snuffed out in committee, diluted before they reached the floor for debate, or filibustered to death in the Senate, which could never muster enough votes to invoke cloture. Even more than these legislative difficulties, however, the dispute over the Negro's role in the armed forces revealed the interplay between the Cold War and civil rights. Triggered by Truman's request for the enactment of peacetime selective service in 1947 and by its passage in 1948, the dispute raised the very issue of loyalty that was on nearly everyone's mind. The controversy can be approached by examining the responses of three prominent blacks and the reception their views received.

Even in 1941, when he had threatened to lead a march on Washington, A. Philip Randolph wanted to end Jim Crow in the armed forces. Having bartered that demand in exchange for Roosevelt's executive order banning discrimination in defense hiring, Randolph thought the time had come in 1947 to realize his original purpose. He called, therefore, for legislation to end discrimination in the military, eliminate segregated facilities for soldiers traveling across state lines, treat attacks on uniformed servicemen as federal offenses, and exempt enlisted men from paying poll taxes in federal elections. When the Selective Service Act did none of these things, Randolph, resorting to a strategy that had succeeded once before, demanded that Truman include them in an executive order. Urging black and white youths to boycott the draft so long as segregation remained in force, Randolph said imprisonment for noncompliance was preferable to "permanent military slavery." Although Randolph added that segregation "is the greatest single propaganda and political weapon in the hands of Russia and international communism today," his stand at the time seemed enormously radical, while his endorsement of the Cold War consensus was widely overlooked.[42]

Paul Robeson probably stood as far outside that consensus as it was possible to get. Unlike Randolph, who condemned communism and asserted that Negroes would be only too happy to serve in an integrated army, Robeson defended the Soviet Union down the line and, while in Paris in early 1949, made a speech that brought down on him an avalanche of criticism. Claiming that American policy toward the people of Africa "is similar to that of Hitler and Goebbels," Robeson added that it was unthinkable "that American Negroes would go to war on behalf of those who have oppressed us for generations" against the Soviet Union, which "has raised our people to full human dignity." Widely condemned as a heretic, Robeson was subjected to the modern equivalent of trial by fire. His career as an actor and singer, already on shaky ground as a result of the blacklist, went into eclipse. In Peekskill, New York, rock-throwing veterans, with the connivance of the police, disrupted a concert at which he was scheduled to appear. FBI agents staked out his home and followed him wherever he went. In 1950 the State Department lifted his passport. The House Committee on Un-American Activities called witnesses to denounce him, one of whom said that Robeson wanted to be "the black Stalin among Negroes."[43]

The most famous person summoned by HUAC in the summer of 1949 was Brooklyn Dodger second baseman Jackie Robinson. Two years after breaking the color barrier in the major leagues, Robinson had lived up to all the expectations of Branch Rickey, who had signed him to a big-league contract. The first Negro in organized baseball, Rickey believed, must be a superior athlete who could not fail to be a star, a man of impeccable morals who could not be touched by scandal, and a person with superhuman self-control who could not be provoked by racial slurs hurled from opposing dugouts. Robinson's appearance before HUAC, which wanted him to "give the lie to statements by Paul Robeson that American Negroes would not fight in case of a war against Russia," would, in Rickey's view, be the ultimate step in solidifying the Negro's place in baseball. With Rickey's help Robinson drafted a statement in which he claimed that segregation was wrong but that "we can win the fight without the Communists and we don't want their help." Robeson, he added, was "still a famous ex-athlete and a great singer and actor," but the statement made in Paris "sounds very silly to me." The next day's headlines announced: JACKIE HITS ROBESON'S RED PITCH.[44]

At the time Robinson testified, the issue of segregation in the armed forces remained only partially resolved. Partly in response to Randolph's protest and partly as an election-year tactic, Truman in July 1948 had issued an executive order stating that equality of treatment in the armed services would be effected as quickly as possible. This went far enough for Randolph to call off his civil disobedience campaign and for Truman to consolidate his hold on black voters, but the new policy encountered one fortress of opposition. While the Navy and Air Force quickly agreed to integrate, the Army did not. In January 1950 it grudgingly accepted an integration plan which it assumed would take years to implement. That assumption was shattered by the Korean War. In the summer of 1950, as white troops suffered heavy casualties, the Army rushed black soldiers in as replacements. Then, in 1951, the Army asked social scientists to evaluate the impact of integration on morale. Their report proved favorable, so the Army consented later that year to abandon segregation.

Yet as the attempt to establish a new Fair Employment Practices Committee revealed, the Korean War provided an insubstantial basis for civil rights advances. Civil rights leaders urged the creation of an FEPC in 1950 "not only because our country can no longer enjoy the luxury of wasted industrial manpower but also because our men in Korea need to know in their hearts and minds that they are not fighting in vain."[45] But if the administration was pulled in one direction by the argument for efficient mobilization, it was pulled just as strongly in the other by its desire for what one official, arguing against the FEPC on the grounds that it would antagonize white southerners, termed "national unity in these perilous times."[46] The tug-of-war ended in a standoff. In December 1951 the President created a Committee on Government Contract Compliance. It had a staff, but a tiny one. It could hold hearings but not subpoena witnesses. It could make recommendations but not issue cease-and-desist orders. Not a single contract was canceled during the Korean War, even though abundant evidence of discrimination was gathered.

It was in February 1951, in the midst of this controversy over discriminatory hiring practices, that *Fortune* published *USA: The Permanent Revolution.* The theorists of pluralism labored mightily to account for the persistence of racial injustice. Conceding that discrimination represented the nation's single greatest failure, the authors concluded that the problem of equal opportunity "is being solved slowly but surely state by state, this method being the best guarantee that when a national FEPC law is passed, it will be a real and enforceable reform, not a paper one."[47] But this confident assumption that things were getting better all the time, so characteristic of the pluralist approach to class and mobility, was not applicable to the problem of racial injustice. The civil rights movement, having done its best to use the Cold War and then the Korean War as weapons in behalf of reform, discovered that anticommunism was wielded more effectively by those who wanted to preserve the status quo than by those who sought to change it.

3.

Communism, in the public mind, has frequently been linked with immigrants, and subversion with the foreign-born. The image of the radical and of the alien have often converged, as, for example, during the Red Scare following World War I and again when fear of fifth-column activities developed in the years preceding World War II. The 1940s and 1950s, however, exhibited a different pattern. The Truman administration certainly attempted to deport aliens it regarded as subversive, and Congress went the administration one step better by erecting barriers to the entry of those whose political views were, by the strict standards of the day, suspect in the least. Yet if the anticommunist impulse was tinged with nativism, it never assumed the character of a crusade against immigrants. That much, if little else, can be said for the most virulent form that impulse took: McCarthyism.

The belief that communist activities in the United States were directed by alien forces was cultivated in hearings before the Subcommittee on Immigration and Naturalization of the Senate Judiciary Committee. Chaired by Senator Pat McCarran of Nevada, the committee in 1949 was searching for a justification to impose additional controls on subversive aliens. The question that intrigued the committee, one it had undoubtedly answered to its own satisfaction before the first witness ever took the stand, was put by its staff director as follows: "Is communism in the United States a local product, or is it a plant or a weed, that is being engendered and developed from abroad?" To no one's surprise, such former communists as Elizabeth Bentley and Louis Budenz, as well as émigrés from Eastern European nations, asserted that communism was not home-grown. "The backbone of the Communist Party in this country," said Bentley, "is an alien backbone"; the party, added Budenz, "is directed exclusively by aliens." Not only did outsiders constitute the bulk of the party's membership and pull all the strings, but according to these witnesses, foreign agents used embassies as espionage bases.[48]

Attorney General Tom C. Clark's testimony before the McCarran committee was designed to make a believer out of the most hardened skeptic. Replying to a question about the extent of foreign-born influence in the Communist party, Clark reported the findings of a 1947 study. The Department of Justice had investigated 4,984 of "the more militant members" of the party, all but 217 of whom were citizens. It had found that 78.4 percent of the subjects were immigrants or the children of immigrants and that an additional 13 percent had husbands or wives of foreign ancestry. This made a grand total of 91.4 percent. "In only 429, or 8.6 percent of the 4,984 cases, were the subject and his parents, and if married the spouse and the spouse's parents, all born in the United States."[49] On the basis of this testimony and that of other witnesses, the committee quickly concluded that communism in America was an alien movement.

Although McCarran suspected that Clark was not acting vigorously enough, the Department of Justice had, in 1948, undertaken a deportation drive against aliens that had met with mixed results. Early that year the Attorney General ordered the arrest of a number of aliens known or suspected to be members of the Communist party. One was Gerhart Eisler, who, Clark said, "had been making speeches around the country that were derogatory to our way of life."[50] Another was Alexander Bittelman, who had emigrated to the United States in 1912 and had been a member of the Communist party since its founding in 1919. Some of those arrested were placed in solitary confinement on Ellis Island and held without bail for several days until the courts ruled that bail could not be denied. The attempt to expel radical aliens, however, foundered on the legal requirement that an alien could be deported to his country of origin only with that nation's consent. Since such consent was usually not forthcoming, the deportation drive was, for the moment, stymied.

In moving to expel aliens, moreover, the government followed administrative procedures which the Supreme Court held unconstitutional in February 1950. The case concerned a Chinese seaman, Wong Yang Sung, who had overstayed his shore leave and tried to remain in the United States, but the ruling applied as well to the cases, then pending in lower courts, involving left-wing aliens. The Immigration and Naturalization Service had claimed that deportation proceedings were exempt from the provisions of a 1946 act which required that in hearings before government agencies the functions of investigation and decision be separated. The Court rejected that claim, stating: "When the Constitution requires a hearing, it requires a fair one, before a tribunal which meets at least currently prevailing standards of impartiality."[51] Procedures that were swift, cheap, and virtually certain to result in a finding of deportability had to be replaced by others that were slower, more costly, and less predictable.

Two cases illustrate how the government could succeed in harassing aliens and naturalized citizens even when it could not actually deport them. The first involved Harry Bridges, the leader of the West Coast longshoremen, who had emigrated to the United States in 1920. Earlier attempts to deport him as a subversive alien on the grounds that he had communist affiliations had apparently been halted in 1945, when the Supreme Court ruled in his favor and Bridges applied for, and was admitted to, citizenship. But in May 1949, in the midst of its drive against aliens, the Department of Justice moved to denaturalize Bridges, charging him—and the two witnesses who had testified to his loyalty—with conspiracy to defraud the government by falsely denying Communist party membership on the citizenship application. The trial, which began in November, ended in April 1950 with a guilty verdict. The judge sentenced Bridges to five years in prison and stripped him of his citizenship. That summer, after the Korean War broke out, the prosecutor demanded the revocation of bail, and the judge complied. After Bridges had spent three weeks in jail, a higher court ordered his release, but it was not until June 1953, four years after his ordeal began, that the Supreme Court set aside the guilty verdict and restored Bridges's citizenship.

The second case involved a highly unlikely individual: a sixty-three-year-old millionaire who had emigrated to the United States in 1910. Charlie Chaplin had become a controversial figure during World War II, when a much-publicized paternity suit had splattered details of his private life across front pages everywhere. The controversy took on a more ominous aspect during the Cold War, when Chaplin criticized American policy and endorsed Henry Wallace's candidacy. It was hard to tell whether his critics objected more to his sexual adventures or to his political views. Chaplin's life "is detrimental to the moral fabric of the nation," sputtered a congressman in 1947; his "public utterances provide a series of eulogies for the Stalinist dictatorship," thundered a senator in 1949.[52] By 1952 the American Legion had brought so much pressure on movie theaters that Chaplin's new film, *Limelight,* was screened in relatively few cities. Since nothing linked Chaplin with subversive activity, the government bided its time until September 1952, when he and his family left to visit Europe. Then, tigerlike, it pounced, rescinding Chaplin's reentry permit and announcing that he could be readmitted only after submitting to a rigorous investigation of his moral behavior and political involvements. Chaplin elected to remain in Geneva.

With the outbreak of the Korean War in June 1950 Congress approved policies that went far beyond those employed in the deportation drive against aliens, the trial of Harry Bridges, or even the later exiling of Charlie Chaplin. In September 1950 Congress passed the Internal Security Act over Truman's veto. The measure required all communist organizations and their members to register with the Attorney General, and it authorized the President, in the event he declared a national emergency, to round up and imprison suspected subversives. Yet if most attention centered on these provisions, the act also affected the foreign-born. It excluded from entry and made liable to deportation anyone who had ever belonged to a totalitarian organization, and it gave the Attorney General something he had sought for years: the power to detain aliens indefinitely pending final determination of their deportability, a determination, indeed, that might take a considerable amount of time.

In March 1952 the Supreme Court approved the constitutionality of the sections of the Internal Security Act relating to aliens. The key ruling came in *Carlson* v. *Landon,* which involved five aliens who were being held without bail while the matter of their deportation was under consideration. The district judge, to whom they had appealed for release on bail, had declared: "I am not going to turn these people loose if they are Communists, any more than I would turn loose a deadly germ in this community." The Supreme Court, in language that was considerably more elegant but that had exactly the same effect, upheld the congressional grant of authority under which the Attorney General had acted. The Court divided 5–4, with Justice Hugo Black's dissent spelling out the issues involved: "Today the Court holds that law-abiding persons, neither charged with nor convicted of any crime, can be held in jail indefinitely, without bail, if a subordinate Washington bureau agent believes they are members of the Communist Party, and therefore dangerous to the nation because of the possibility of the 'indoctrination of others.' "[53]

Yet the anticommunist impulse, while it could exploit fears of a foreign conspiracy and produce administrative, legislative, and judicial action aimed at aliens, did not flow primarily along nativist channels. Even those most inclined to associate radicalism with the foreign-born defended the patriotism of the great majority of immigrants. Observers agreed that the 1.3 million immigrants who entered the United States between 1945 and 1952 met with a friendly public reception and that the various agencies devoted to helping them adjust to life in America did a remarkably effective job. *Fortune*'s *USA: The Permanent Revolution,* the pluralist manifesto which so nicely revealed attitudes toward class and race, also illustrated the salubrious climate respecting ethnic diversity: "Here is a town addicted to schottisches, another whose social life centers around a Norwegian Harmony Club, another that features Czech gymnastic festivals. Here is a town with a Chinese restaurant; over there a town with German *verein;* over there a town, redolent of frijoles, that speaks mostly Spanish." The authors could barely contain their ecstasy: "All cultures are cherished—interwoven—modified."[54]

One reason for this approving response was that a large number of immigrants were themselves the victims of Soviet expansionism. These exiles not only supped at the table of Cold War anticommunism but made themselves veritable trenchermen. It was only logical that immigrants, attempting as they did to move the United States toward a policy of facing down the Russians and liberating Eastern Europe, would come to be identified with the far right rather than with the far left. Anticommunist refugees from Poland, Czechoslovakia, and other nations that had fallen under Soviet control, however, often found themselves torn by conflicting emotions. Forced to emigrate against their will, cut off from the kinds of contacts immigrants normally maintain with friends and relatives who stay behind, and determined to return to their homelands in the not-too-distant future, when, they supposed, those nations would be liberated, these refugees sought to preserve their ethnic identity even as they found it necessary, for practical reasons, to adapt to American ways. Many persisted in the belief that they had, in effect, purchased a round-trip ticket to the United States long after it had become apparent that they would never make the return voyage.

The controversy over the admission of displaced persons, which lasted from 1947 to 1950, illustrated the tension between the older perception of immigrants as radicals and the emerging recognition that they were more likely to be strongly anticommunist. In 1947 hundreds of thousands of people who had been uprooted by World War II were still living in special camps, their numbers augmented by hundreds of thousands more, many of them Jews, who had fled from Eastern Europe after the installation of communist governments. The Truman administration urged Congress to admit 400,000 displaced persons over a two-year period and to do so outside the regular quota system. Congress responded in June 1948 by admitting 205,000 such refugees, but only those who had left their homelands by the end of 1945. The measure also provided for mortgaging the number of immigrants against each nation's future quota and for giving preference to immigrants from the Baltic nations of Latvia, Lithuania, and Estonia. During the debate the standard anticommunist argument was used by some representatives, notably Congressman Ed Gossett of Texas, who objected to admitting displaced persons on the grounds that the Russians had planted "a few chosen disciples to infiltrate with the hope that they would plant the seeds of communism elsewhere, where they might flourish and grow."[55]

That argument, however, sounded increasingly like a relic from a remote, if well-remembered, past. By 1949, when Truman asked Congress to liberalize the law, many people had come to believe with Republican Senator Alexander Wiley of Wisconsin that a less restrictive bill would serve as a "weapon in our ideological war against the forces of darkness, the forces of Communist tyranny."[56] In 1950 Congress agreed to increase the number of displaced persons who would be admitted, to admit refugees who had fled Eastern Europe after 1945, and to eliminate the preference for the Baltic states. To be on the safe side, the Displaced Persons Commission enforced what it termed "the most rigorous system of security and intelligence investigations in the history of American immigration."[57] By 1952, when the program ended, the United States had admitted 390,000 displaced persons, more than 70 percent of whom were born in countries then in the Soviet orbit. What Congress refused to do was to tamper with the quota system. Displaced persons counted against future quotas even when the results defied common sense. Seven nations had to mortgage their quotas into the twenty-first century, and Latvia, with an annual quota of 236, into the year 2274.

The McCarran-Walter Act of 1952 demonstrated that the fear of communism, while it embraced the foreign-born, was not essentially directed at them. The act rightly earned the contempt of liberals, including the President, over whose veto it was passed, because it reaffirmed the system of quotas based on national origins, a system that could be defended only on the grounds that some nationalities were superior to others. Nor was any attempt made to bring quotas up to date by basing them on the current rather than the past makeup of the population. Moreover, Congress paid due homage to anticommunist sentiment by strengthening the Attorney General's authority to deport aliens suspected of harboring subversive views. But Congress also liberalized existing practices in several respects. It repealed the Oriental exclusion law, set a small annual quota for each Asian nation, and removed racial qualifications for citizenship. More important, Congress elected to admit immigrants who had belonged to communist organizations in the past if their membership was inadvertent or involuntary or if they had, over a five-year period, taken an anticommunist position. This was an exemption that, until the act passed, the Department of Justice had granted past members of fascist groups but not of communist groups.

By 1952, when Congress passed this measure, anticommunism in America had become very nearly synonymous with the name of Senator Joseph R. McCarthy of Wisconsin. Two years earlier, in February 1950, he had made a speech at Wheeling, West Virginia, that catapulted him to national attention. For years thereafter, certainly until his censure by the Senate late in 1954, McCarthy strode like a giant across the anticommunist landscape, applying the label of "subversive" to those no less anticommunist than he and miraculously making it stick. Although McCarthy came to prominence shortly before the Korean War began and remained influential for some time after it ended, his ascendancy coincided for the most part with that war, and his success would have been unthinkable without it. A great admirer of Douglas MacArthur's—he once praised a statement of the general's as one of "the most intelligently clear-cut, irrefutable and valuable documents which has been brought to the attention of the public for many months"—McCarthy brilliantly exploited the frustrations many Americans experienced in waging a limited and, one might add, unsuccessful war.[58] Condemning the "Communists and queers" who had wormed their way into the State Department, the senator lambasted the Truman administration for failing to defend American interests in Asia.

In his Wheeling address, McCarthy made a point to which he often returned: "It has not been the less fortunate or members of minority groups who have been selling this nation out, but rather those who have had all the benefits . . . —the finest homes, the finest college education, and the finest jobs in Government we can give."[59] Radical immigrants, subversive aliens, foreign-born agitators—such picayune prey was not the quarry

McCarthy hunted. He was after bigger game, and he found it in persons who, by any reasonable standard, had to be considered pillars of the establishment. Anglo-Saxon ancestry, an Ivy League degree, and a home in Georgetown seemed the attributes most likely to attract McCarthy's attention. He lit out, for example, after Secretary of State Dean Acheson, the "Red Dean of the State Department," with his "cane, spats, and tea-sipping little finger." He delivered a wild 60,000-word assault on Secretary of Defense George C. Marshall, who had served as Army Chief of Staff in World War II. "Unless we understand the record of Marshall," he said, "it will be impossible . . . to foretell the next move on the time-table of the great conspiracy."[60] A journal sympathetic to the senator, in describing those who had defended Alger Hiss as "the American respectables, the socially pedigreed, the culturally acceptable," succinctly caught the main drift of McCarthyism.[61]

Jews have frequently served as the target of anticommunist extremists, but there appears to have been no affinity between McCarthyism and anti-Semitism. Two of the senator's closest aides, Roy Cohn and G. David Schine, were Jewish, and McCarthy himself was so far removed from the world of professional anti-Semites that one called him "a crypto Jew" who was undoubtedly using an alias.[62] Although certain events that occurred during McCarthy's heyday, such as the conviction of Julius and Ethel Rosenberg on charges of conspiring to transmit atomic secrets of the Soviet Union during World War II, fueled the fantasies of anti-Semites, McCarthy "did not invoke the Jews—or any other clearcut population group—in his attempt to construct a conspiracy theory."[63] What is more, public opinion polls revealed that those who said they would be more inclined to vote for a candidate for public office if he was Jewish expressed more favorable attitudes toward

McCarthy than those less likely to vote for such a candidate. Among both Protestants and Catholics, regardless of educational level and political affiliation, an inverse relationship existed between support for McCarthy and anti-Semitism.

By adopting a pro-McCarthy posture, certain immigrant groups managed to do what had to be done in an anticommunist era to prove their credentials as loyal Americans. That they supported McCarthy with this purpose in mind is unlikely, but whatever their reasons Irish, Polish, and Italian Catholics rallied in large numbers to the senator's side. Catholics as a whole were more likely than any other religious group to back McCarthy, although those who were Republicans were more likely to do so than those who were Democrats. Yet the extent of McCarthy's support in the Catholic community can easily be exaggerated.[64] Like public opinion in general, Catholic opinion was sharply divided and tended to fluctuate over the years. Although he always found sympathetic audiences at meetings of the Catholic War Veterans and the Holy Name Societies, McCarthy also was roundly criticized by liberal Catholics.

The road to assimilation during the Cold War was paved with anticommunist intentions, and the road crew, it sometimes seemed, was working a double shift. It is easier in retrospect than it was at the time to point out that McCarthysim sanctioned vicious smear campaigns, created harmful pressures for conformity, and rode roughshod over individual rights, all of which was antithetical to American ideals, if not atypical of American practices. But from another perspective McCarthy in particular, and the mood of anticommunism in general, offered many immigrants the means to scale the walls of ethnic prejudice. The unpleasant truth is that for many immigrants, joining the Cold War consensus was the surest means of affirming their patriotism.

[4]
The Suburban Nation

William Levitt, the builder whose name became a generic synonym for the American suburb, once remarked: "No man who owns his own house and lot can be a communist. He has too much to do."[1] The image Levitt evoked—that of the suburban homeowner struggling, in spare moments, to clear the lawn of crabgrass, the attic of screens, and the driveway of tricycles—while surely oversimplified, nevertheless reflected certain underlying realities. During the 1950s suburban growth transformed American life. Although that growth had begun long before and would continue long after the decade ended, it was during the 1950s that the most pronounced shift from the central cities to the surrounding rings took place. By 1960 as many people lived in suburbs as in cities. This process, which saw new communities sprout like so many mushrooms across the land, altered patterns of class structure, ethnic assimilation, and, above all, race relations. Just when the federal government and the civil rights movement appeared to be moving the nation toward integration, the flight to the suburbs was pulling it even more strongly in the opposite direction.

1.

In the 1950s the urbanization of America came to a virtual halt, and the march toward suburbanization hit full stride. From 1950 to 1960 fourteen of the fifteen cities with more than 1 million inhabitants actually shrank in size while the suburbs around those cities grew at an astonishing speed. New York City's population declined by 2 percent, and Chicago's remained the same; but New York City's suburbs grew by 58 percent, and Chicago's by 101 percent. While St. Louis, Philadelphia, Cleveland, Minneapolis, and Detroit were experiencing small but significant population losses, the suburban rings around those five cities were experiencing gains, respectively, of 51 percent, 92 percent, 94 percent, 105 percent, and 131 percent. The only urban growth of significance occurred in the South and West, and in those sections, too, it lagged far behind suburban expansion. The Census Bureau reported that the population of "standard metropolitan statistical areas" jumped during the decade from 95 to 120 million. Central cities grew by 11 percent, from 54 to 60 million, while suburbs grew by 46 percent, from 41 to 60 million.

Startling as these statistics may be, they nevertheless understate the magnitude of the trend toward suburbanization. The Census Bureau defined a "standard metropolitan statistical area" as a place having a city of at least 50,000 inhabitants. Americans who lived on the outskirts of slightly smaller cities, therefore, were not classified as suburban dwellers. Nor were those who resided in "detached suburbs," in communities separated from cities by more than one and one-half miles of sparsely settled land. Finally, census data often masked the suburban growth that occurred in outlying areas annexed by the cities. During the 1950s many cities extended their territorial boundaries, absorbing large tracts and thereby converting some 4.8 million people, for statistical purposes at least, from suburban to city dwellers. This peripheral expansion accounted for much of the urban growth in the South and West. For the nation as a whole, when adjustments are made for such boundary changes, suburbs during the 1950s grew not four times as fast as central cities but forty times as fast.

Sociologists offered a variety of explanations to account for this population shift, of which the simplest turned out to be the best. Some interpreted suburbanization as a social movement inspired by an unconscious search for community and corresponding revolt against technocracy. Yet the evidence to support this view was flimsy, consisting largely of bucolic names—such as Peppermill Village, Woodbury Knoll, or Park Forest—that developers gave to their communities. Other scholars, taking their cue from advertisements which importuned people to "escape to Scarborough Manor. Escape from cities too big, too polluted, too crowded, too strident to call home," viewed suburbanization as a flight from urban problems.[2] This came much nearer the truth, but it, too, exaggerated the degree of dissatisfaction with city life. When sociologists asked newly established suburbanites their reasons for moving, most simply talked about the advantages of homeownership: the "need for more space"; "comfort and roominess for family members in new house"; "privacy and freedom of action in owned home." For four out of five families moving to Levittown, New Jersey, one investigator reported, "the house was the major reason for coming."[3]

The general contours of suburban development were shaped by the expansion of the automobile industry, the creation of a national highway system, the federal approach to insuring home mortgages, the application of mass-production techniques to the housing industry, and the decision of businessmen to decentralize their operations. The relationship between these social, economic, and technological changes, on the one hand, and suburban growth, on the other, was nothing less than symbiotic. The car, the highway, the Veterans Administration mortgage, the Levittown Cape Codder, and the shopping center—all complemented suburban growth and were, often, the beneficiaries of that development.

Automobiles were the lifeblood of the suburbs. Although critics of the automobile industry's devotion to size, horsepower, and chrome may have been right in diagnosing a severe case of blood poisoning, few suburbanites seemed to exhibit any signs of distress. Following World War II the automobile industry enjoyed a boom period that lasted until the late 1950s and coincided with the most rapid suburban expansion. General Motors, Chrysler, and Ford offered consumers an ever-wider choice of engines, colors, and accessories and, as the industry grew increasingly oligopolistic, a steadily narrower choice of prices. Production of passenger cars nevertheless rocketed from 2 million in 1946 to 8 million in 1955, and registrations followed suit, increasing from 25 million in 1945 to 40 million in 1950, 51 million in 1955, and 62 million in 1960. Nearly nine out of ten families living in the suburbs owned a car, compared to six out of ten urban families, a reflection not only of differences in income but of obvious differences in need. By 1960 nearly one-fifth of suburban families owned two cars, and two out of every three persons in the United States drove to work each day in an automobile.

Cities, states, and the federal government built new roads and repaired old ones at a nearly fast enough pace to accommodate the automobiles using them. Hundreds of thousands of miles of highways were reinforced, widened, and extended during the early 1950s, but such improvements constituted small steps compared with the giant step taken in 1956, when the Interstate Highway Act was passed. This measure provided for the construction of 41,000 miles of express highways at a cost of more than $100 billion. The federal contribution, to be raised through new taxes on gasoline, oil, tires, buses, and trucks, would amount to $31 billion. Sold to skeptical congressmen partly on the grounds that modern highways would provide a speedy means of evacuating the cities in case of an atomic attack, the program had its major impact not on urban refugees but on suburban commuters, who became heavy users of the nearly 6,000 miles of freeways built within metropolitan areas. A writer in *Architectural Forum*, noting the effect all this would have on commuting patterns, predicted that the measure would produce environmental changes "on a scale so mammoth as to dwarf all previous public works projects and indeed all manmade physical enterprises except war."[4]

Programs of the Federal Housing Administration and the Veterans Administration similarly transformed patterns of homeownership. Before World War II, banks and other lending institutions adhered to a mortgage policy that, in retrospect, would have done justice to an Ebenezer Scrooge. They ordinarily demanded a large down payment—50 percent as a rule—and required repayment within a short time—ten years at the most. Reducing their risk to a discreet minimum, banks also locked out of the housing market millions of would-be purchasers who lacked substantial resources. The FHA and VA stood this system on its head by insuring mortgages on terms that would have appealed to a Bob Cratchit. The FHA insured thirty-year bank mortgages of 90 to 95 percent, and the VA of 100 percent. The VA alone enabled 3.75 million ex-servicemen to buy homes, often with a token $1 down payment. The two agencies were insuring 36 percent of all new nonfarm mortgages by 1950, and 41 percent by 1955. Once bankers realized that the risk involved in granting liberal terms was not substantially higher than it had been before, they reacted like men who had glimpsed the Ghost of Suburbia Future. They increasingly made the more generous terms available even to buyers whose mortgages were not federally insured.

It was precisely in the suburbs that the new mortgage policies had their greatest effect. Congress, responding undoubtedly to public pressure, directed the FHA to give preference to buyers of single-family, detached houses, precisely the kinds of houses which could most readily be built in the suburbs. People who wanted to buy such homes could therefore obtain more favorable terms than people who wanted to improve older homes. Moreover, both the FHA and the VA primarily assisted middle-income buyers who were interested in houses ranging in price from $7,000 to $10,000; again, those were the people most likely to be attracted to the suburbs. The FHA rated each residential area on the basis of how great a risk the agency believed it would incur by insuring a loan in that area. Suburban communities invariably achieved higher ratings than urban neighborhoods, which often were "redlined," or labeled undesirable, on the agency's maps. It became virtually impossible to obtain a federally insured mortgage to buy an older home in the city. The deck was stacked in favor of those who wanted to buy a new home in the suburbs.

No one perceived this more quickly or acted on that perception more successfully than William Levitt. Always ready to take a gamble, Levitt, observing people eager to move into their own homes and federal agencies equally eager to help them do so, regarded suburban development as the surest of bets. "How could we lose?" he asked. But to rake in all the chips, Levitt realized, would require a new approach, quite unlike the one he had followed in the 1930s. Then he had built houses for the well-to-do in a community called Strathmore-at-Manhasset. The houses had sold for $9,100 to $18,500.

His experience during World War II, when his firm had erected houses for war workers in Norfolk, Virginia, taught Levitt the advantages of mass production. He built the first Levittown, a community of more than 17,000 homes at Hempstead, Long Island, in the late 1940s; a few years later another Levittown of 16,000 homes arose in Bucks County, Pennsylvania; and a third Levittown of 6,200 homes appeared in Willingboro, New Jersey, in the late 1950s. Levitt's operations provided "the foremost examples of volume and organization in an industry distinguished for neither." The individually designed custom-built house, Levitt said, was a thing of the past: "The reason we have it so good in this country is that we can produce lots of things at low prices through mass production."[5]

Levitt did not make his houses in a factory, but he did the next best thing: he made "a factory of the whole building site."[6] When construction proceeded on schedule, a house was completed in Levittown every sixteen minutes. All materials, precut and preassembled, were moved to each site according to a fixed timetable. All operations were broken down into their constituent parts, and gangs of workers, each performing a single function, moved from one site to the next. Levitt did not deal with unions. Labor, most of which was unskilled, was provided by subcontractors, who were paid a predetermined fee and therefore had every incentive to increase efficiency. Levitt did not deal with middlemen if he could help it. He bought his own forests to provide lumber, and he set up his own supply company to obtain electrical appliances. He cut construction costs at Levittown, Long Island, to $10 a square foot at a time when $12 to $15 was common. A standard Cape Cod house, with a kitchen, a living room, two bedrooms, and an expansion attic, sold for $7,990. The night before the houses went on sale, buyers lined up as they would for World Series tickets. It was no small part of Levitt's entrepreneurial genius that he made the purchase of a house—once a time-consuming procedure involving lawyers and bankers—almost as simple as going out to the ball park.

It was only a matter of time before commerce and industry followed people to the suburbs. A strong trend toward such relocation marked the fifteen years from 1948 to 1963. During that period, in the nation's twenty-five largest cities, manufacturing and trade employment each declined by 7 percent, while in the suburbs of those same cities, employment rose by 61 percent in manufacturing and by 122 percent in trade. The only area in which the cities gained jobs was in service employment, but even there the suburbs gained at a rate more than four times as great. Commuting patterns in Levittown, Long Island, served as a barometer of change. In the late 1940s only one of every four Levittowners worked in surrounding Nassau County, and the other three commuted to New York City. By the early 1960s, however, the proportion was nearly, if not exactly, reversed, with six of ten residents holding jobs in Nassau County.

The most visible symbol of this economic metamorphosis was the suburban shopping center. The first shopping center opened in Kansas City in the early 1920s, but at the end of World War II there were still only eight in existence. Then, like the measles, they spread, dotting the suburban landscape and producing a feverish level of construction, the appearance of one seeming only to herald the appearance of others. After seventeen regional shopping centers had opened their doors in three months in 1957, one observer commented that "at times it seemed they must be coming off a hidden assembly line."[7] Eastland opened in Detroit in 1957, Mayfair in Milwaukee in 1958, Big Town in

Dallas in 1959, and Penn Square in Oklahoma City in 1960. By then there were an estimated 3,840 shopping centers, and they occupied as much land as all the central business districts in all the cities. Geared to the convenience of suburban dwellers, with ample parking space and late-evening hours, shopping centers altered the nation's buying patterns and retail structure. A new breed of builders appeared, as confident of their knowledge of consumer psychology as of their ability to forecast regional growth trends. Don M. Casto, who built the Miracle Mile outside Columbus, Ohio, explained that his success depended largely on the choice of location. "People have path-habits," he said, "like ants."[8]

Commercial developers were not the only ones to discover antlike qualities in the behavior of suburbanites. With the care one might expect to find only among a society of entomologists, Americans during the 1950s scrutinized suburbanization and all that accompanied it—the cars, highways, housing tracts, and miracle miles. Perhaps because of their very visibility, the suburbs became a favorite subject for sociologists, psychologists, architects, planners, political scientists, and, to a lesser extent, novelists. With a few important exceptions these writers assumed a decidedly critical stance toward suburbia and what they took to be its uniformity, blandness, and plasticity. Sociologist David Riesman's essay "The Suburban Sadness," while conceding the diversity to be found, held that the "ideal-typical suburb" stunted its inhabitants' sense of visual imagery and capacity for personal growth. In one mordant sentence Riesman captured the prevalent tone of the criticism: "The suburb is like a fraternity house at a small college in which like-mindedness reverberates upon itself."[9]

The critical literature about the suburbs was extensive, but three books summed up in their very titles the chief elements in the indictment: John Keats's *The*

Crack in the Picture Window (1957), Richard Gordon's *The Split-Level Trap* (1960), and William H. Whyte's *The Organization Man* (1956). Keats wrote about a fictitious suburban couple, the Drones, who, upon moving into a "box," find they have the Amiables, the Faints, and the Fecunds as next-door neighbors. In what was largely an attack on real estate developers (the initials of one of them conveniently spelled SOB), Keats claimed that the all-seeing picture window afforded a family about as much privacy as a waiting room in a railroad station.[10] *The Split-Level Trap* ostensibly discussed the emotional problems that the author, a psychiatrist, observed in Bergen County, New Jersey. Suburbia, he thought, might better be termed "Disturbia," for it harbored "haggard" men, "tense and anxious" women, and "the gimme kids," who, on unwrapping the last Christmas present, "look up and ask whether that is all."[11] Whyte's target was in some respects the broadest of the three: the emerging "social ethic," which he defined, in part, as "a belief in 'belongingness' as the ultimate need of the individual." His study of Park Forest, Illinois, convinced him that the residents experienced a subtle but overpowering pressure to conform, a pressure illustrated by the woman who stopped telling her friends she enjoyed listening to *The Magic Flute,* declaring, "I began to learn that diaper talk is important to them and I'm not so highbrow about it now."[12]

The novelist who most successfully utilized the suburban locale was John Cheever. *The Wapshot Chronicle,* which won the National Book Award in 1957, traced the progress of Coverly Wapshot (and his brother, Moses) from his childhood in the "old river town" of St. Botolphs, Massachusetts, to a post–World War II suburb. Coverly and his wife, Betsey, settled in "a rocket-launching station called Remsen Park . . . a community of four thousand identical houses." There they rented a house "furnished even to the pictures on the walls" and later found that their best friends' house was furnished exactly like theirs, "including the Picasso over the mantelpiece." The boredom of Betsey's daily routine was relieved only by telephone calls, visits from the vacuum cleaner salesman, and trips to shopping centers and supermarkets "not because she needed anything but because the atmosphere of the place pleased her. It was vast and brightly lighted and music came down from the high blue walls. She bought a giant jar of peanut butter to the strains of the 'Blue Danube' and then a pecan pie."[13] Cheever's novel and the collection of his short stories published the following year, *The Housebreaker of Shady Hill,* while anything but polemical in their approach, nevertheless helped authenticate the popular image of suburbia as a place that was humdrum, complacent, and devoid of taste.

The longer sociologists studied suburbia, however, the more clearly they realized how difficult it was to generalize about it and how much the popular image distorted reality. Some of the qualities critics attributed to the suburbs characterized American society as a whole. Commuting, for example, was surely more visible in the suburbs than in the cities but not significantly more common. "Traveling regularly to work is not a peculiarly suburban pattern at all," concluded one study. "It is a characteristic of metropolitanism in particular but of American society in general."[14] Many of the other qualities critics ascribed to the suburbs—their social homogeneity, pervasive conformity, and widespread transiency—seem not to have characterized them at all. One sociologist claimed, with good reason, that the "ideal-typical suburb" was a theoretical figment of the imagination that did not describe the real world. "Suburbs differ greatly in the circumstances of their creation, in the price and use of their real estate, their degree of transiency, their size and institutional complexity, and the income, life style, occupation, and educational level of their residents."[15]

One of the most enduring myths regarding the suburbs was that they served as political rivers Jordan, into which urban émigrés waded, bone-dry, as Democrats only to emerge, dripping wet, as Republicans. In suburbia, the notion went, one "buys the right car, keeps his lawn like his neighbor's, eats crunchy breakfast cereal, and votes Republican."[16] That myth derived from what appeared at the time to be a strong Republican showing in the suburbs in the elections of 1952 and 1956. From 1948 to 1952 the Republicans pluralities in the suburban counties of the fifteen largest metropolitan areas more than doubled, from 773,000 to nearly 1.7 million, and these pluralities increased still further in 1956. In 1952 Democratic candidate Adlai Stevenson carried New York City, Chicago, Cleveland, and Boston; but in every instance Dwight Eisenhower's suburban pluralities wiped out this advantage, and New York, Illinois, Ohio, and Massachusetts went Republican. Political pundits assumed that the old cleavage between urban and rural America, in which demographic trends favored the former, was being replaced by a new division between the cities and the suburbs, in which time was on the side of the latter. Jacob Arvey, the Democratic boss of Chicago, summed it up succinctly on election night in 1952: "The suburbs were murder."[17]

Arvey might more accurately have attributed his party's reverses to Eisenhower's popular appeal than to suburban growth. The shift to the Republicans in the 1950s was, contrary to the conventional wisdom at the time, actually less pronounced in the suburbs than in the cities, and the shift in both areas was less to the Republicans as a party than to Eisenhower as a candidate. In 1952, by winning 55 percent of the total vote and carrying thirty-nine states, Eisenhower increased the Republican share of the vote in the nation's twelve largest cities from 38 to 44 percent; that represented a proportionately greater increase than Republicans achieved in the suburbs. Eisenhower carried San Francisco, Los Angeles, Bridgeport, Buffalo, Rochester, Minneapolis, and Seattle, cities the Democrats had held in their hip pockets for a generation. By 1960, however, with Eisenhower no longer heading the ticket, it became apparent that voters who had moved to the suburbs had not necessarily converted to Republicanism. As the suburbs expanded, so, too, did the Democratic portion of the suburban vote, a change that reflected, in part, the class and ethnic composition of the suburban electorate.

2.

After observing the community of Park Forest, Illinois, William H. Whyte reported that "it is classless, or, at least, its people want it to be." The suburbs, added another scholar, were becoming "the ultimate melting pot."[18] Both remarks expressed the conviction, widely held in the 1950s, that the suburbs were places in which class distinctions dissolved and ethnic attachments evaporated. A visitor to Levittown, Long Island, noting that everyone looked about the same age, wore the same kind of clothing, and lived in houses that were hard to tell apart, could not resist the ultimate comment on standardization: "Each set of parents has exactly two offspring in tow, and the offspring are, respectively, exactly 32 and 36 in. high."[19] The notion of uniformity accorded well with the belief that America was itself in the process of becoming increasingly homogeneous. The process, it seemed, revealed itself most starkly in the burgeoning new suburbs.

Sociologists who set out to discover the relationship

between social class and suburbanization in the 1950s faced problems unknown to their predecessors who, in the 1930s and 1940s, had studied such cities as Newburyport, Massachusetts, Morris, Illinois, and Natchez, Mississippi. In examining the suburbs, they were quite often examining the kinds of communities in which they themselves lived, and in writing about suburbanites, they were, similarly, writing about people very much like themselves. Maintaining one's scholarly detachment was considerably more difficult when talking about Park Forest than when talking about what David Riesman termed "a New England museum for the upper class, such as Yankee City, or a small and rather parochial town in the South or Midwest, such as Jonesville."[20] Then, too, sociologists more frequently came across respondents who, as college graduates, anticipated just what they were supposed to say. "Well, the class structure of this community is quite homogeneous. It is distinctly middle-class but with a scattering of upper-middle-class people," one woman told a startled, if crestfallen, investigator. "I took quite a few sociology courses. That's where I learned about these things."[21] For these reasons, studies of suburban life often left much to be desired.

There were, of course, exceptions to the rule, most notably Herbert Gans's *The Levittowners.* Gans, a professor at the University of Pennsylvania, bought a home in Levittown, New Jersey, in 1958 and lived there for two years, informing people he was studying the community but not admitting he had moved there for just that purpose. "Actually," he reflected, "it would not have occurred to them that I was not simply interested in a good low-priced house and the chance to enjoy suburban living."[22] Gans's work, and that of other scholars, make it apparent that class distinctions did not disappear in the suburbs. The range of classes was considerably narrower, however, and the means of telling them apart somewhat more difficult. And the disputes that most clearly exposed class distinctions often involved local institutions, particularly the public schools.

The class structure of postwar suburbia was, in certain respects, unique. A description of one such community provides a reasonable description of many of them: "There was no elite, no wealthy, prestigious, powerful upper class. There were no shanty families, no clusters of the ethnically 'undesirable.' "[23] The very poor did not live in the new suburbs, and neither, as a rule, did the very rich (whose suburban homes were more often found in older, established areas). What remained were the three classes sociologists designated "upper-lower," "lower-middle," and "upper-middle." Many suburbs had a preponderance of only one of these classes, but a large number contained a mixture of the three. In Levittown, New Jersey, Gans reported that professionals accounted for 18 percent of the work force, white-collar workers for 56 percent, and blue-collar workers for 26 percent. Within the blue-collar category, however, 7 percent were foremen, 10 percent skilled workers, and only 9 percent semiskilled or unskilled workers. In the suburbs, just about everyone lived on the right side of the tracks.

Disparities in income between suburban communities might be large, but such disparities within a particular community were usually small. A 1959 survey of Levittown, Long Island, showed that only 12 percent of the families earned under $5,000 and only 4 percent earned more than $15,000. Two-thirds of the residents had annual incomes between $5,000 and $10,000. The range of occupations was a good deal wider than the range of incomes. On one street in Levittown, for example, a sociologist found twelve families representing twelve different lines of work: house painter, college professor, automobile mechanic, plumber, salesman, blue-collar worker, skilled worker, factory foreman, clerk, research physicist, semiskilled worker, and Wall Street "customer's man." Yet it seems probable that the twelve families' incomes varied less than these job descriptions might imply and that their incomes fairly reflected those of the community as a whole.

If each of the Levittowns was, to varying degrees, heavily middle-class, other suburbs had a decidedly working-class complexion. Such communities arose near every major industrial center, but the one subjected to the most careful study was located in Milpitas, California, fifty miles outside San Jose. Its character as a working-class suburb was fixed in 1955, when a Ford plant moved there, followed by many workers. Milpitas was a community composed not of white-collar workers but of blue-collar workers, not of college graduates but of junior high school and high school graduates, not of young adults and small children but of people of all ages. Suburban by virtue of its location, near universality of homeownership, and reliance on the automobile, Milpitas was not a temporary way station for junior executives seeking room at the top but a permanent home for automobile workers who understood that their lives—although not, they hoped, those of their children—would be spent on the assembly line. Although earning good wages—weekly take-home pay averaged between $80 and $120—and owning their own homes, most did not claim membership in the middle class. One worker, however, made a slightly different claim. "Around here," he said, "the working class *is* the middle class."[24]

In suburban communities more diversified than Milpitas, the older bases of social demarcation proved less and less helpful. Family ancestry, for example, traditionally a badge of rank, counted for little, since no one necessarily knew who anyone else's parents were and since many suburbanites diligently avoided the subject of their origins. Another basis of classification, the kind of home in which one lived, also lost much of its dependability because houses within a given suburb did not vary significantly in price or quality, much less in age. In Levittown, New Jersey, houses ranged from $11,000 to $14,500, but many considerations, including, most importantly, family size, might dictate the purchase of a more expensive model. The kind of work a person did still provided the most reliable guide to class position, but not so reliable a guide as in the past. Rapid technological change itself laid down a false trail. As Gans reported: "Many were working in new and unfamiliar technical jobs, for example, as computer programmers, whose status could not easily be judged by traditional indices."[25]

With kinship, property, and occupation less useful as indicators of status, new measuring devices soon were assembled. The length of time a family had resided in a community often helped determine who was who, with so-called pioneers constituting a self-anointed upper class. Taking an active part in the community and, better yet, acquiring a position of leadership in it were also common means of climbing the social ladder. To be chosen an officer of a civic or fraternal organization, to be elected a member of the school board, or to become known as an articulate advocate of popular causes at public forums—each signified that one had reached another rung. Distinctions, therefore, emerged in the suburbs, and if they were somewhat less sharply etched and more fluid than in older communities, they were by no means less real.

The sharpest conflicts within these communities often occurred over issues involving the public schools. This was hardly surprising, given the child-centered orientation of suburban families, the importance a school district's reputation played in the choice of a home, and the astonishing rate at which schools expanded as a consequence of the postwar "baby boom." It was not at all uncommon during the 1950s for the number of children in a district to double, to triple, or even to quadruple, with the result that new schools could not be built quickly enough, teachers hired rapidly enough—or, some residents grumbled, taxes raised sharply enough. Often controversies arose over the nature of the curriculum itself, and social class had much to do with determining the side on which one stood. The upper middle class tended to support educational innovations even if they were costly. Working-class and lower-middle-class parents, on the other hand, showed considerably less enthusiasm for such innovations. Social class could be gauged with great accuracy when one's position was known on such questions as the age at which children should be admitted to kindergarten, the grade in which the study of foreign languages should be introduced, and the degree of permissiveness students should be allowed. It was precisely over such questions that class attitudes surfaced.

Just as class distinctions persisted in the suburbs, but in a markedly different form, so, too, did distinctions based on ethnicity. To be sure, the suburbs exhibited no single pattern with respect to ethnic adaptation. One observer could point to "suburban districts which have become as heavily Jewish or Italian or Irish in family ancestry as were the ghettos of 'Little Italys' or 'New Erins,'" while another, with no less justice, could assert that "the sheer concentration of ethnic, racial, and national communities in central cities has no similar expression in terms of frequency and magnitude in the suburbs."[26] Yet insofar as it is safe to generalize, it appears that, as in the case of social classes, the suburbs were typified by a narrowing of the range of ethnic groups but not by any diminution of an awareness of differences within that range.

Suburban migration was an ethnically selective process. Immigrants were less likely to move to the suburbs than their children, and the children, in turn, were less likely to move than the grandchildren. Suburbs, in addition, attracted members of some ethnic groups, of whatever generation, more than members of others. The more highly concentrated and residentially segregated an ethnic group in a city, the smaller the proportion of its members who migrated outward. Nonetheless, group differences were surely less important than individual preferences within each group. People who maintained strong ties to the ethnic community in the city understandably found suburban life less attractive than those who were more completely assimilated. Even though people representing nearly every nationality group moved to Levittown, New Jersey, "most came from acculturated homes . . . with little evidence of ethnic culture remaining except among Jews and a handful of Greeks, Chinese, and Japanese."[27]

A waning sense of ethnic attachment in the suburbs mirrored a declining sense of ethnic awareness in the nation as a whole. Issues that had once provoked passionate responses now evoked tired yawns. With a minimum of debate, Congress relaxed immigration quotas, not by modifying the national origins system but by creating new categories of admissible aliens. The Refugee Relief Act of 1953, for instance, authorized the entry over a three-year period of 214,000 people who had fled from communist lands. Of the total, 90,000 were to be of German, 60,000 of Italian, and 17,000 of Greek ancestry. Congress later voted to admit thousands of refugees from the Hungarian Revolution of 1956, removed restrictions on the entry of orphans under the age of fourteen whom American families wished to adopt, and reinstated the quotas mortgaged under the displaced persons program. The new immigrants acquired citizenship in record time. In 1946 it had taken aliens, on the average, more than twenty-three years to become citizens; by 1956 it required only seven years. The Immigration and Naturalization Service sponsored a mass citizenship induction on Veterans' Day in 1954. In what officials termed an "amazing spectacle," 55,000 aliens were naturalized, 7,500 of them in the Hollywood Bowl and 8,200 in the Polo Grounds.[28] In the 1950s, it seemed, the melting pot bubbled cheerfully, a far cry from the pressure cooker it had at times resembled in the past.

With this in mind, many commentators played down the role of ethnicity and emphasized the importance of religion. That, at least, was the argument of Will Herberg's *Protestant-Catholic-Jew* (1955). Citing case studies which indicated that ethnic intermarriage was increasing while religious intermarriage was not, Herberg asserted that religion was replacing nationality, language, and culture as the chief basis of social differentiation. Religious identification, Herberg said, permitted third-generation Americans to have the best of both worlds: they could affirm a connection with both the immigrant past and the American present. Immigrants and their descendants were not expected to relinquish their religious beliefs, although they were, for example, expected to give up their native languages. "The people in the suburbs want to feel psychologically secure, adjusted, at home in their environment," Herberg claimed. "Being religious and joining a church is, under contemporary American conditions, a fundamental way of 'adjusting' and 'belonging.'" As each religious community absorbed "ethnic interests, loyalties, and memories," religion itself became, in the words of another writer, whom Herberg quoted approvingly, "the focal point of ethnic affiliations."[29]

Although Herberg may have exaggerated the decline of ethnic distinctions, religion often did constitute the most obvious basis of social cleavage in the suburbs. The relationship between Catholics and Protestants in "Westwood," an affluent middle western suburb, provided a case in point. A community with about the same number of Catholics as Protestants, Westwood appeared on the surface to be without deep social divisions, but appearances were, in fact, deceiving. "People dressed alike, earned the same kind of income, lived in the same homes, rode the same commuter trains, but occupied two very different worlds." As youngsters Catholics and Protestants went to different schools, played ball in different schoolyards, attended different social functions, and generally kept their distance. As adults they joined the same country club and even arranged informally for the presidency to rotate between the faiths, but they rarely had much to do with each other. The very choice of golf partners, one sociologist claimed, indicated that friendships seldom crossed religious lines: "Even on the links it was a rare foursome which contained members of both groups. . . . The invisible walls of the ghetto cut across the fairways of Westwood Country Club instead of being coterminous with its fences."[30]

If Protestants and Catholics in Westwood kept each other at arm's length, Jews and Gentiles in "Lakeville," another middle western suburb, seem to have lived on opposite sides of a religious Grand Canyon. Jews accounted for much of the community's postwar growth and by 1958 constituted about one-third of its population. Jews and Christians reported that they felt distinctly uncomfortable in each other's presence. They weighed their words more carefully, behaved in a more inhibited fashion, and found fewer areas of common interest. Consequently, friendship circles were to a considerable extent religiously constricted, and even when they were not, the quality of friendship between a Jew and Gentile "rarely matches in warmth, intimacy, interest, spontaneity, and trust the friendliest relationship that respondents have developed with someone of their own faith." In Westwood, Protestants and Catholics at least belonged to the same country club. In Lakeville, however, "the more formally organized country or city clubs are predominantly Jewish or Gentile. So are the garden clubs, the sports groups, the bridge clubs, and especially the informal social groups." Outwardly amicable, the relations between religious groups were marked by an underlying suspicion and by an unyielding tendency to think in stereotypes. When asked to explain the absence of overt religious conflict, one man replied: "No mixing, so there's little chance for strain."[31]

People who moved to the suburbs often became more deeply involved in religious activities, partly for the reason Herberg advanced but for other, more important ones as well. Suburban families were, typically, rearing school-age children, and most Americans, even if not themselves devout, have traditionally wanted to give their children a sense of religious identity as well as an opportunity to meet other children of the same faith. Since suburban churches and synagogues were newer than those in the city, many people felt more of a proprietary sense toward them and more of a need to support them. This was particularly true of people who left urban areas in which their religious group had been dominant and who suddenly found themselves a religious minority in the suburbs. After a while community expectations played a part. Jews who moved to St. Louis Park, Minnesota, a suburb of Minneapolis, could have commuted to a synagogue in the city, but they decided to build a new one, partly to enable their children to obtain a Jewish education but also to relieve "the surprise (and shock) of their non-Jewish neighbors, who had *expected* them to build at least a modest synagogue."[32]

The return to religion in the suburbs attracted a good deal of attention, much of it sharply critical. Suburban churches, the argument ran, were too secular, too complacent, too remote from pressing social problems. "How can you preach repentance for a way of life which has obviously brought to people a resounding success?" asked a writer in the *Christian Century*.[33] Theologians worried about the "suburban captivity of the churches" and about the implications of that captivity: the existence of religious institutions warmly receptive to the superficial but hermetically sealed against any concern with poverty, injustice, or wrongdoing. Some writers carried their attack to extreme lengths. According to the most spleenful critic, the suburban church and the shopping center were becoming indistinguishable, for each catered to materialistic values. "On weekdays one shops for food, on Saturdays one shops for recreation, and on Sundays one shops for the Holy Ghost."[34] Havens for bored suburbanites seeking bingo games, the churches in this view had ceased to be homes for troubled souls seeking salvation.

These accusations, like the indictment of suburbia in general, were surely overstated. There is little evidence to support the view that a shallow religiosity characterized the suburbs any more than it did the cities or small towns. It was in the suburbs, however, that one could most easily observe the process by which religion came to play an increasingly larger role, and ethnicity a smaller one, in the way people defined their identities. This process involved at most a shift in the relative importance people attached to nationality and religion rather than a replacement of one by the other, and it obviously did not affect all suburbanites to the same degree. Gans indicated the subtlety of the process in *The Levittowners:* "Although no one paid much attention to them, some of the traditional ethnic differences remained; German names were prominent in the Lutheran church and only slightly less so than Irish ones in the Catholic parish."[35] The key phrase—"no one paid much attention to them"—supported as well as anything Herberg's contention that a "triple melting pot" was boiling down a multitude of ethnic loyalties and recasting them along religious lines.

3.

During the 1950s, as white Americans moved from cities to suburbs, black Americans, largely from southern rural areas, took their places. Nearly 1.5 million Negroes left the southern states, making their way, for the most part, to large cities in other parts of the country. From 1950 to 1960 the nation's twelve largest central cities lost 3.6 million whites but gained 4.5 million nonwhites. By 1960 more than half of the black population, compared with only one-third of the white population, resided in central cities. Yet in the suburbs whites outnumbered blacks by a ratio of more than thirty-five to one. The nation at times seemed to be the scene of a gigantic game of leapfrog, with white migrants to the suburbs one or two jumps ahead of black migrants to the cities.

Although the black suburban population increased during the decade from 1 to 1.7 million, in 1960, as in 1950, Negroes accounted for somewhat under 5 percent of all suburban residents. But if blacks lived in suburban communities, those communities were often suburban in name only. Many Negro farmers whose homes were situated on the outskirts of southern cities fitted the Census Bureau's definition of suburban but did so solely by virtue of geographic location, not for reasons of income or occupation. Moreover, many blacks lived in older all-Negro or virtually all-Negro suburban communities. The St. Louis suburb of Kinloch, the Chicago suburb of Robbins, the Cincinnati suburb of Lincoln Heights, and the Miami suburb of Richmond Heights, to name but a few, were inhabited almost exclusively by blacks. Relatively few Negro suburbanites lived in places bearing any resemblance to the modern postwar developments.

The social characteristics of black suburbanites reflected, in a curiously inverse fashion, those of whites. By and large, whites who moved to the suburbs held more prestigious jobs, earned higher incomes, had more education, and lived in more comfortable homes than whites who remained in the cities. Just the opposite was true of Negroes. Suburban blacks were even less likely than urban blacks to work in managerial, professional, or technical positions but were, indeed, more likely to be poverty-stricken. In 1959, 51 percent of Negro suburbanites, compared with 41 percent of Negro city dwellers, lived below the poverty level (a consequence, in part, of classifying as suburban a certain number of southern black farmers). Suburban blacks in the 1950s had typically completed fewer years of school than had urban blacks. In the black suburbs, unlike the white suburbs, a large proportion of homes were in a deteriorating or dilapidated condition.

Most Negroes could not afford to purchase homes in the more affluent suburban communities. Of those who could, some preferred to live in the cities, and others found it impossible to leave even if they wanted to. Often real estate agents would refuse to deal with black families who showed an interest in moving to a white suburb. As if by magic, houses that had been on the market vanished into thin air, and down payments that had seemed reasonable soared out of sight. As one observer remarked: "Every routine act, every bit of ritual in the sale or rental of a dwelling unit can be performed in a way calculated to make it either difficult or impossible to consummate a deal."[36] As modern-day Houdinis, however, bankers outperformed realtors, making mortgages that had been available to whites disappear in a flash when blacks applied. So large suburban tracts were closed to Negroes, and the pattern found to exist outside Columbus, Ohio, was, in fact, quite common: "Negro buyers, regardless of affluence, education, or credit rating, would be refused and discouraged if they should attempt to purchase a home in the new developments which cater to the white market."[37]

During the 1950s many suburban communities adopted zoning regulations which, if not so effective as moats around medieval castles, offered some protection against a feared incursion by unwanted groups. These regulations boosted the price of homes by requiring that they be built on large lots, that they contain large livable floor areas, and that they be constructed of fairly expensive materials. Small houses, on quarter-acre lots, with plumbing made of plastic rather than copper could not meet the restrictive specifications. Other ordinances excluded apartment houses and multiple-dwelling units. Designed to preserve property values, maintain health standards, prevent overcrowding, and hold down taxes, these regulations also made it difficult for low-income groups, especially for Negroes, who constituted a disproportionate share of the poor, to acquire suburban homes. Although these ordinances served a number of useful purposes, their actual effect, however euphemistically phrased, was to encourage racial exclusivity.

In a survey taken in sixteen municipalities near Philadelphia nearly four out of five residents frankly stated that they favored "using zoning laws to keep out of [their] community the type of people who usually build cheaper houses on small lots."[38]

The myth of racial homogeneity in the suburbs, therefore, rested on so firm a factual foundation that it can scarcely be considered a myth at all. One of the more striking features of this racial bifurcation is that it occurred at the very moment when, in the nation as a whole, the legal foundations of segregation were beginning to dissolve. Four developments played an especially crucial role in that dissolution: the Supreme Court's decision in *Brown* v. *Board of Education,* the Montgomery bus boycott, the Civil Rights Act of 1957, and the Little Rock school desegregation crisis. The process of suburbanization, it turned out, was strengthening the de facto basis for racial segregation even as judicial rulings, militant protest, congressional action, and executive intervention were weakening its de jure basis.

In 1954 public schools were segregated in twenty-one states and the District of Columbia. One of those states was Kansas, where, in the city of Topeka, Oliver Brown's daughter, Linda, had to travel a mile by bus to reach a black school, although walking to the bus stop she passed a nearby white school. Brown challenged the constitutionality of this arrangement, but in June 1951 a three-judge panel ruled against him on the grounds that segregated schools met the requirements of the separate-but-equal doctrine handed down in 1896 in *Plessy* v. *Ferguson.* The Supreme Court heard arguments in the case in December 1952 and again a year later. In May 1954 the Court unanimously declared that "separate educational facilities are inherently unequal." To separate grade-school children "from others of similar age and qualifications solely because of their race generates a feeling of inferiority as to their status in the community that may affect their hearts and minds in a way unlikely ever to be undone."[39] The Court's ruling eventually became the basis for a series of decisions striking down segregationist ordinances in virtually all areas of southern life.

In reaching its decision the Court relied on law, psychology, and history, although none provided as clear a justification as the justices may have preferred. Legal precedent was especially shaky, for while the Court had recently upheld the argument of blacks who challenged segregated schools, it had never done so in a case that squarely tested the separate-but-equal doctrine. In 1950 the Court had ruled that Texas could not deny a Negro admission to the University of Texas Law School by creating, on a moment's notice, a black law school, for such an institution could not reasonably be considered the equivalent of a well-established one. Similarly, the justices decided that a black educator, admitted to a doctoral program at the University of Oklahoma, could not be required to read at a separate desk in the library, eat at a separate table in the cafeteria, and sit in a separate classroom, for again, such arrangements obviously deprived him of educational opportunities white students enjoyed. Both cases, however, concerned problems peculiar to institutions of higher education. In 1954 the clearest precedent with respect to separate public schools derived not from these 1950 cases but from the original 1896 ruling.

Psychology provided no firmer a foundation than did precedent. Advocates of integration claimed that separate schools harmed black children by damaging their sense of self-esteem and by distorting their image of reality. As evidence, the NAACP introduced two studies by psychologist Kenneth Clark. In one, Negro children were given dolls, some with light and some with dark skins, and asked which they thought were "nice" and which they would like to play with; in the other, Negro children were given crayons and asked to color pictures of themselves as they would like to be. Finding that they often preferred the white doll and often colored the pictures of themselves white, Clark concluded that the children "have been definitely harmed in the development of their personalities; . . . the signs of instability . . . are clear."[40] The Supreme Court cited Clark's studies in its opinion, but his findings were at best inconclusive. For one thing, black children attending integrated schools in the North demonstrated an even lower sense of self-regard, as Clark defined it, than black children in segregated schools. For another, tests of preschool-age children gave the same results as those of older children whose personalities should have been altered for the worse by their experience. One of the Court's law clerks, whose advice was, however, not heeded, summed up the justices' own reservations: "Sociology and psychology appear to be poor foundations for a decision such as this."[41]

Not entirely satisfied to rest its decision on either precedent or psychology, the Supreme Court asked the opposing sides to search the historical record to determine the intentions of those who had framed the Fourteenth Amendment. Passed in 1866 and ratified in 1868, the amendment prohibits any state from abridging the "privileges and immunities of citizens," depriving anyone of "life, liberty, or property without due process of law," or denying anyone "the equal protection of the laws." The historical record, however, could be interpreted in antithetic ways. Lawyers for the southern states pointed out that the Congress which had passed the Fourteenth Amendment had also provided for segregated public schools in the District of Columbia and that many northern states in the late 1860s sent blacks and whites to separate schools. Lawyers for the NAACP, on the other hand, contended that the purpose of the Reconstruction amendments, broadly construed, was to "revolutionize the legal relationship between Negroes and whites, to destroy the inferior status of the Negro and to place him upon a plane of complete equality with the white man." In its opinion the Supreme Court noted that the historical record was "inconclusive," adding that education played so crucial a role in a modern society that it would be wrong to "turn the clock back to 1868 when the Amendment was adopted, or even to 1896 when *Plessy* v. *Ferguson* was written."[42]

The Court's ruling, then, depended more on the justices' perception of morality than it did on legal precedent, social science, or historical interpretation. Earl Warren, who had been appointed Chief Justice in 1953, at a time when the Court was bitterly divided over the issue, convinced those of his colleagues who needed convincing that whatever the situation in the past, segregation rested on a discredited theory of racial supremacy and could no longer be tolerated. With eight of the justices prepared to overturn *Plessy,* the ninth, Stanley Reed, decided to concur for the sake of unanimity. To persuade the nation to eliminate segregation, Warren reasoned, would require not only a unanimous decision but one that would allow for gradual, orderly change. Accordingly, the Court set no timetable for desegregation and even its second *Brown* ruling, in 1955, merely used such phrases as "prompt and reasonable start" and "all deliberate speed." Conceding that problems of administration, personnel, and transportation could not be solved overnight, the Court left all details to the local federal courts.

Southern reaction to the *Brown* decisions more than justified Earl Warren's worst fears. Although some communities in the border states made a start toward compliance, the Deep South adopted diehard tactics of massive resistance. These tactics included the use of economic pressure to intimidate blacks who advocated equality, the assertion of a doctrine of state interposition to rationalize defiance of federal law, and the enactment of measures to harass civil rights organizations by requiring them, for example, to register and provide the names of their members. Among the more successful techniques used to maintain public school segregation were pupil placement laws which authorized local school boards to assign students to schools on the basis of their scholastic aptitude, "mental energy," psychological qualifications, capacity to adjust to new environments, or "morals, conduct, health, and personal standards." The Supreme Court upheld Alabama's pupil placement law in *Shuttlesworth* v. *Birmingham Board of Education* (1958). Refusing to sanction southern plans which overtly defied the *Brown* ruling, the Court nevertheless accepted subtle strategies, like pupil placement laws, the actual effect of which was to maintain a school system as rigidly segregated as that which the justices had declared unconstitutional.

However ineffectual it was in bringing about integration, the 1954 decision helped create a different climate in the South, one manifested clearly in Montgomery, Alabama. In December 1955, after an incident in which a black woman refused to give up her seat on a bus to a white man and was fined for violating the city's Jim Crow ordinance, black leaders hit on the idea of a bus boycott. For nearly a year the city's 50,000 Negroes walked, arranged car pools, or rode in black-owned taxicabs or station wagons provided by supporters. The boycott presented a study in contrasts: between the philosophy of nonviolence preached by Dr. Martin Luther King and the murderous tactics—including the bombing of homes and the dynamiting of churches—practiced by segregationists; between the unity within the city's black community and the divisiveness among whites, a minority of whom favored granting concessions; between the commonly held view of King as a dangerous radical and his actual program. King and his followers were extremely cautious, demanding not that blacks be given the right to sit wherever they pleased but only that seating on buses be on a first-come, first-served basis, with blacks seating themselves from the rear to the front and whites from the front to the rear.

Perhaps the most intriguing contrast of all was that between the broad social basis of the Montgomery bus boycott and the narrow legal basis of its ultimate victory. All during 1956 city officials harassed the movement's leaders, indicting them for violating the state's antiboycott law and charging them with trumped-up traffic violations. In November 1956 the city narrowed its sights and took dead aim at the movement: it enjoined the use of car pools, claiming they constituted both a public nuisance and an unlicensed private enterprise. The city won the case, and the boycott would surely have failed had not the Supreme Court, in the guise of a deus ex machina, intervened. In November the justices affirmed a lower court's ruling which had held that Alabama's laws requiring segregation on buses were unconstitutional. A month later Montgomery's buses were integrated, although not without several acts of violence by white segregationists. Like Apollo in Euripides's *Orestes,* the Supreme Court was advising blacks and whites to "reconcile all strife." Unlike the ancient Greeks, however, southerners in the 1950s were less than willing to accept a satisfactory resolution from on high.

The Supreme Court acted out of a conviction that law did not merely reflect a society's existing level of morality but could itself contribute in important ways to raising that level. This conviction, however, never commended itself to Dwight Eisenhower. In 1948, commenting on segregation in the armed forces, Eisenhower said: "If we attempt to force someone to like someone else, we are just going to get in trouble."[43] His critics might sensibly argue that whether whites liked blacks had little relevance to whether they would sit next to them on buses, but Eisenhower always believed that progress in race relations would occur only when whites wanted it to occur and that action by Congress or the courts would, by inflaming the atmosphere, only retard that progress. Eisenhower therefore refused to place his personal prestige or that of the presidential office behind the *Brown* ruling. Indeed, he came to regret that he had ever appointed Earl Warren to head the Supreme Court. When it came to changing people's values, Eisenhower told Booker T. Washington's daughter, "we cannot do it by cold lawmaking, but must make these changes by appealing to reason, by prayer, and by constantly working at it through our own efforts."[44]

Given this outlook, it was a matter of some wonder that any civil rights legislation emerged during Eisenhower's years in office. That it did was less a testament to Eisenhower's efforts than to those of Attorney General Herbert Brownell. Like most principled individuals, Brownell was offended by the flagrant mockery of democratic procedures in the South, as, for example, when a registrar in Forrest County, Mississippi, disqualified a Negro who sought to vote for failing to answer the question "How many bubbles are in a bar of soap?"[45] But Brownell also had political motives. Introduction of a civil rights bill, he believed, would kill three political birds with one stone: it would enable the Republicans to capture a larger share of the Negro vote, splinter the Democratic party by exposing its southern wing as the chief stumbling block to reform, and embarrass Lyndon Johnson, the Senate majority leader, who obviously had an eye on his party's nomination in 1960. The Republicans expected to reap these benefits whether or not a bill actually passed.

The Civil Rights Act of 1957, however, neither helped the Republicans nor hurt the Democrats. Eisenhower squandered an opportunity to improve his stature among blacks by disowning the House version of the bill, which was designed both to protect the right to vote and to implement court orders desegregating transportation facilities and public schools. "I personally believe if you try to go too far too fast in laws in this delicate field that has involved the emotions of so many millions of Americans, you are making a mistake," the President told a press conference.[46] In the Senate, Johnson's skill as a legislative tactician shielded his party's reputation. The Senate first stripped the bill of all provisions but those relating to voting rights; this made the measure infinitely more palatable to southerners. Then Johnson won approval of a provision for a jury trial for a registrar charged with abridging a citizen's right to vote by disobeying a federal court order. Everyone assumed that southern juries would never convict such defendants. In its final form the act merely created a Commission on Civil Rights with the power to investigate, appraise, and report, and it authorized the Justice Department to seek injunctions against interference with the right to vote. Too emasculated to register a tangible impact in southern polling booths, the bill, as the first civil rights measure to pass in eighty-two years, nevertheless marked a significant milestone.

Eisenhower's misgivings about judicial rulings and legislation did not prevent him from acting, however hesitantly, when states directly flouted federal authority. Such a challenge arose in Little Rock, Arkansas, where school officials had worked out a plan of token desegregation that they hoped to introduce, at three-year intervals, into the high schools, junior high schools. and elementary schools. In August 1957 segregationists demanded that Governor Orval Faubus block the admission of nine black pupils to Central High School, and when the Eisenhower administration refused to accept in advance any responsibility for maintaining order, Faubus ordered the National Guard to turn the children away. The soldiers' duty, he claimed, was "to maintain or restore order and to protect the lives and property of citizens."[47] The situation festered for nearly three weeks until a federal judge enjoined the state from obstructing desegregation. Faubus re-called the National Guard and predicted violence, a prediction that, under the circumstances, had the force of self-fulfilling prophecy. An angry mob gathered outside the school and forced the Negroes to leave. Responding to an urgent appeal from Little Rock's mayor, Eisenhower reluctantly ordered in federal troops, who escorted the blacks to their classrooms and dispersed the demonstrators. Not to have acted, Eisenhower realized, would have been "tantamount to acquiescence in anarchy and the dissolution of the union."[48]

The Little Rock crisis had all the elements of high drama, involving, as it did, a vehement challenge to federal authority, an angry mob hungry for trouble, and armed troops sent to enforce desegregation. The crisis, moreover, did not end in 1957. Troops remained at Central High School throughout the year, and in 1958 the city voted to close its high schools rather than open them on an integrated basis. For a year, only one activity was made available to high school students: football. Not until 1959, after the Supreme Court had disallowed an attempt to convert the schools into "private," and therefore assuredly segregated, academies, did the high schools reopen. In the meanwhile, bitterly contested school board elections further polarized the community. Yet if national attention focused on Little Rock anotl er crisis over integration, less intense to be sure, was brewing at precisely the same time. It occurred, however, not in the South but in a model northern suburban community, and it showed that racial problems were by no means peculiarly southern.

In 1957 some 60,000 people lived in Levittown, Pennsylvania, not one of whom was black. Levitt had always refused to sell houses to Negroes on the ostensible grounds that to do so would frighten away potential white buyers. In August, however, William Myers, Jr., a black World War II veteran employed as a refrigeration engineer, purchased a home from its white owners. His wife was expecting a child, and the family needed more room. The Myers' appearance in Levittown at first caused little apprehension, for the neighbors assumed that he was a house painter, and his wife a maid, and that they were preparing the home for its new white owners. When the residents learned the truth, some of them undertook a campaign of persecution. Hostile mobs milled around outside the house; someone threw a rock, shattering the picture window. Automobile caravans, flaunting Confederate flags, raced by the house. Midnight telephone calls, when answered, resulted only in frightening silences. "Myers' opponents," one scholar observed, "were almost wholly recruited from the ranks of the relatively uneducated urban proletariat in the process of uncertain transit to the suburban middle class."[49] Finally, the state obtained a court order prohibiting further acts of harassment, and the governor made it clear that violations would be severely punished. After two months of agitation Levittown returned to normal, and no issue arose afterward when other blacks moved into the community.

It would be several years, however, before Levitt himself sold houses to Negroes, and he agreed to do so only under duress. In 1958 two blacks who wished to live in Levittown, New Jersey, brought suit against the builder on the grounds that discrimination in the sale of homes purchased with FHA-insured mortgages was unconstitutional because such insurance, in effect, constituted government support. The case dragged on until late in 1959, when an appellate court ruled that public hearings should be held. To avoid the adverse publicity that would inevitably result, Levitt capitulated, announcing in March 1960 that Negroes could buy homes in Levittown. The most elaborate precautions were taken to prevent disorder. Ministers agreed to announce their support, newspaper editors to limit their coverage, and the police to make necessary preparations in advance. More than that, Levitt screened black purchasers to ensure they were solidly middle-class, and he dispersed black families across the development so that no two ever occupied adjacent homes. Wherever possible, he arranged for Negroes to buy the last house on the street (which, typically, was located on the most desirable lot) so as to reduce their visibility. In June 1960, thirteen years after the first white family bought a house in a Levittown office, the first black family bought one.[50]

The desegregation of Levittowns in Pennsylvania and New Jersey reflected, in part, the changed climate of opinion resulting from Supreme Court rulings, political initiatives, and the militancy of the civil rights movement. Yet what is striking about desegregation in those communities is not that it occurred, but that it was so slow in coming, that it proceeded so grudgingly, and that it affected so few blacks. Compared with the number of whites who moved to the new suburban developments in the 1950s, the number of blacks was infinitesimal. Suburbanization encouraged the growth of a racially segmented society, offering a classic example of how demographic trends could work at cross-purposes with constitutional, political, and social change.

[5]
The Age of Reform

Ambrose Bierce once defined reform as "a thing that mostly satisfies reformers opposed to reformation." As a comment on John F. Kennedy's first two years in office, that definition is remarkably apt. So difficult was it either to discern a clear line of reform policy or to win congressional backing for what policy there was that one liberal commented plaintively in July 1962: "The President is the leader of the New Frontier Administration, but what is the New Frontier?"[1] By 1963, however, this situation had begun to change. First under Kennedy and then under Lyndon Johnson, the nation underwent a brief but intense interlude of reform as liberals attempted to end racial injustice, eradicate poverty, and eliminate ethnic discrimination. Those attempts by no means met with unqualified success, but by 1965 only inveterate cynics would maintain that Bierce, in *The Devil's Dictionary,* had said the last word on reform.

1.

The story goes that a man was asked, on the eve of the 1960 election, "Are you going to vote for Kennedy because he is a Catholic?" "No," he replied, "because I am." Apocryphal or not, the story captured an underlying political truth: Ethnicity in general and religion in particular had a powerful impact on how people voted in 1960. "There is no doubt," one observer wrote with evident disapproval, "that millions of Americans,

Protestant and Catholic, voted in 1960 primordially out of instinct, kinship and past."[2] Yet Kennedy did much to ensure that religion would never again play so large a role in future national elections. His approach as President to highly charged issues of church and state went far toward dispelling anti-Catholic fears and thereby brought Catholics even more firmly into the American mainstream.

In the summer of 1960 it appeared entirely possible that his Catholicism would cost Kennedy the election. A number of Protestant groups, the largest and most influential of which was the 9-million-member Southern Baptist Convention, publicly declared their opposition to any Catholic presidential candidate. That opposition was often couched in crude and bigoted language, as in the case of some Alabama Methodists who detected in Kennedy's candidacy "the political machinations of a determined, power-hungry Roman hierarchy."[3] But many Protestant critics expressed more substantial concerns. Those concerns were put to Kennedy by the editor of the Dallas, Texas, *Baptist Standard*. He argued, first, that the Catholic Church determined its adherents' position on moral issues and, second, that "government is a moral matter." The conclusion seemed to him inescapable: a Catholic President could not remain in good standing in his church and at the same time "be absolutely free to exercise his own judgment." Such susceptibility to outside influence might crucially affect policies toward, among other things, birth control, censorship, divorce, and aid to parochial schools.[4]

Recognizing that the election could well hinge on his ability to answer this argument, Kennedy, to the consternation of his advisers, accepted an invitation in September to address the bitterly hostile Ministerial Association of Greater Houston. These advisers, viewing

Kennedy's appearance with no less trepidation than King Darius observing Daniel's descent into the lions' den, were no less astonished to witness the candidate emerging unscathed. Indeed, Kennedy handled the religious issue so skillfully as to remove it from public discourse for the remainder of the campaign. In Houston he reiterated his support for the strict separation of church and state, noted that he had opposed direct federal aid to parochial schools as unconstitutional, condemned all forms of religious intolerance, and promised that if elected, he would decide all issues on the basis of "what my conscience tells me to be in the national interest, and without regard to outside religious pressure or dictate." Should a conflict arise between conscience and public duty, a conflict he did not consider remotely possible, Kennedy pledged to resign his office. "I believe in an America that is officially neither Catholic, Protestant nor Jewish," he asserted, "where no religious body seeks to impose its will directly or indirectly upon the general populace."[5]

Kennedy's views were patterned after the liberal Catholicism of John Cogley, the editor of *Commonweal,* and John Courtney Murray, the Jesuit scholar who taught at Woodstock College in Maryland, both of whom had made suggestions for the Houston speech. Father Murray's *We Hold These Truths,* published, appropriately, in 1960, provided a classic exposition of the Catholic ecumenical doctrine. In a pluralist democracy such as the United States, Murray reasoned, the separation of church and state and the guarantee of religious freedom in the First Amendment served as "articles of peace" which ensured the church's stability and protected its legal position. Consequently, Catholics "benefited by our free institutions, by the maintenance, even in exaggerated form, of the distinction between church and state." That distinction meant that "the Church is entirely free to define herself and to exercise to the full her spiritual jurisdiction." To be sure, in applying these principles to particular cases, Murray did not always arrive at the same conclusions as Kennedy. Murray, for example, favored public support for parochial schools. Yet the two men shared the conviction that Catholic doctrine was entirely compatible with the values central to the American consensus.[6]

Kennedy's adept handling of the religious issue succeeded in disarming even so caustic a critic of the Catholic Church as Paul Blanshard. The author of *American Freedom and Catholic Power* (1949), a book that sold more than 300,000 copies, Blanshard had, over the years, insisted that the church's "authoritarian-minded hierarchy" threatened the liberty of all Americans. Should Catholics ever constitute a majority and follow the dictates of the church, he prophesied bleakly, they would repeal the First Amendment and replace it with one stating: "The United States is a Catholic Republic, and the Catholic Apostolic and Roman religion is the sole religion of the nation." Yet even Blanshard, while not endorsing Kennedy's candidacy, viewed it with uncharacteristic sympathy. In *God and Man in Washington* (1960) he wrote that Kennedy "should be given due credit for challenging the most reactionary view of his own Church's hierarchy." The issue of federal aid to parochial schools provided the best test of a Catholic candidate's credentials, and Kennedy passed with flying colors. Kennedy's stand in favor of the separation of church and state was "quite remarkable for its candor and breadth," so remarkable, to Blanshard's mind, that he entitled a section of his book "A Candidate Versus His Church."[7]

Despite these efforts to minimize the religious issue, it decisively influenced the way millions of people cast their ballots. Not surprisingly, people who attended church most regularly were most likely to vote along religious lines. The effect was considerable: a Protestant Democrat, it was estimated, would have got about 63 percent of the Catholic vote; Kennedy received 80 percent of it. On the other hand, a Protestant Democrat would have got nearly half the Protestant vote, but Kennedy received 38 percent of it. In the trade-off Kennedy lost more votes than he gained; but he lost them primarily in certain southern states which he did not need to carry, and he gained them in northern states, such as Illinois and Michigan, without which he could not have won the electoral-college majority needed to defeat Richard Nixon. Religious preferences did not obliterate class patterns of voting but were superimposed upon them. Although Kennedy's share of the vote increased among both Catholics and Protestants as one descended the economic ladder, there remained striking variations in his levels of support, at each rung, among the two church groups.

Democratic support among Catholics varied along class lines more predictably than it did along ethnic lines. Kennedy achieved levels of support among non-Irish as high as, and sometimes higher than, among Irish Catholics. He received the votes of four of every five Italian Americans in Providence, five of every six Polish Americans in Buffalo, and nine of every ten Spanish-speaking Mexican Americans in Los Angeles. Catholics of German ancestry resisted this trend, but even they, while not providing pluralities of the same magnitude, voted more heavily Democratic than in the past. Because Kennedy won by only 118,000 votes of a total of 68.3 million cast, and because he carried several key states by razor-thin margins, virtually every Catholic group, of whatever ethnic origin, could claim some credit for his triumph. Yet others could no less justifiably make the same claim. Jews voted for Kennedy in almost the same proportion as Catholics, and however great his appeal to religious minorities, Kennedy received more votes from Protestants than from Catholics and Jews combined.

During Kennedy's years in the White House the Catholic issue swiftly subsided. This happened, in part, because most of the remaining differences between Catholics and non-Catholics affected policies at the state and local rather than at the national level. When spokesmen for the Catholic Church, for example, exerted pressure to maintain strict laws against divorce, the targets invariably were state legislatures. Again, Catholics in Massachusetts and Connecticut lobbied on behalf of laws limiting or forbidding the prescription of birth control devices. The National Office for Decent Literature, established by church leaders in 1955 "to organize and set in motion the moral forces of the entire country . . . against the lascivious type of literature which threatens moral, social, and national life," continued its efforts to blue-pencil books, films, and television scripts.[8] Yet censorship, birth control, and divorce, all inflammable issues, did not come before Congress or require the President to take a stand one way or the other.

Federal aid to parochial schools was one issue that did have nationwide repercussions, and here Kennedy bent backward to demonstrate his freedom of action. The President undoubtedly recognized that no matter how firm a stand he took against the church, he ran little risk of losing the support of Catholic voters, and he realized as well that unless he took a strong stand, he stood no chance of allaying the suspicions of non-Catholics. Who could fail to appreciate the irony of a Catholic President who, of necessity, had to be less sympathetic to the church than a Protestant President could have been? As one adviser wrote, aid to parochial schools "is the first real test of the question of whether or not under a Catholic President, the Church would have an inordinate influence. . . . Out of a battle with the Catholic Church leaders," he added, Kennedy would "go far toward neutralizing the religious issue in the country." In proposing an aid-to-education bill, one that would have provided $2.3 billion over a three-year period to build new schools and raise teachers' salaries, Kennedy, citing Supreme Court decisions, noted that "the Constitution clearly prohibits aid to . . . parochial schools."[9]

The Court's rulings, however, were more ambiguous than this statement implied. The three relevant cases, in which only a constitutional virtuoso could have found certainty of meaning, were *Everson* v. *Board of Education* (1947), *McCollum* v. *Board of Education* (1948), and *Zorach* v. *Clauson* (1952). In the first, the Court ruled that New Jersey could reimburse parents for the cost of busing children to parochial schools because such payments did not constitute direct aid to the school. Affirming that "no tax in any amount, large or small, can be levied to support any religious activities or institutions," the majority nevertheless accepted a child-benefit theory under which a state did not need to deprive students who attended religious schools of benefits available to other children. A year later the Court struck down an Illinois ordinance under which children could receive religious instruction, during a released-time period, in public school buildings. But in 1952 the justices approved a New York City provision under which Catholic children attended released-time classes outside school property on the grounds that Americans were "a religious people whose institutions presuppose a Supreme Being."[10]

If these rulings meant that direct aid to religious schools violated the First Amendment, they did not necessarily mean, or so Catholic leaders believed, that long-term, low-interest loans were similarly unconstitutional. It was a dispute over the size and number of such loopholes that led to the rupture between Kennedy and the church. For a time, in 1961, it appeared that a middle course might be safely navigated, one that would satisfy non-Catholics by omitting from the education bill any aid for parochial schools, yet would satisfy Catholics by attaching an amendment to the National Defense Education Act granting $375 million in loans for improvement of the science, language, and mathematics facilities of those schools. The middle course proved more treacherous than imagined; at the twelfth hour a Catholic Democrat from New York City deserted ship and cast a deciding vote that buried the bill in the House Rules Committee. Flimsy to begin with, the craft all too easily capsized, and aid to education was lost overboard. What remained, over the next two years, was the unusual spectacle of Francis Cardinal Spellman anathematizing the President's bill while southern Baptists gave it their blessing.

More than anything else, Supreme Court decisions banning prayer in the public schools kept religious issues alive but in a way that minimized sectarian tensions. The two crucial cases came just a year apart. In *Engel* v. *Vitale* (1962) the Court ruled that it was unconstitutional for students to say a short nonsectarian prayer written by the New York State Board of Regents. Although children could ask to be excused, they nevertheless faced "indirect coercive pressure" to recite the prayer. In *Abington* v. *Schempp* (1963) the justices banned Bible reading in the schools at a time when twelve states made such reading mandatory and thirty others encouraged it. Justice William Douglas explained: "Through the mechanism of the State all of the people are being required to finance a religious exercise that only some of the people want and that violates the sensibilities of others."[11] Controversial though they were, these rulings drew fire from conservatives in both the Protestant and the Catholic communities. One school official in Tennessee, surely overstating the extent of public dissatisfaction, characterized the anti-Court constituency in sweeping terms: "I am of the opinion that 99% of the people in the United States feel as I do about the Supreme Court's opinion—that it was an outrage. . . . The remaining 1% do not belong in the free world."[12]

The Kennedy administration helped remove most vestiges of anti-Catholicism: the fear that a Catholic President would appoint an ambassador to the Vatican, or show religious favoritism in his appointments, or attend mass in the White House, or, when visiting Rome, kneel before the Pope. Changes in the church undoubtedly eased Kennedy's task. By the time Vatican II met, Catholics placed much greater value on dialogue with non-Catholics, and Pope John XXIII's encyclicals emphasized the church's role in achieving world peace and social justice. After Kennedy's death, a Baptist newspaper could assert that "Southern Baptists have had no better friend in the White House. He defended the principle of religious liberty." The assassination itself hastened the Catholic sense of identification with America, for, in John Cogley's words, "now American Catholics have their own 100 percent tragic American hero representing their group in the pantheon of American heroes."[13] Kennedy's belief that politics was a secular matter, that ideology was to be shunned in favor of a rational, problem-solving approach would later be subjected to considerable criticism. For the first Catholic to have become President, however, this approach did have its advantages.

2.

In 1959 historian Arthur Schlesinger, Jr., wrote a memorandum entitled "The Shape of National Politics to Come" which came to Kennedy's attention. Maintaining that American politics follow a cyclical pattern in which periods of reform alternate with those of conservatism, Schlesinger predicted that the passivity of the Eisenhower era was drawing to an end. It was destined to be followed by "a time of affirmation, progressivism, and forward movement." The change would occur, if the rhythm held, "about 1961–62." This view, Schlesinger later wrote, "evidently corresponded to things which Kennedy had for some time felt himself." The historian's forecast proved reasonably accurate, although no one, of course, could have foreseen that Kennedy would only initiate the process of reform and that Lyndon Johnson would preside over its enactment. The years after 1963 witnessed the most powerful surge of social reform since the New Deal, culminating, in 1965, when the Eighty-ninth Congress "brought to a harvest a generation's backlog of ideas and social legislation."[14]

The seeds of that harvest were sown, in the first instance, by economic growth, the signs of which were unmistakable. From 1953 to 1960 the gross national product grew at a yearly rate of 2.1 percent; from 1961 to 1965, even when adjusted for inflation, it grew at more than twice that rate, or 4.5 percent annually. Unemployment declined steadily until by 1965 only 4.5 percent of those looking for jobs could not find them. In the fall of 1961 there were twenty-five areas with unemployment levels higher than 7 percent, but four years later only two such areas remained, both in Puerto Rico. The weekly buying power of a worker with three dependents, again adjusted for inflation, increased by 4 percent from 1955 to 1960 but by 13 percent from 1961 to 1965. At the same time corporate profits after taxes ballooned under Kennedy and Johnson by nearly 67 percent. This expansion, moreover, caused hardly an inflationary ripple. From 1961 to 1965 consumer prices rose, on the average, only 1.3 percent a year.

Puffing up their chests, administration economists crowed loudly over these figures. Convinced that planned budget deficits would stimulate economic growth, they had, not without difficulty, persuaded political leaders to accept a compensatory fiscal policy. The keystone in this Keynesian arch was a $13.5 billion tax cut, proposed by Kennedy in 1963 and enacted under Johnson in 1964, which provided an immense stimulus to consumer purchasing power. The pivotal brick in this structure was considerably less reformist in shape and dimension than one that was rejected: increased expenditures for social welfare programs. Spending billions on such programs, some economists thought, would be no less effective and would do more to advance social justice than would a tax cut which provided the greatest relief to those with high incomes. But it was hard to quarrel with success. By 1965 the Council of Economic Advisers had lost much of its remaining modesty: "Federal policies have made a major and continuing contribution to the great achievements of the American economy during the past four years."[15]

The conviction that this growth was man-made had an intoxicating effect on social reformers, and no one seemed more flushed with the knowledge than Daniel Patrick Moynihan. An Assistant Secretary of Labor under Kennedy and an adviser to Johnson, Moynihan believed that economic planning was rapidly "approaching the status of an applied science." It did not seem unreasonable to suppose that John Maynard Keynes's

"General Theory" explained as much about the laws of the marketplace as Isaac Newton's "Mathematical Principles" did about the laws of gravity. Since a "near quantum change" had occurred in the kinds of information available to government agencies, and since "computer technology [had] greatly enhanced the possible use of such data," the "simulation of social processes" would permit economists to predict the rate at which the GNP would rise as surely as physicists could predict the speed at which an object would fall. The prospects made reformers' heads swim. The question, Moynihan wrote in 1965, was not whether the federal government could discover means of dealing with old problems but whether it could find new problems to make use of the means at its disposal. It seemed that "the immediate *supply* of resources available for social purposes might actually outrun the immediate *demand* of established programs."[16]

No less than these rosy prospects, the easing of Cold War hostilities also cleared a path for reform. After the Cuban missile crisis of October 1962 both the United States and the Soviet Union moved cautiously toward disengagement, finally reaching agreement on a partial nuclear test ban treaty in the summer of 1963. Although the treaty did not ban underground detonations and did not limit either nation's right to manufacture or stockpile nuclear weapons, it marked a first step toward détente and was accompanied, no less importantly, by a deescalation of inflammatory rhetoric on both sides. As the Soviet Union and the United States reached their first major accord since 1945, the Soviet Union and China reached a public parting of the ways. Mao Tse-tung denounced Nikita Khrushchev for signing the treaty, and Khrushchev, for his part, blasted Mao as a warmonger. By the fall of 1963, then, two Cold War tenets had begun to appear somewhat more dubious:

that Russia could never be trusted to live up to its promises and that international communism was a monolithic force.

With the relaxation of international tension, Americans shifted their attention to domestic problems and became, on the whole, increasingly receptive to social criticism. It became first possible, then fashionable to acknowledge faults, to point out defects, to admit that everything was not for the best in the best of all possible nations. Joseph Heller's *Catch-22* offered a case in point. Through the character of Yossarian, a combat flier in World War II whose "only mission each time he went up was to come down alive," the novel sought to expose the immorality of war, the illusion of nationalism, and the institution that symbolized both: the United States Army. The Army, in truth, was filled with madmen, who, with "their loveless faces set immutably into cramped, mean lines of hostility," regarded enlisted men as so much cannon fodder and cared only for their own advancement. The perfect outsider, Yossarian saw things no one else could: "Appleby was a fair-haired boy from Iowa who believed in God, Motherhood and the American Way of Life, without ever thinking about any of them, and everybody who knew him liked him. 'I hate that son of a bitch,' Yossarian growled."[17] Published in 1961 and issued as a paperback in September 1962, the book went through fifteen printings in the next three years. Its popularity reflected, in part, a new willingness to question institutions once held sacrosanct.

The Supreme Court, itself one of the most sacrosanct of institutions, played the unfamiliar role of reform catalyst in the 1960s. The Court's reformist inclinations, evident since Earl Warren's selection as Chief Justice, were confirmed in 1962 by the appointment of Arthur Goldberg to replace Felix Frankfurter, who had been the most influential voice for judicial restraint. The new spirit of judicial activism led the Court to broaden the constitutional rights of citizens and, at the same time, to sanction governmental efforts to remove barriers to social equality. These decisions infuriated many Americans and led, inevitably, to scurrilous attacks on Earl Warren and his associates. Yet fair-minded critics had a valid point in noting that the Court had come to consider itself "a general haven for reform movements." Justice John Marshall Harlan, often, in these years, the odd man out in Court decisions, complained that his brethren seemed to believe that "every major social ill in this country can find its cure in some constitutional 'principle,' and that the Court should 'take the lead' in promoting reform when other branches of government fail to act."[18]

The Court's reform instincts found an outlet in the field of criminal justice. The landmark cases—*Mapp* v. *Ohio* (1961), *Gideon* v. *Wainwright* (1963), *Escobedo* v. *Illinois* (1964), and *Miranda* v. *Arizona* (1966)—expanded the due process clause of the Fourteenth Amendment to protect citizens against infringement, by either the states or the federal government, of certain rights. Often the result of split votes, these decisions nevertheless laid down clear guidelines: a person charged with a felony (as well as a capital crime) was entitled to legal representation; a person too poor to hire a lawyer must be provided with one; a person who was the focus of a criminal investigation must be informed, at the start of the interrogation, of the right to legal counsel and the right to remain silent; a person who waived these privileges must have done so knowingly if the confession was to be used in court. Applicable to anyone who ran into trouble with the law, these rulings naturally had their greatest impact on the poor, on those least able to afford lawyers, least familiar with the

Bill of Rights, and least likely to challenge police procedures.

The Court may have done most for the cause of reform in its decisions on legislative reapportionment. For years the justices had refused to rule on such cases, reasoning, with Felix Frankfurter, that they led into a "political thicket." But by the 1960s the growth of cities and suburbs had created glaring inequities in representation in state legislatures and Congress, inequities that invariably favored rural at the expense of urban areas. In 1962, in *Baker* v. *Carr,* the Court took a flying leap into the thicket it had so long avoided, agreeing that a man in Memphis who thought his vote counted less than that of a rural resident of Tennessee had a justiciable claim. Within two years the Court had handed down decisions requiring that seats in both houses of state legislatures and the House of Representatives be apportioned on the basis of "people, not land or trees or pastures."[19] The "one person, one vote" formula had seismic repercussions over the years, for it strengthened the political clout of the cities and suburbs, the natural constituencies for reform.

In the short run reformers added to their strength in Congress primarily as a result of the Republican debacle in the 1964 election. Senator Barry Goldwater of Arizona received his party's nod that year partly because few other Republicans believed their chances of election good enough to pursue the nomination and partly because many Republicans imagined that a subterranean stream of rock-ribbed conservative voters would surface when a worthy candidate appeared. If anyone deserved such a vote, it was Goldwater, for not only was he a true conservative, but he had the uncanny knack of sounding more conservative than he truly was. The Democrats, hardly able to believe their good fortune, derided Goldwater as a dangerous extremist. They successfully painted Goldwater's acceptance speech ("Extremism in the defense of liberty is no vice. . . . Moderation in the pursuit of justice is no virtue!") as an endorsement of radical-right groups like the John Birch Society, his foreign policy pronouncements ("We will never reconcile ourselves to the Communists' possession of power of any kind in any part of the world") as an invitation to nuclear war, and his criticism of the welfare state ("My aim is not to pass laws but to repeal them") as a death knell for Social Security.[20] If, as Yeats said, "there is safety in derision," the Democrats stood on the safest possible ground in 1964.

In going down to defeat, Goldwater dragged his party with him. Johnson, with 61.1 percent of the vote and a plurality of nearly 16 million votes, carried forty-four states and in thirty-two of them won a majority in every congressional district. Johnson's coattails were commodious enough to carry many Democrats to victory. The party gained 2 seats in the Senate and 37 in the House, so that when Congress convened in 1965, the Democratic majorities of 68–32 and 295–140 in the two bodies were the largest since 1937. The House counted 71 first-term Democrats who were, for the most part, ready to show the President their gratitude, willing to accept his leadership, and able to provide crucial votes. All this enabled the House leadership to add a number of liberal Democrats to key committees—Ways and Means for one, Appropriations for another—and thereby overcome the ability of Republicans and southern Democrats to sabotage reform legislation. The power of the Rules Committee, which is to say the power of its conservative chairman, Howard Smith of Virginia, was diminished when the speaker of the House was authorized to bring to the floor any bill the committee had held for twenty-one days. Observing these changes with evident delight, a presidential aide exulted that "half the battle of enacting the Johnson program is over."[21]

The other half of the battle would be won by Johnson's use of presidential power, a use fully congruent with existing liberal theory. Reformers in the 1960s took it for granted that a strong chief executive was a good thing. On every count, the presidency seemed superior to Congress: one was modern and efficient; the other, archaic and ungainly. Where the President was an advocate of the national good, congressmen were too often slaves of parochial interests. Such was the argument, to one degree or another, of three books published in 1960—Rexford Tugwell's *The Enlargement of the Presidency,* Herman Finer's *The Presidency,* and Richard Neustadt's *Presidential Power*—and of another, the most widely read of all, that appeared a year later: Theodore White's *The Making of the President, 1960.* White went so far in his apotheosis as to say that Kennedy, on election night, was "still half-man, half-President," as if to suggest that by the next morning, or surely by the day of his inaugural, no longer a mere mortal, he would feel as much at home on Mount Olympus as in the White House. When Kennedy called the presidency "the vital center of action," he was voicing a generally accepted view in reform circles, one with which Lyndon Johnson fully agreed.[22]

A past master at calling in political debts accumulated over the years, at exploiting a man's fears and ambitions, at finding acceptable formulas for compromise, Johnson faced a Congress that, by usual standards, was as malleable as putty. He therefore had a much easier time than Kennedy in winning approval for his program. Indeed, Johnson went far toward blurring the distinction between executive and legislative functions. "He blended and obscured the usual relationship between the President and the Congress," one scholar has noted, "mingling previously distinct functions together until he involved each branch in both proposing and disposing of legislation." Johnson dragooned congressmen into the process of drafting bills, determined which congressmen would sponsor the bills, decided which committees would consider the bills, and demanded regular reports from Cabinet members on the standing of the bills. Doing more than his fair share of ear bending and arm twisting, Johnson laid it on thick when a congressman did his duty: "You did the U.S. a great service. You're a gentleman and a scholar and a producer and I love you."[23]

Johnson had once likened the Senate to "a dangerous animal that you're trying to make work for you. Push him a little bit, and he'll go. Push him a little bit harder and he may go or he may balk and turn on you. . . . If you lose your feel for him, he's going to turn around and go wild."[24] In 1965, it might be said, Johnson exhibited the skill of a Clyde Beatty, cracking presidential influence as if it were a whip, while congressmen, purring like so many big cats and only rarely flashing their claws, passed Great Society legislation in the fields of medical care, education, housing, civil rights, poverty, and immigration. The last three were of particular importance. The reform impulse owed as much to a growing national concern with the divisions associated with race, class, and ethnicity as it did to anything else. The civil rights movement, the war on poverty, and, to a lesser extent, the opposition to national origin quotas defined the parameters of reform in the 1960s.

3.

On February 1, 1960, four black college students sat down at a segregated lunch counter in Greensboro, North Carolina, and refused to leave until they were served. After an hour the management closed the counter, and the students departed. The civil rights movement launched that day would, over the next five years, refashion race relations in America. With a complete cast of heroes and villains, an anthem, a slogan, and a list, tragically long, of martyred dead, the movement produced moments of high tension: James Farmer leading freedom riders into the Deep South in May 1961; James Meredith seeking admission to a riot-torn University of Mississippi in September 1962; Police Commissioner Eugene "Bull" Connor turning fire hoses on protesters in Birmingham in May 1963; Governor George Wallace vowing to block integration at the University of Alabama in June 1963; 200,000 participants in the March on Washington, arms linked, singing "We Shall Overcome" in August 1963; college students trooping to Mississippi to organize voter registration drives in July 1964; Martin Luther King leading marches from Selma to Montgomery in March 1965. The movement came to fruition on August 6, 1965, when President Johnson signed the Voting Rights Act.

The civil rights struggle witnessed the most successful application of civil disobedience in the nation's history. In breaking the laws which upheld segregation or prohibited demonstrations, blacks undertook to observe a special kind of discipline. It seemed essential, to civil rights leaders, that demonstrators behave nonviolently, accept the legal consequences of their acts, and direct their protest against injustices so blatant that the movement's idealism could not be questioned. "One who breaks an unjust law must do so openly, lovingly," Martin Luther King explained, "and with a willingness to accept the penalty." Yet King also warned whites that should his approach fail, black extremists were waiting in the wings: "Millions of Negroes will, out of frustration and despair, seek solace and security in black-nationalist ideologies—a development that would inevitably lead to a frightening racial nightmare."[25] Guided by King and others, the civil rights movement adopted new, militant tactics to achieve long-standing goals: equal access to places of public accommodation, the right to vote, and equal opportunity in employment, education, and housing.

By countering hatred with love and brute force with sweet reason, nonviolence would, the theory went, convert even the most hardhearted of segregationists. King had said in 1958 that the Negro's willingness to endure suffering would lead to "redemption and reconciliation . . . the creation of the beloved community."[26] But by the early 1960s, as it became apparent that the hearts of all too many southern whites were hearts of stone, nonviolent protest came to serve a somewhat different, if unstated, purpose: to provoke a series of crises and thereby mobilize white opinion across the nation behind civil rights legislation. To gain presidential and congressional support for such legislation seemed, however, an awesome task. That it was achieved can be attributed partly to the creation of a new organizational base in the black community and partly to the backing the movement acquired in the media, the churches, and the courts.

For fifty years the National Association for the Advancement of Colored People and the Urban League had pursued what one scholar has called a "strategy of assertive accommodation." To a generation of blacks coming of age in 1960 the devotion to gradual and orderly change within the law seemed scarcely assertive and overly accommodating. Three organizations worked to redress the balance: the Congress of Racial Equality, the Student Nonviolent Coordinating Committee, and the Southern Christian Leadership Conference. Although differing in emphasis and structure, each endorsed direct action and civil disobedience in the conviction that "nonviolence as it grows from the Judaic-Christian tradition seeks a social order of justice permeated by love."[27] For a few years these groups achieved parity with the two older organizations, not in finances or membership but in influence and importance. The civil rights campaigns on which national attention centered were, in most cases, initiated by CORE, SNCC, and the SCLC.

Those campaigns received extensive and sympathetic coverage on television. The civil rights movement coincided with the emergence of television as the chief source from which Americans obtained the news, and in the fall of 1963, at once exploiting and solidifying this newfound influence, both CBS and NBC expanded their evening news programs from fifteen to thirty minutes. Stirring, absorbing, and easily grasped, civil rights demonstrations created juxtapositions—prayer, nonviolence, and brotherhood on one side; profanity, malevolence, and discrimination on the other—that were particularly suited for television coverage. Many newsmen credited network news programs with the movement's victories. "Before television," an NBC correspondent remarked, "the American public had no idea of the abuses blacks suffered in the South. We showed them what was happening; the brutality, the police dogs, the miserable conditions. . . . We made it impossible for Congress not to act."[28] One need not accept such claims in their entirety to recognize that television helped legitimize the cause of civil rights by forming a national consensus behind it.

Many institutions, including labor unions, business organizations, and civic groups, contributed to the building of that consensus, but none was more important than the churches. If, as many religious leaders confessed, it was still the case that "Sunday morning at church is the most segregated time in America," religious institutions nevertheless served as spearheads of reform in the 1960s. The National Council of Churches exemplified the new spirit by calling on the church "to confess her sin of omission and delay, and to move forward to witness to her essential belief that every child of God is a brother to every other." Churchmen did more than profess their faith. Priests, nuns, ministers, and rabbis marched in many civil rights demonstrations and served as observers at others, hoping, by their presence in clerical garb, to ward off violence. In a remarkable display of interfaith harmony, religious leaders went to Washington to lobby for civil rights legislation. "For the first time in American history," a writer in *Religious Education* noted, "the United States Congress was presented with a united testimony by Catholics, Protestants and Jews . . . [in favor of] the passage of a strong civil rights law."[29]

The civil rights movement received even more substantial support from the Supreme Court than from the media and the churches. The Court's role was particularly vital in protecting the right to demonstrate because southern law enforcement officials had at their disposal an arsenal of statutes regulating trespass, disorderly conduct, unlawful assembly, obstruction of traffic, and breach of the peace. Handing the police a virtual blank check for repression, courts in Louisiana had construed breach of the peace as meaning "to agitate, to arouse from a state of repose, to molest, to interrupt, to hinder, to disquiet."[30] The Supreme Court, however, insisting on the states' obligation to protect the expression of unpopular views, repeatedly rejected convictions based on these statutes. The justices refused to uphold guilty verdicts based merely on demonstrators' refusals to obey an order to disperse, demanding, instead, proof of their disorderly or tumultuous behavior. In all, the Supreme Court reversed lower court rulings unfavorable to black defendants better than 90 percent of the time.

By 1963 the three streams—religious, judicial, and informational—were beginning to converge and reinforce one another. January 14: More than 650 delegates representing Protestant, Catholic, and Jewish organizations convened in Chicago to discuss ways in which religion could contribute to racial justice. After listening to pleas from clergymen who quoted everyone from the prophet Isaiah ("Seek justice, undo oppression") to the poet Lawrence Ferlinghetti ("I am waiting/for the American Eagle/to really spread its wings/and straighten up and fly right") the delegates resolved: "Racism is our most serious domestic evil. We must eradicate it with all diligence and speed."[31] May 21: The Supreme Court struck down a Greenville, South Carolina, ordinance requiring segregated seating in restaurants (at "a distance of at least thirty-five feet"). As agents of states, cities could not discriminate between citizens on racial grounds without violating the Constitution's equal protection clause. September 2: NBC broadcast a three-hour documentary, *American Revolution, 1963,* devoted to the civil rights movement. A "drama-packed tapestry of pride, courage, hatred, violence and hope," the program left few viewers in doubt about which side the network was on.[32]

But the most auspicious development in 1963, one that marked a turning point in the civil rights movement, was the awakening of the Kennedy administration from a two-year period of hibernation. If the administration had not been soundly asleep throughout 1961 and 1962, it had nevertheless succeeded in shutting its eyes to the moral urgency of the problem. Indeed, the prospect of sponsoring civil rights legislation was enough to give Kennedy and his advisers bad dreams.

Given southern Democratic strength in Congress and seniority on key committees, such a battle not only would be futile but, worse yet, might well torpedo the rest of the New Frontier program. Kennedy still thought it possible to do what he had done in 1960: retain the loyalty of both northern blacks and southern whites. So his early actions—appointing blacks to federal office, speaking out in favor of integration, introducing an equal employment program in the civil service—were designed to solidify his standing with civil rights activists without antagonizing southerners any more than necessary.

Two cases illustrated the administration's circumspection in this area. The first involved the freedom rides. In the spring of 1961 teams of black and white activists rode buses into Alabama and Mississippi in an attempt to desegregate the facilities in terminals. Brutally attacked by angry whites, they received no protection from the police. Faced with the spread of violence, Attorney General Robert Kennedy dispatched 500 United States marshals to Montgomery, Alabama. But he neither endorsed the freedom riders' purpose nor protested against their imprisonment; rather, he viewed their arrest as an acceptable alternative to mob rule. Later in 1961 the Interstate Commerce Commission ordered an end to segregation in interstate depots, and the Justice Department worked to obtain full compliance. A second case grew out of Kennedy's promise during the 1960 campaign to issue an executive order banning discrimination in housing. Fearing the adverse political and economic consequences, the President did not act until after the midterm elections in November 1962 and then sharply limited the order's scope. Although it covered public housing and federally guaranteed mortgages, it was not made retroactive, and it did not cover privately insured mortgages. In both housing and transportation, the administration had followed the most cautious route compatible with preserving its credibility with the civil rights movement.

Spokesmen for the movement, while not regarding Kennedy as an adversary, did not consider him an advocate of the cause. But that changed in 1963, and it changed as a result not only of the developing consensus behind civil rights but also of the pressures generated by the movement. In the spring of 1963 those pressures focused on Birmingham, where Martin Luther King's strategy was put to its sharpest test. Civil rights organizations laid the ground carefully, training volunteers in the methods of nonviolence, screening out those who by temperament or inclination seemed unsuitable, and staging "socio-dramas" to prepare blacks "to resist without bitterness; to be cursed and not reply; to be beaten and not hit back." The "non-violent army," as King called it, engaged in marches, sit-ins, even pray-ins and, when its ranks were depleted by arrests, recruited grade-school children despite the risks.[33] The danger was real enough: state troopers, on more than one occasion, unleashed police dogs on demonstrators or attacked them with fire hoses powerful enough to skin the bark off a tree. Weeks of turmoil produced a sense of national revulsion at the police tactics, an agreement by Montgomery businessmen to desegregate stores and upgrade black workers, and, not least, a recognition on Kennedy's part that his civil rights policies were inadequate.

During the Birmingham crisis Kennedy commented that a photograph of a German shepherd leaping at a black woman made him "sick." But other considerations also dictated his change of course: a belief that the racial crisis was tarnishing the nation's image abroad, a fear that blacks would resort to violence if the government could not respond to their entirely legitimate grievances, and a conviction that as President he must, as Theodore Sorensen put it, "lead and not be swamped" by the civil rights movement.[34] On June 11, 1963, after having had to send federal marshals to enable two black students to register at the University of Alabama, Kennedy made a television address which moved his administration from the periphery to the center of the civil rights drive. The issue of racial justice, he said, posed a "moral crisis" which "patience and delay" could not solve. "A great change is at hand, and our task, our obligation, is to make that revolution, that change, peaceful and constructive for all." Kennedy pledged to ask Congress to commit itself to the proposition "that race has no place in American life or law."[35]

In the next few months the administration proceeded along three lines. First, it cultivated grass-roots support for voluntary integration by arranging White House meetings with labor, business, religious, legal, and women's groups, seeking to create what one aide termed "a new, powerful and virtually invulnerable political and moral force against segregation." Second, Kennedy endeavored to harness the energy of the civil rights movement to his own purposes. When its efforts to cancel an August march on Washington failed, the administration ensured that the speeches were moderate in tone and, in effect, converted the demonstration from a protest against federal inaction into a rally in favor of its own civil rights bill. Introduced in June, the bill would have eliminated segregation in all public places, prohibited discrimination in any state program receiving federal aid, and removed racial barriers to employment and union membership. To garner bipartisan support for the measure was the administration's third objective. Recognizing that a bill could pass only if the Senate invoked cloture against a filibuster and that the sixty-seven votes needed for cloture could be obtained only with Republican help, Democrats worked closely with Minority Leader Everett M. Dirksen. Without his support, they believed, the effort to pass a bill would "be reduced to an absurdity."[36]

By the time the civil rights bill reached the floor of Congress in February 1964 Lyndon Johnson had assumed the presidency. Civil rights was to Johnson as a southerner what aid to parochial schools was to Kennedy as a Catholic: a test of his credentials as a reformer and a national leader. "If I didn't get out in front on this issue," Johnson recalled, the liberals "would get me. They'd throw up my background against me, they'd use it to prove I was incapable of bringing unity. . . . I had to produce a civil rights bill that was even stronger than the one they'd have gotten if Kennedy had lived. Without this, I'd be dead before I could ever begin."[37] That explains why Johnson, who usually leaned toward compromise as a seedling bends toward light, refused to make any concessions to southern Democrats, thereby resisting an instinct for accommodation so strong, in his case, as to constitute a positive tropism.

The Civil Rights Act of 1964 passed the House with the support of 152 Democrats and 138 Republicans, and in June, after Dirksen had delivered the promised votes for cloture, the measure cleared the Senate by a margin of 73 to 27. The act barred racial discrimination in theaters, gas stations, hotels, restaurants, and other places of public accommodation. It authorized the Attorney General to eliminate segregation in public schools, libraries, museums, hospitals, and playgrounds. It provided for the withholding of funds from federally assisted projects which failed to desegregate. It prohibited discrimination by businesses with 100 employees or trade unions with 100 members, and it stipulated that within three years the prohibition would extend to smaller concerns. The Supreme Court quickly upheld the constitutionality of the act's most controversial sections, those relating to public accommodations, with some justices basing their decision on the power of Congress to regulate interstate commerce and others resting their argument on the Fourteenth Amendment. Whatever the grounds, the purpose of the act was, in Justice Goldberg's words, "the vindication of human dignity."[38]

The act, however, proved ineffective in safeguarding the right to vote. While it made a sixth-grade education a presumption of literacy and prevented the rejection of applicants for slight errors on their registration forms, it permitted southern registrars a wide area of discretion. In 1965, therefore, the civil rights campaign centered on voting rights and, more specifically, on Selma, Alabama. Located in Dallas County, where 2.1 percent of the eligible blacks were enrolled but where the election board remained open two days a month and processed applications at a snail's pace, Selma had, in the person of Sheriff Jim Clark, who ordered his men to use electric cattle prods on demonstrators, the embodiment of southern intransigence. By February 1965 the city had arrested 2,000 blacks, and the following month, when the state could not guarantee the safety of demonstrators who planned to march from Selma to Montgomery, the President federalized the National Guard. Just as Birmingham had forced Kennedy's hand, so Selma forced Johnson's. On March 15 the President, stating that Selma "lay bare the secret heart of America itself," went before Congress to request a strong voting rights bill.[39]

Five months later, in the same room in which Abraham Lincoln had signed the Emancipation Proclamation, Johnson signed the Voting Rights Act of 1965. Enacted with bipartisan support, the act declared a moratorium on literacy tests in states or counties which required them and in which less than half the population had voted in 1964. The Civil Service Commission would assign federal registrars to enroll voters. Affecting Alabama, Georgia, Louisiana, Mississippi, South Carolina, Virginia, and parts of North Carolina, the act, in Johnson's words, was "one of the most monumental laws in the entire history of American freedom."[40] It had an instantaneous effect. On August 14, in Selma, federal registrars enrolled 381 blacks, more than the number registered in the previous sixty-five years. In 1964, 35 percent of southern blacks were registered; in 1969, that figure had risen to nearly 65 percent. The deepest of Deep South states saw the most dramatic changes, with the percentage of registered blacks increasing from 19 to 61 in Alabama, from 7 to 67 in Mississippi, and from 27 to 60 in Georgia.

On signing the Voting Rights Act, Johnson, with characteristic overoptimism, said that "today the Negro story and the American story fuse and blend." Yet while the nation had traveled a remarkable distance, it had not reached the Elysian Fields. Even as the civil rights forces were scoring their most impressive legislative victories, signs were appearing of the discord that would fracture the movement and the consensus on which it rested. By 1965 many blacks had begun to question integration as an ultimate goal, and many more, including some who had served in the forefront of the struggle, had begun to doubt the worth of nonviolence. Then, too, as activists turned their attention to conditions in the North, where the target was de facto rather than de jure segregation, whites who had supported civil rights when protest was confined to the South grew distinctly cooler to black demands. Ghetto rioting had already erupted, first in New York City in 1964 and then, only a week after Johnson spoke of fusion and blending, in the Los Angeles ghetto of Watts. The flames that rose skyward from the charred buildings in Watts signaled the direction that events would thereafter take as surely as the first sit-in, five years before, had ushered in the civil rights movement.

4.

Social reform in the 1960s dealt with class as well as with racial inequality. After tiptoeing carefully around the problem of poverty, as it had that of race, for two years, the Kennedy administration in 1963 claimed the issue as its own. Within a year Congress enacted legislation to effectuate what Lyndon Johnson termed a "redistribution of wealth . . . from those who have it, to those who don't have it." Yet the concern with poverty differed in a fundamental respect from the concern with race. Unlike the civil rights movement, which generated powerful mass pressures and thereby forced politicians to take action, the antipoverty program remained "a movement of reform in search of its constituency."[41] The program did not arise out of a loud public demand but from a quiet professional one. Economists, both within and outside the federal government, made the most effective case for a war on poverty.

For that case to obtain a cordial hearing there had to be, as a minimum, public recognition that poverty constituted a serious national problem. No such awareness existed in the 1950s. When John Kenneth Galbraith's *The Affluent Society* (1958) attempted to show that poverty, if no longer "a massive affliction," was nevertheless a hurtful one, few seemed to take notice. This complacency was rattled in March 1962 by publication of Michael Harrington's *The Other America*, which called for "a crusade against this poverty in our midst," and it was further shaken by Harry Caudill's *Night Comes to the Cumberlands* (1963), a portrait of the coalfields of eastern Kentucky, which pointed to "medieval stagnation in the midst of twentieth-century prosperity and progress."[42] By January 1963 Dwight Macdonald, reviewing several newly published studies of poverty for *The New Yorker,* could observe: "In the last year we seem to have suddenly awakened, rubbing our eyes like Rip van Winkle, to the fact that mass poverty persists." In April 1963 the Swedish economist Gunnar Myrdal delivered a series of lectures at the University of California which were published as *Challenge to Affluence.* The title, appropriately, seemed a rejoinder to Galbraith, and there was no mistaking Myrdal's message: "There is an ugly smell rising from the basement of the stately American mansion."[43]

On October 20, 1963, the New York *Times* published a report by Homer Bigart on conditions in the Kentucky coalfields. Bigart wrote of "the pinched faces of hungry children, the filth and squalor of cabins, the unpainted shacks that still serve as schoolhouses." He pictured creeks littered with garbage and hills gouged out by bulldozers. The welfare system may have prevented people from starving to death, but it had a fatal effect on their self-respect. "Gone is the frontier bravado, the sense of adventure, the self-reliance that once marked the Kentucky mountaineer." Communities were "whipped, dispirited," the children "pot-bellied and anemic," the unemployed "too listless, too beaten to be capable of political activism." Muckraking journalism of the first order, Bigart's article, whether intentionally or not, brought together the three most important concepts underlying the new perception of poverty.[44]

The first was that of white Appalachia as the archetype of a region in need. Public concern centered on the coal-mining communities of eastern Kentucky, northern Tennessee, and West Virginia for several reasons: a wildcat strike by miners in the summer of 1962 had erupted in violence; torrential rains in March 1963 had produced devastating floods that made a bad situation worse; and strip-mining operations strikingly dramatized the ravaging of a once-beautiful landscape. Producers of television documentaries discovered a gold mine of visual images in Appalachia and, according to one resident, soon began to "vie with one another in ferreting out the most woebegotten of our citizens to place before their cameras."[45] For those who favored an antipoverty program Appalachia had an obvious appeal. Not only did focusing on it offer a means of winning southern Democratic support in Congress, but it also suggested that poverty was, if anything, as American as Davy Crockett, Daniel Boone, and the Cumberland Gap. An antipoverty program might aid Harlem as much as, or more than, Harlan County, but those who backed the program had little, if any, reason to announce that fact.

A second concept—poverty as a cycle—could be found, in one of two versions, in every work on the subject. Impoverished people were trapped in a vicious circle: since they lived in slums, ate unnutritious food, and received poor medical care, they got sick more often and stayed sick longer than did others; they were therefore more likely to forfeit their pay and lose their jobs; they were then forced to live in even worse slums, eat even less well, and call the doctor even less frequently, with the prospect always of being swept downward in the spiral. Children as well as adults drowned in this tragic vortex: lacking parental support and encouragement, the children of the poor started school at a disadvantage, fell behind in their work, lost interest in their studies, and dropped out; lacking either skill or self-confidence, they were engulfed in the same maelstrom as their parents and bequeathed a similar legacy to their own children.

Poverty, in either case, was self-perpetuating, and what

was being perpetuated was nothing more or less than a full-fledged culture, "a way of life which is passed down from generation to generation along family lines."[46] The concept of a culture of poverty was borrowed from the work of anthropologists. Oscar Lewis, who formulated the idea in 1959 and later expanded it in *La Vida* (1966), a study of a Puerto Rican family in New York City, reasoned that the culture of poverty consisted of "some seventy interrelated social, economic and psychological traits," including an unstable, authoritarian, and matriarchal family structure, "a strong feeling of marginality, of helplessness, of dependence and of inferiority," an inability to defer gratification, a capacity for spontaneity and adventure, and "a sense of resignation and fatalism." Transcending national boundaries, these characteristics, Lewis held, were commonly found among the poor in less advanced nations. In the United States, however, only one-fifth of the poor revealed "characteristics which would justify classifying their way of life as that of a culture of poverty." Michael Harrington and others appropriated Lewis's general idea but left out his qualifications. "To be impoverished is to be an internal alien, to grow up in a culture that is radically different from the one that dominates this society," Harrington wrote. "The poor are not like everyone else. They are a different kind of people."[47]

The notion of a culture of poverty seemed to serve reformers' purposes well. It absolved the poor of any blame for their condition, since children, by the time they were six or seven, had "absorbed the basic values and attitudes of their subculture" and were therefore locked involuntarily into the same dismal lives their parents led. It justified outside intervention, since the poor were too inarticulate and unorganized to act for themselves. It also suggested the need for a broad-gauged program, one capable of substituting a "human environment for the inhuman one that now exists."[48] The only hitch was the absence of empirical evidence that an autonomous culture of poverty actually existed. Many critics pointed out that the concept itself, although expressed in scientific terminology, only reflected and reinforced "ethnocentric middle-class stereotypes of the poor." Despite this criticism, the concept of a culture of poverty, like the image of Appalachia and the belief that poverty follows a cyclical pattern, shaped the direction of government policy.[49]

The conversion of the Kennedy administration to the antipoverty cause was gradual. As late as December 1962 the prevailing dogma held that poverty was diminishing, that insofar as it still existed, it was best remedied by policies designed to stimulate general economic growth, and that "to the extent it is peculiarly associated with nonwhite color, widowhood, and old age" it might "be harder to overcome than the more generalized poverty of earlier generations." By the spring of 1963, however, the transition to a new set of beliefs had begun, propelled by studies prepared for the Council of Economic Advisers which effectively made two points: despite the economy's good health, poverty was diminishing more slowly than had been assumed and, in view of that good health, more slowly than was necessary. Moreover, the civil rights movement encouraged a recognition that racial problems were often economic in nature and amenable only to an economic solution. The President himself finally sensed a need for a bold program around which Democrats could unite. In the fall of 1963, with the zeal of a true believer, Kennedy said that "the time has come to organize a national assault on the causes of poverty, a comprehensive program across the board."[50]

Once the conversion of the federal government was complete, ideas formerly regarded as heretical speedily acquired the aura of revealed truth. Nothing better illustrated the process of legitimization better than the

Council of Economic Advisers' *Economic Report of the President* for 1964, which virtually paraphrased Michael Harrington's views on the poverty cycle and its cultural manifestations. "Poverty breeds poverty. A poor individual or family has a high probability of staying poor. Low incomes carry with them high risks of illness; limitations on mobility; limited access to education, information, and training," the council noted. "Thus the cruel legacy of poverty is passed from parents to children." Again: "The poor inhabit a world scarcely recognizable, and rarely recognized, by a majority of their fellow Americans. It is a world apart, whose inhabitants are isolated from the mainstream of American life and alienated from its values." Similarly, the 1964 report of the President's Appalachian Regional Commission echoed Harry Caudill or, to be more exact, provided a mass of facts and figures that substantiated his claims.[51]

In the space of eight months in 1964 the Johnson administration framed an ambitious antipoverty program and secured its enactment. R. Sargent Shriver, who was put in charge of defining the program's scope and direction, faced pressures from two directions. Nervous about the potential cost, the President was willing to request only $462.5 million, which, when added to the $500 million earmarked for existing programs, would produce a war on poverty with a price tag of nearly $1 billion. (When Michael Harrington, who was consulted in drafting the bill, protested that this sum amounted to "nickels and dimes," Shriver replied, "Perhaps you've spent a billion dollars before, but this is my first time around.")[52] Shriver operated under administrative as well as fiscal constraints, for the Secretaries of Labor and HEW, arguing against the creation of a separate antipoverty bureaucracy, sought control over many of the new programs. Congressional Democrats, if not exactly jubilant about declaring war on poverty, had little inclination to cross the President in an election year and on an issue defined in partisan terms. Republican votes, vital for civil rights, were not needed and not solicited. Congress passed the Economic Opportunity Act by a comfortable margin, and Johnson signed it in August 1964.

The act aided impoverished young people, hard-pressed small businessmen, marginal farmers, and welfare recipients, but the Community Action Program, housed in a newly created Office of Economic Opportunity, best exemplified the administration's approach. Nursery schools, remedial reading courses for adults, job training for teenagers, consumer education classes, legal aid services, neighborhood recreation centers—within eighteen months the OEO had funded some 1,000 such programs. Their most striking feature was the requirement that in both planning and administration they obtain the "maximum feasible participation" of the poor. Although it may well be true that "nobody in 1964 knew the meaning of these three words" and although it is certainly true that Congress paid no attention to the provision in its debate, it was generally assumed by those who drafted the act that involvement of the poor would help overcome the alienation, despair, and helplessness that, it was also assumed, characterized the culture of poverty.[53]

The antipoverty formula provided a perfect rationale for other ambitious federal programs, many of which had been bottled up in Congress for years but were approved in 1965. The Elementary and Secondary Education Act, for example, sidestepped the controversy over aid to parochial schools by making such aid available to all schools in districts in which a certain proportion of children came from low-income homes. The Housing Act provided rent subsidies for poor families that were displaced by urban renewal projects or could not find suitable public housing. Medicare and medicaid provided health insurance for the elderly and the indigent, the former by covering 80 percent of the hospital expenses of anyone over the age of sixty-five and the latter by helping poor people, regardless of age, pay their doctors' bills. The Appalachian Regional Development Act pumped billions of dollars into the area, much of it to modernize highways and attract new industry.

All this, especially the Economic Opportunity Act, was "unabashedly class legislation, designating a special group in the population as eligible to receive the benefits of the law."[54] But who qualified as poor and was consequently eligible? The government at first operated under a rule-of-thumb assumption that the poverty line, for an urban family of four, was $3,000, but in 1964 an economist in the Social Security Administration, Mollie Orshansky, undertook to find a more precise measure. She began with several premises: a person could manage on three meals a day at a total cost of 70 cents; a family needed one-third of its income for food; a rural family, which could grow some of its own food, required 40 percent less cash than an urban family. It then became a matter of simple multiplication to determine that the poverty line for an urban family of four was $3,130, and for a farm family, $1,925. By this standard, 34.6 million people lived in poverty, 15.6 million of them under the age of eighteen and 5.2 million of them over the age of sixty-five. Recognizing that each of her premises was, in fact, open to question, Orshansky defended the standard on the grounds of plausibility. "Few could call it too high," she asserted. "Many might find it too low."[55]

The poor, now having been defined, were expected to participate in community action programs, but their participation virtually ensured that the OEO would become a hornet's nest of controversy. It was no easy task to select residents of impoverished communities who would fairly represent their neighbors on the boards of community action agencies, partly because elections ordinarily attracted tiny turnouts and partly because there was an overabundance of self-appointed spokesmen who, recognizing a good thing when they saw it, viewed antipoverty funds as an excellent thing indeed. A few ill-conceived programs, calculated, it seemed, to offend local political leaders, were instituted. In Syracuse, New York, for example, the antipoverty office first called for protest marches against the mayor and then used its funds to bail the demonstrators out of jail. Mayors, even those who were not so directly assailed, naturally preferred City Hall to be the channel for federal funds and therefore regarded antipoverty officials as rival sources of patronage and power. The OEO also fought day-in, day-out skirmishes with the Department of Labor for jurisdiction over job-training programs. To add to these troubles, Republicans attacked the war on poverty in the same partisan spirit in which Democrats had enacted it. The "greatest boondoggle since bread and circuses in the days of the ancient Roman empire," intoned Senator Dirksen, adding ominously, "when the republic fell."[56]

With these forces ranged against it, within a year or two the OEO found Congress limiting its flexibility, curtailing its activities, and subjecting it to a much greater degree of gubernatorial and mayoral influence than at first. Then, too, as escalation of the war in Vietnam made more insistent demands on the federal budget, the President edged away from his commitment to the antipoverty program. The OEO found itself on a treadmill, fighting a losing battle each year merely to stay in place. The OEO expected to spend $3.5 billion in its second year but received just half that amount, and the next year its budget was sliced to $1.5 billion. Not only did these cuts hobble the agency, but more and more of its time had to be spent in trying to decide which programs to barter for congressional votes in order to prevent further cuts.

The OEO represented only one flank in the war on poverty, and despite the agency's difficulties, total federal outlays to assist the poor rose substantially from $13.4 billion in 1964 to $23.9 billion in 1969. During Johnson's years in office poverty was reduced. From 1964 to 1967 the number of people whose incomes placed them below the poverty threshold declined from 34.6 to 25.9 million, although how much of the decline should be attributed to the war on poverty and how much to general prosperity—unemployment dropped in the same period from 5.2 to 3.8 percent—is difficult to say. The success of federal programs can best be measured by the impact on the poor of cash transfers under federal income-support programs. In 1965 there were 16 million households with incomes below the poverty line before such transfers were made. Two-thirds of those households received some assistance from government programs, and this aid lifted 4.7 million individuals above the poverty line. The war on poverty produced a gradual, incremental advance but not the unconditional surrender and spectacular victory that Johnson had promised.

5.

Less controversial than either civil rights legislation or the war on poverty, the reform of immigration policy was nevertheless a fundamental goal of the New Frontier and the Great Society, and it, too, was partially realized. The Immigration Act of 1965 did not substantially increase the number of people who were granted entry into the country each year, and while it eliminated vestigial forms of ethnic and racial discrimination, the new law also introduced a new distinction by limiting, for the first time, immigration from nations of the Western Hemisphere. But the importance of the reform, if largely symbolic, should not be underestimated. Congress in 1965 finally recognized that the ideal of cultural assimilation, to which the law had paid homage since 1924, was no longer appropriate.

Beyond the Melting Pot was, in fact, the title of an influential book published in 1963 by Nathan Glazer and Daniel Moynihan. By no means a call for liberalization of immigration policy, the book nevertheless described patterns of ethnic adjustment in New York City in a way that could not but help support critics of assimilation. Although "powerful assimilatory influences" had undermined the foreign-language press, broken up immigrant quarters, weakened fraternal societies, and cut immigrants' ties to their native lands, the result, the authors contended, was not the melting down of immigrant groups, their alchemization into a native American gold. Instead, while the grandchildren of Italian, Irish, and Jewish immigrants spoke the same language and were, to outward appearances, alike, they remained "distinct and identifiable." They "voted differently, had different ideas about education and sex, and were still, in many essential ways, as different from one another as their grandfathers had been."[57]

The grandson of one Irish immigrant, John F. Kennedy always thought that the national origins system had "strong overtones of an indefensible racial preference."[58] Kennedy expressed an interest in reforming the immigration laws in the summer of 1962, and his interest may well have deepened that fall after the Democratic party lost ground among immigrant voters. In July 1963 the President called on Congress to eliminate immigration quotas over a five-year period by reducing each nation's quota by 20 percent annually and by allotting the excess places to applicants on a first-come basis. Eventually, all immigrants—up to 165,000 a year—would be considered without regard to national origin. Kennedy also proposed that Congress retain the quota exemption for immigrants from Western Hemisphere nations and for other special cases. These recommendations met with stubborn resistance in Congress, but by January 1965, when Johnson made the same recommendations, the prospects appeared substantially brighter.

From February to August 1965, as subcommittees on immigration of the House and the Senate Judiciary committees held hearings on Johnson's proposal, it became apparent that the balance on those committees had swung toward reform. Just as clearly, however, leading Democrats, notably Congressman Michael Feighan of Ohio and Senator James Eastland of Mississippi, remained bitterly antagonistic. When an officer of the Daughters of the American Revolution, testifying against the termination of national origin quotas, pointed in terror to "a collapse of moral and spiritual values if nonassimilable aliens of dissimilar ethnic background and culture are permitted gradually to overwhelm our country," Eastland was very pleased. "You have made a very fine, sensible statement, very able statement," he said.[59] Joining the DAR in its stand against reform were such groups and quasi groups as the League of Christian Women, the American Legion, the Sons and Daughters of Liberty, and the Sons of Union Veterans of the Civil War.

Spokesmen for the Johnson administration as well as for organizations representing labor, religious, liberal, and immigrant groups defended reform on practical and philosophical grounds and pointed also to opinion polls which showed that the public, although not favoring an increase in immigration, considered place of birth less important in determining admissibility than an immigrant's occupational skills or familial ties to American citizens. Advocates of change claimed, above all, that they merely wished to make the law conform with actual policy. In the thirteen years since passage of the McCarran-Walter Act, they noted, 3.5 million immigrants had entered the United States, but two-thirds of them had done so outside the quota system. All sorts of imaginative ploys had been devised to get around an antiquated law, one which established larger quotas for Britain and Germany than for all the other nations of the world combined. By enacting special dispensations to expedite nonquota admissions, Congress had, over the years, "abandoned the national origins system without repealing it. It was dead."[60]

Senator Sam Ervin of North Carolina made the most diligent attempt to breathe new life into that system. The quota, he said, was "like a mirror reflecting the United States," for it "brings people to this country similar to those who have already got in here, and they are more easily assimilated into our population. . . . Those who are most alike live together in the greatest tranquility." When, during the course of the hearings, Ervin declared that certain immigrants, notably those from England, had made the greatest contribution to American life, he was challenged by Senator Robert Kennedy of New York: "I think . . . the people from all these countries have made major contributions to the United States, and I do not think any Senator is in a position to say one country or one people has made more of a contribution . . . than people of another country."[61] By the fall of 1965, realizing that no form of artificial respiration could revive the national origins system, Ervin swung his support to reform, but not before exacting a stiff price.

Centering his fire on the existing quota exemption for nations of the Western Hemisphere, an exemption dating from 1924, Ervin gave the bill's sponsors a heavy dose of their own medicine. If, as the administration claimed, the quota system discriminated against some nations in favor of others, was not the exemption of Western Hemisphere nations open to the same objection? And if, as the administration said, there was no danger of a massive influx of immigrants from Canada, Mexico, and South America, was anything to be lost by setting an upward limit, just to be sure? Thrown on the defensive by these arguments, the administration barely beat back an attempt in the House to limit immigration from the Western Hemisphere only to lose a key vote in the Senate when the subcommittee of the Judiciary Committee accepted Ervin's proposal by a margin of 5 to 3. Fearing no bill could pass without the amendment, Johnson decided not to seek its elimination, and in September the Senate passed the Immigration Act of 1965.

The act revamped existing procedures. It abolished the national origins system as of July 1, 1968; until then unused portions of quotas would be pooled, and thereafter quotas would no longer exist. A total of 170,000 immigrants—but no more than 20,000 from any one nation—would be admitted each year on a first-to-apply basis. Relatives of American citizens would be admitted separately. The act repealed the provision for an "Asia-Pacific Triangle," under which Asian immigrants were counted against quotas according to their racial ancestry rather than their place of birth. The act imposed a ceiling of 120,000 on immigration from the Western Hemisphere, a limitation to take effect on July 1, 1968, unless Congress decided in the interim not to implement it. At the time nearly 125,000 such immigrants were entering the United States each year, 70,000 of them from Canada and Mexico. Finally, the act gave preference in admission to immigrants with professional training and highly developed skills.

These provisions altered the composition of the immigrant stream. More immigrants came from Asia and fewer from Europe until, by the early 1970s, Asian immigration exceeded European. Of European immigrants, relatively more were from Mediterranean nations and relatively fewer were from Britain and Germany. After 1965 the countries contributing the largest number of immigrants were Mexico, the Philippines, Cuba, and Korea. The characteristics of the newcomers as well as their countries of origin underwent a change. Because the act granted priority to people with specially needed skills, it ensured that the proportion of professionals among those granted entry would nearly double. This contribution to the "brain drain" led one journalist to suggest that Emma Lazarus's verse on the Statue of Liberty needed revision: "Give me your gifted, your educated few yearning to strike it rich."[62]

It was at the Statue of Liberty, on October 3, 1965, that Lyndon Johnson signed the Immigration Act. His remarks, for the most part, concerned immigrant contributions to America, the injustices of the national origins system, and the improvement promised by the new legislation. Then, suddenly, Johnson said: "This year we see in Viet Nam" men dying, "men named Fernandez and Zajac and Zelinko and Mariano and McCormick. Neither the enemy who killed them nor the people whose independence they have fought to save ever asked them where they or their parents came from. They were all Americans."[63] Those sentences deserved more attention than they received. In the fall of 1965 an era of reform was drawing to an end, one that had seen an attempt, only partially successful, to bridge the distance between races, classes, and ethnic groups. An era of war had already begun, one that would see the distance widen once again.

[6]
Vietnam

In 1967 a Defense Department official observed worriedly that "the increased polarization that is taking place in the United States" contained the "seeds of the worst split in our people in more than a century."[1] He by no means exaggerated the severity of the polarization resulting from the war in Vietnam. From 1965, when Lyndon Johnson first made a large-scale commitment of American forces, until 1973, when Richard Nixon finally negotiated a cease-fire agreement, the nation was intermittently torn by internal divisions. Undercurrents of rage, outbursts of violence, and social discord, although varying in intensity, characterized the entire Vietnam era. Many of the catchphrases of the period—"the silent majority," "Black Power," "the new ethnicity"—indicated that the fissures occurred, in large measure, along the fault lines of class, race, and ethnicity. The result, to borrow a phrase Edmund Wilson once used in another context, was an "American Earthquake."

1.

World War II and to a lesser extent the Cold War had encouraged feelings of unity, stimulated a sense of national purpose, and generated pressures for domestic accommodation. The war in Vietnam produced the very opposite: fragmentation, alienation, confrontation, what the editors of *Time* would call "the loss of a working consensus, for the first time in our lives, as to what we think America means." The discord resulted from several things: the discrediting of the assumptions that led the United States to intervene in Vietnam, the way in which the Johnson administration first escalated and then prosecuted the war, the images of the conflict that the news media presented to the public, and the policies adopted by the Nixon administration when withdrawing from the war. Each contributed importantly, if not in equal volume, to the disharmony. Each helps explain why George F. Kennan, drawing on both his knowledge of history and diplomacy, would ultimately pronounce the war in Vietnam "the most disastrous of all America's undertakings over the whole two hundred years of its history."[2]

The decision to intervene in Vietnam derived from assumptions Lyndon Johnson shared with Secretary of State Dean Rusk, Secretary of Defense Robert McNamara, Special Assistant for National Security Affairs McGeorge Bundy, and nearly all his other advisers. Rooted in a conviction that events in Southeast Asia in the 1960s mirrored those in Europe in the 1930s, these assumptions fitted together as tightly as the pieces of a jigsaw puzzle, but unlike those pieces, once in place they could not be dislodged. The conflict in Vietnam resulted primarily from Communist aggression, from a North Vietnamese attack on South Vietnam. The attack, the argument continued, was instigated by Communist China as part of a broader aggressive policy. A firm stand, not appeasement, was the only safe reply, and the United States possessed the military power to make such a response. To act, and act decisively, would ensure the blessings of liberty for the people of South Vietnam. To back away, Johnson believed, would fatally undermine the credibility of the United States. The communists would then foment wars of national liberation throughout Asia, and the dominoes would begin to tumble, until the United

States was directly imperiled. If the President ever questioned these assumptions, and there is no evidence he did, his advisers dispelled his doubts. Journalist Tom Wicker said of Johnson's decision to intervene: "He would look around him and see in Bob McNamara that it was technologically feasible, in McGeorge Bundy that it was intellectually respectable, and in Dean Rusk that it was historically necessary."[3]

The history of America's involvement in Vietnam is, in one sense, the history of the erosion of those assumptions about what policies were feasible, respectable, and necessary. A far better case was ultimately made for a diametrically opposed set of assumptions: that the conflict in South Vietnam originated in an internal revolution, that North Vietnamese leaders treasured their nation's independence of China, that American air power was ill-suited to a campaign against guerrillas, and that American values were no more exportable to Vietnam than Vietnamese traditions would be to the United States. Far from enhancing American prestige, the long and debilitating war in Vietnam dealt it a serious blow. If there is no way of knowing how many people finally rejected the technological, intellectual, and historical assumptions that produced the war, public opinion polls leave no doubt that the administration's central claim—that a communist victory in South Vietnam would directly threaten the United States—grew less plausible with each passing year.

Governments are seldom entirely candid, especially in time of war, but the deception practiced during the war in Vietnam was singular. The Johnson administration denied any intention of intervening in Vietnam even though it desired to do so; it denied enlarging the war even as it undertook a massive military buildup; it denied suffering setbacks even while weekly casualty lists mounted ominously; it denied that the war would exact domestic costs even as these costs became all too apparent. The denials stemmed from the worst and best of motives. On the one hand, Johnson feared that the public would not support the war if it knew the truth, and on the other, he believed that by concealing the truth, he could blunt any efforts to slash spending for domestic reforms. "We are a rich Nation and can afford to make progress at home while meeting obligations abroad," Johnson said. "For this reason, I have not halted progress in the great and vital Great Society programs in order to finance the cost of our efforts in Southeast Asia."[4]

The administration continued the masquerade in taking the three steps that set the United States on the road to war. The first occurred in the summer of 1964, when President Johnson reported that North Vietnamese vessels had, on August 2 and 4, fired at American destroyers in the Gulf of Tonkin. The ships, the President said, were minding their own business and were sailing in international waters. After ordering swift retaliatory air raids against North Vietnamese naval bases, Johnson easily obtained a congressional resolution empowering him "to take all necessary measures to repel any armed attack against the forces of the United States and to prevent further aggression." The truth emerged only later. The United States had provided logistical support for commando raids on the coast of North Vietnam. On August 2 North Vietnamese ships had fired at an American vessel which, at the time, was surveying North Vietnamese naval activity and radar systems in aid of the South Vietnamese. An attack on August 4 probably never occurred, although an American ship, believing it might be in danger, fired retaliatory torpedoes at radar blips. "For all I know," Johnson later confessed, "our Navy was shooting at whales out there."[5] Nevertheless, the President skillfully used the crisis to win broad congressional authorization for whatever step he wished to take next.

It proved to be momentous: the air bombardment of North Vietnam. Having considered such action in the fall of 1964. Johnson authorized it on February 13, 1965, after the North Vietnamese attacked an American base at Pleiku, killing 8 "military advisers" and wounding 100 more. The administration believed air strikes would sap North Vietnam's resolve to carry on a protracted war and would bolster South Vietnam's sagging morale. At the same time military planners realized, as McGeorge Bundy put it on his return from an inspection visit to Vietnam, that "without new U.S. action defeat appears inevitable."[6] Bundy expected at first to relate each bombing raid to specific "outrages" committed by North Vietnamese forces, but he also understood that the need for such tit-for-tat justifications would diminish as the scale of operations on both sides intensified. The attack on Pleiku, therefore, was more a rationalization than a reason for the sustained air assaults that began on March 2. Officials had known that such an incident would come along, sooner or later, if they were patient enough. Bundy conceded as much when he said, "Pleikus are like streetcars."[7]

The third step, the decision to send American troops into ground combat, followed from the second with deadly predictability. Within a week after the bombing raids began, marines landed in Vietnam in order to secure airfields and other installations. They were under very strict orders not to undertake offensive operations, but only to protect vital enclaves. These orders, however, were remanded almost before the ink on them had dried. American officers saw no point in "a rather inglorious static defensive mission" which put them in the unhappy position of waiting to be attacked, beating back the attack, and waiting to be attacked again.[8] Why not permit the marines to drive Vietcong and North Vietnamese forces from surrounding areas? By April the administration had authorized such "search-and-destroy" missions and, by June, the use of American troops in an all-out land war. This, in turn, signified a change in overall strategy: the United States was no longer merely trying to force the Vietcong and North Vietnam to negotiate a settlement but was now intent on defeating the opposing forces.

"Remember," Senator Mike Mansfield of Montana warned the President in July 1965, "escalation begets escalation."[9] That seems to have been the first thing Johnson forgot. Like an addict craving an ever-larger fix, the administration, once it had committed ground forces to battle, steadily increased the number of fighting men stationed in Vietnam. That number, which stood at 25,000 on January 1, 1965, had grown to 184,000 by 1966, 385,000 by 1967, 485,000 by 1968, and 536,000 by 1969. Yet subterfuge characterized the escalation no less than it did the extraction of the Gulf of Tonkin resolution and the response to the attack on Pleiku. In July 1965, for example, the President announced a troop buildup from 75,000 to 125,000 (but did not announce a planned buildup to 200,000). A reporter asked whether this implied "any change in the existing policy of relying mainly on the South Vietnamese to carry out offensive operations and using American forces to guard installations." Johnson replied: "It does not imply any change in policy whatsoever."[10]

The desire to conceal the costs of Vietnam explains Johnson's reluctance to call up reserve units. Ordering such a mobilization, which military leaders considered essential, would, the administration thought, open a Pandora's box of plagues, many of them political. Robert McNamara informed Defense Department aides in February 1966 that "the political aspects of a Reserve call-up are extremely delicate," since it was proving "a very difficult and delicate task for the Administration to mobilize and maintain the required support in this country to carry on the war properly." Similarly, Under-Secretary of State Nicholas deB. Katzenbach noted in May 1967 that "Congressional and public debate on the reserve call-up would be divisive and give comfort to Hanoi."[11] A general mobilization could trap the administration in a crossfire: doves would use it as an excuse to demand withdrawal, and hawks as a pretext to call for even harsher military action. Despite these fears, by March 1968 Johnson saw no alternative to a modest reserve call-up. Even then he refused to order a full-scale mobilization.

Johnson approached economic policy in much the same manner. Faced with a choice of financing the war through taxes or inflation, the President in effect chose the latter in the belief that if he requested a tax hike, the public would reject his policy and Congress would cut back domestic programs. So from 1965 to 1967, while defense expenditures rose from 7.2 to 9.2 percent of the gross national product, setting off powerful inflationary tremors, Johnson did not ask for an increase in taxes. When he finally did, the chairman of the House Appropriations Committee, Wilbur Mills of Arkansas, confirmed Johnson's fears by calling for "major slashes in domestic spending."[12] In June 1968 Congress enacted a one-year 10-percent surcharge on personal and corporate income taxes, but it acted too late to dampen the accumulated inflationary pressures of three years. The rate of inflation climbed to 4.2 percent in 1968, to 6.1 percent in 1969, and the United States soon faced the prospect of double-digit inflation.

The official pretense that accompanied the nation's entrance into the war, the escalation of the fighting, the raising of troops, and the financing of the conflict extended as well to pronouncements about the war's progress. In rhetoric worthy of a Dr. Pangloss, military and civilian spokesmen predicted imminent victory. If Americans were never so gullible as a nation of Candides, they had little basis for challenging those rosy estimates until the Tet offensive of early 1968. Attacking on the last day of January, Vietcong and North Vietnamese forces struck at thirty-nine of South Vietnam's forty-four provincial capitals, captured the city of Hue, and proved that after three years of intervention even the American Embassy in Saigon was not secure. Coupled with General William Westmoreland's request for an additional 206,000 troops, Tet precipitated a major policy review in Washington as well as an awareness that overly optimistic statements had strained the government's credibility past the breaking point. In March 1968 the newly appointed Secretary of Defense, Clark Clifford, ordered Westmoreland to adopt "a sober and conservative attitude." Years later Westmoreland would complain: "I was being told not to be optimistic when I was trying to make an objective appraisal of the situation."[13] Voltaire's definition of optimism—"the passion for maintaining that all is right when all goes wrong with us"—never seemed more fitting.

The Tet offensive jolted the public, in part because of the way television covered the story. Although newscasts had carried images of the war into American homes on a daily basis ever since 1965, those images, before Tet, tended to suggest a routine, mechanized war, dislocated in time and disengaged in space. The requirements of network news programs were largely responsible. Since it was ordinarily too costly to transmit film by communications satellite (and such film, arriving shortly before a broadcast, would afford producers much less control over program content), most footage was at least three days old when it was shown. Television film crews were therefore instructed to focus on routine operations, such as helicopter patrols or search-and-destroy missions, which were continually taking place, were virtually interchangeable, and would not seem dated by newspaper reports. Moreover, television had emphasized American rather than South Vietnamese actions. "It's not a Vietnamese war," said an NBC producer. "It's an American war in Asia, and that's the only story the American audience is interested in."[14] News coverage was also influenced, however subtly, by army brass who made things easy for correspondents who would cover what the military thought fit to report.

All this changed during the unnerving days of Tet, when the networks concentrated on specific events, covered the South Vietnamese in greater detail, and showed scenes that had never before been screened. The war quickly lost its detached and impersonal quality when marines garrisoned at Khe Sanh, surrounded, isolated, and pounded by continuous artillery fire, were interviewed nightly. On the evening of February 2, NBC news broadcast the most sensational report of the war when it presented a film showing the chief of the South Vietnamese National Police, General Nguyen Ngoc Loan, holding a pistol to the head of a Vietcong captive, then shooting him. The cameraman who filmed the event succinctly described the execution: "Loan pulls out his pistol, fires at the head of the VC, the VC falls, zoom on his head, blood spewing out." Recognizing a scoop, however gory, when they saw it, the newsmen arranged to process the film speedily and beamed it to New York by satellite. John Chancellor, who viewed it shortly before air time, was so shaken that he "could hardly speak." NBC executives cut the final terrifying seventeen seconds so that, as shown and viewed by 20 million people, the film ran for only six seconds after the killing.[15] But the effect was devastating, and a few weeks later Walter Cronkite of CBS summed up the lessons of Tet as perceived by the networks: "For every means we have to escalate, the enemy can match us. . . . To say that we are mired in stalemate seems the only realistic, yet unsatisfactory, conclusion."[16]

During the Tet offensive the domestic toll the war had taken was made clear to American policy makers. It was not that a majority of people opposed the war in 1968, but rather that key groups, with influence disproportionate to their numbers, had withdrawn their support. This emerged clearly during the broad policy review carried out under Clark Clifford's direction and most clearly of all at a meeting of the so-called wise men on March 25 and 26. Fourteen pillars of the Cold War establishment, including Dean Acheson, Omar Bradley, Douglas Dillon, John McCloy, Matthew Ridgway, and Cyrus Vance, assembled in Washington to receive briefings on the war. At the end, nearly all of them advised the President to discontinue the escalation. First angry, then incredulous, finally resigned, Johnson felt he had little choice but to accept the group's wishes. Rejecting any substantial escalation, Johnson also halted the bombing of much of North Vietnam and announced his withdrawal from the presidential race. Clifford explained: "Major elements of the national constituency—the business community, the press, the churches, professional groups, college presidents, students, and most of the intellectual community have turned against this war." Cyrus Vance put it most succinctly: "The divisiveness in the country was growing with such acuteness that it was threatening to tear the United States apart."[17]

The war in Vietnam, however, ended neither with Lyndon Johnson's retrenchment in March 1968 nor with Richard Nixon's inauguration the following January.

Nixon slowly withdrew American troops—the level fell to 467,000 by 1970, 335,000 by 1971, 157,000 by 1972, and 24,000 by 1973—and the television networks contributed to the declining public awareness of the war by emphasizing stories that, in the words of an ABC executive, were "pegged to the eventual pull-out of the American forces."[18] Yet at the same time, goaded by his belief that if the United States acted "like a pitiful, helpless giant, the forces of totalitarianism and anarchy will threaten free nations and free institutions throughout the world," Nixon raised the tempo of the war.[19] He authorized secret bombing raids against Cambodia in 1969, initiated an invasion of that country in the spring of 1970, ordered an air and ground war against Laos in 1971, and stepped up the assault on North Vietnam in 1972, mining the harbor at Haiphong in May and carpet-bombing Hanoi in December. By then American airplanes had pulverized large portions of North Vietnam, South Vietnam, Laos, and Cambodia with more than 7 million tons of bombs.

If anything, Nixon carried the deception practiced by his predecessor to new lengths. "When President Johnson escalated the war," Jonathan Schell has observed, "the public had at least known that the war was being escalated, though it did not know by how much, whereas when President Nixon escalated the war, the public, owing to his assurances, believed that the war was coming to an end."[20] The Nixon administration resorted to doctoring Air Force records so that congressmen would not learn about the bombing of Cambodia and to falsifying casualty reports so that mothers and fathers would not discover their sons had met their deaths in Laos. This took place, moreover, in an atmosphere clouded by two disclosures, each in its own way appalling. In November 1969 correspondent Seymour Hersh broke the story of the massacre by an American battalion of

300 Vietnamese civilians in the hamlet of My Lai in March 1968. In June 1971 Daniel Ellsberg released the *Pentagon Papers,* a classified Defense Department study of American policy in Vietnam to 1968. Both undermined official explanations of why the United States had intervened and how much good that intervention had done.

The less credible the war, the more willing the government to curb the civil liberties of those who opposed it. The Central Intelligence Agency's domestic spying program, Operation CHAOS, which was introduced in 1967 ostensibly to determine whether antiwar groups received funding from foreign governments, expanded after 1969. CHAOS eventually collected 300,000 names for HYDRA, its computerized index file, and compiled dossiers on 7,200 American citizens even though the agency's charter forbade such domestic operations. "This thing is illegal as hell," the director of security said, but the CIA proceeded to open mail, tap telephone wires, bug hotel rooms, and burglarize offices. Not to be outdone, the Federal Bureau of Investigation stepped up its own program, known as COINTELPRO, which it had instituted in the 1950s. The FBI did thoroughly what the CIA had done by halves, attempting, for example, to wreck the marriages of antiwar dissidents by writing poison-pen letters to one spouse accusing the other of infidelity. A congressional committee later concluded: "Careers were ruined, friendships severed, reputations sullied, businesses bankrupted and, in some cases, lives endangered."[21]

By the time these acts were revealed the public's capacity for indignation was largely, if not entirely, exhausted. It was not surprising that after entering a war the justification for which many came to perceive as at best morally ambiguous, after carrying on this war in a manner that demonstrated the inadequacy of American military power, after withdrawing from the war in a way that exposed the disproportion between the lethal means employed and the ends sought, many people came to regard deception in high places as the rule rather than the exception. But Vietnam produced more than an estrangement from the government, for, as Daniel Bell has argued, "the rejection of the government led many to reject the nation."[22] The rejection was undoubtedly most apparent on some campuses and in most communes. But the estrangement also had class, racial, and ethnic dimensions that were equally important.

2.

In the fall of 1967 a coalition of antiwar groups organized a demonstration in Washington. More than 75,000 people attended a rally at the Lincoln Memorial, with perhaps half then proceeding to the Pentagon, where, according to a spokesman for the Episcopal Peace Fellowship, they sought to "disrupt the center of the American war machine. In the name of humanity we will call the warmakers to task." For much of the afternoon and evening of October 21 the protesters, most of them college students, confronted a cordon of military policemen stationed at the Pentagon, alternately taunting the troops and inviting them to break ranks and join the demonstration. Observing that the soldiers and students facing each other so distrustfully were of a like age, Norman Mailer noted: "They looked across the gulf of the classes, the middle classes and the working classes." In his extraordinary account of the event, *The Armies of the Night,* Mailer went on to wonder at "this middle class condemnation of an imperialist war in the last Capitalist nation, this working class affirmation."[23]

The view that support for the war was anchored in the working class appeared to receive confirmation a year later in George Wallace's presidential campaign. Running in 1968 at the head of the newly formed American Independent party, Wallace chose as his running mate retired General Curtis E. LeMay, who spoke unblushingly of the need to bomb North Vietnam "back to the Stone Age." Hawkish on Vietnam, Wallace took a strong stand for law and order and against antiwar demonstrators. Sensing that large numbers of people were becoming alienated from the political system, Wallace voiced the generalized resentment of those who felt themselves powerless and put upon. "Liberals, intellectuals, and long hairs have run the country for too long," Wallace declaimed; "the average American is sick and tired of all those over-educated ivory tower folks with pointed heads looking down their noses at us." To attract support beyond his natural constituency in the rural areas and small towns of the South, Wallace adopted a platform with a strong populist flavor. It called for federal job-training programs, safeguards for collective bargaining, a higher minimum wage, protection of workers "in the event of adversity or unemployment," and policies to ensure that "in this land of plenty, no one should be denied adequate medical care because of his financial condition."[24]

Wallace directed his overtures to "this average man on the street, this man in the textile mill, this man in the steel mill, this barber, this beautician, the policeman on the beat, they're the ones—and the little businessman," and polls taken in the weeks before the election indicated he had found a receptive audience.[25] A survey of trade unionists in September 1968 showed 25 percent favoring Wallace, 32 percent for Richard Nixon, and 34 percent for Hubert Humphrey. Although the pull of party loyalties and the fear of wasting a vote ultimately cost Wallace some of this support, his showing in the election was remarkable. More than 9.9 million voters, 13.5 percent of the total, voted for him, with the result that Nixon, with a plurality of only 43.4 percent of the popular vote, narrowly defeated Humphrey. The vote for Wallace evidenced a clear class pattern. Professionals, businessmen, and white-collar workers gave him 9 percent of their votes; manual workers, however, gave him 17 percent. Outside the South, Wallace's proportion of the vote was lower, but the pattern remained the same: nonmanual workers gave him 5 percent of their votes, and manual workers 9 percent. Sociologists who interviewed white males in Gary, Indiana, found not only that Wallace had the greatest support among blue-collar workers but also that the more strongly a man identified with the working class, the more likely he was to support Wallace.

What Wallace in 1968 had called "the average American," Nixon in 1969 would term "the great silent majority." Similarly, Wallace's fulminations against "sissy-britches intellectual morons" would be translated in Nixon's White House into harangues, less folksy, if no less bitter, against "elite groups" and "the Establishment." Yet the focus remained the same: the Nixon administration based its political strategy on the dual conviction that the war in Vietnam had produced a new "social" issue and that most American workers, standing as they did on the conservative side of that issue, were potential converts to Republicanism. The social issue, which political analysts Richard M. Scammon and Ben Wattenberg defined as "a set of public attitudes concerning the more personally frightening aspects of disruptive social change," involved a backlash against rising crime rates, antiwar protest, campus disorders, black militancy, and moral permissiveness. These issues, Republicans believed, were as good as gold. Beguiled by visions of an electoral El Dorado, they set out, as Jeb Stuart Magruder said, "to recruit Middle

America, the Silent Majority, or whatever we choose to call it, into our camp."[26]

The task of recruitment had several dimensions. The administration first adopted the social issue by denouncing protest, pot, and pornography, by condemning the busing of schoolchildren for the purpose of achieving integration, by affirming a law-and-order posture, and by welcoming the divisions such rhetoric encouraged. As Vice President Spiro Agnew announced: "If, in challenging, we polarize the American people, I say it is time for a positive polarization."[27] Next, the Republicans endeavored to prove that they could be trusted not to dismantle the welfare state but rather to extend its benefits. Nixon eventually sponsored economic policies remarkably similar to those favored by the Democrats. He accepted planned budget deficits to counteract rising unemployment and, for a time, imposed a partial system of mandatory controls, including wage and price ceilings, to bring down the rate of inflation. The demon of Barry Goldwater exorcised, Republicans looked forward confidently to capturing what one strategist, Kevin Phillips, described as "an increasing portion of the Northern blue-collar electorate."[28]

By the early 1970s it was commonly assumed that American workers, whether for patriotic or chauvinistic reasons, were among the most ardent supporters of Nixon's Vietnam policies. In May 1970, as if to confirm that assumption, a contingent of construction workers set out to disrupt an antiwar parade in New York City. Carrying signs that read "Don't worry, they don't draft faggots" and screaming, "Get the hippie! Get the traitor!" the workers—described by one liberal journalist as "burly super patriots," "frenzied hard-hats" with "bellies bulging defiantly"—chased the demonstrators and pummeled those they caught.[29] Incensed at Mayor John Lindsay for having ordered flags flown at half-mast in memory of four students who had been killed a few days earlier by the Ohio National Guard at Kent State University, the workers marched on City Hall and demanded that the flag be raised. Soon after, the head of the construction workers' union, Peter Brennan, visited the White House, presented Nixon with a hard hat, and pinned an American flag on his lapel. Articles then began to appear with such titles as "Why Hard Hats Hate Hairs," and the writer on labor affairs for the New York *Times* claimed: "The typical worker—from construction craftsman to shoe clerk—has become probably the most reactionary political force in the country."[30]

The motion picture *Joe,* which opened in the summer of 1970, authenticated the emerging cultural stereotype of the hard hat. The film revolves around Joe Curran, a balding foundry worker, who, hating liberals, blacks, dissenters, and "hippies," represents "the ultimate hard-hat: outraged, terrified, violent and more than a little envious, lashing out blindly at threatening forces that he only dimly understands." Having accidentally discovered that a well-heeled advertising man, Bill Compton, has murdered a "hippie" or, more precisely, a drug dealer who gave his daughter an overdose of amphetamines, Joe enters into a pact to preserve the secret. But that guilty knowledge is virtually all that the $160-a-week worker and the $60,000-a-year executive have in common. Everything else reveals insurmountable class barriers: how they talk and what they talk about, how they dress and where they live. As with so many films of the Vietnam era, *Joe* concludes in a paroxysm of violence, with the two men united in the end, as in the beginning, only by a murderous rage. But Joe's soliloquy, delivered, characteristically, to a bartender, expresses the values many came to attribute to the silent majority: "And the college kids, they're acting like niggers. They got no respect for the President of the United States. A few heads get bashed and the liberals behave like Eleanor Roosevelt got raped. The liberals. Forty-two percent of the liberals are queer —and that's a fact. Some Wallace people took a poll."[31]

Nothing could have more clearly revealed television's unique capacity to exploit cultural stereotypes than the appearance, early in 1971, of *All in the Family*. Archie Bunker, if not brutal and depraved like Joe Curran, was no less prejudiced or xenophobic. He represented, one reviewer said, "your friendly neighborhood bigot, the American workingman as CBS conceives of him." That same reviewer, however, went on to complain that the series, by emphasizing its hero's humorous and endearing side, left the dangerous impression that he was "certainly incapable of roughing up antiwar demonstrators." An instant hit, the program seemed not in the least offensive to its satirical targets. "The show has connected in a way no family series ever has," *Life* reported. The magazine then interviewed a family, living in a small town in Oregon, whose members proudly identified, in one way or another, with the Bunkers. Even the son, who published an underground newspaper, commented somewhat uncharitably: "My father *is* Archie Bunker." A railroad worker, according to *Life,* admitted that the program voiced his own biases: "You think it, but ole Archie he *says* it, by damn."[32]

The image of a socially conservative working class seemed compelling to many, if not all, radicals in the late 1960s. As in the case of many New Left formulations, this one owed much to the philosopher Herbert Marcuse. The industrial proletariat, Marcuse wrote, was "no longer qualitatively different from any other class and hence no longer capable of creating a qualitatively different society."[33] Given the left's long-standing infatuation with the working class, the disillusionment, when it came, was marked by bitterness. With the sourness of a jilted suitor, a radical journalist in the *Berkeley Barb* described a prowar parade in 1967: "A hundred thousand workers marched down Fifth Avenue. . . . Seamen, Teamsters, Longshoremen, Auto Workers, Carpenters, Bricklayers, and many others. . . . Anyway, the next time some $3.90 an hour AFL type workers go on strike for a 50¢ raise, I'll remember the day they chanted 'Burn Hanoi, Not Our Flag,' and so help me I'll cross their fucking picket line." The repudiation of the working class as an agent of revolution reached a culmination in a statement issued by the Weathermen, a faction of Students for a Democratic Society, in June 1969. Unionized workers, especially those holding skilled jobs, gained "short-range privileges from imperialism" and had "a strong material basis for racism and loyalty to the system." Consequently, "we do not put any emphasis on reaching older employed workers from this strata at this time."[34]

In place of the working class, these New Left activists proposed to muster the poor, the black, and the young, all groups, it was supposed, that were not "ideologically conditioned members of the society." Above all, emphasis was placed on young people, among whom, the Weathermen maintained, "there is less of a material base for racism—they have no seniority, have not spent 20 years securing a skilled job . . . and aren't just about to pay off a 25-year mortgage on a house which is valuable because it's located in a white neighborhood."[35] The flaws in this reasoning, as many radicals themselves pointed out, were that poor people, blacks, and students constituted a distinct minority of the population, and in no way a revolutionary minority. The New Left, however, was itself largely a class phenomenon, drawing support primarily from upper-middle-class college students, many of whom found it easy enough to reject the working class as an instrument of social progress.

The low esteem in which some of the New Left held

workers led Irving Howe, speaking for an older socialist tradition, to assail the "nasty elitist notions" that "workers are clods whose only interests are guzzling beer, staring at the boob tube, and whistling at girls." By the early 1970s many radicals were beginning to question the validity of the hard-hat image, especially as it concerned the issue of war and peace. Pointing out that "not one systematic study has ever been done of class and the opinion 'data' on the war in Vietnam," these critics analyzed what meager evidence there was and arrived at conclusions directly at variance with the prevailing mythology. Opposition to the war, they found, tended to be greatest among blacks, women, and the elderly. Polls purporting to show that workers endorsed the war had simply overrepresented young white males, whose opinion had as much as or more to do with their age, race, and sex than with their social class. Further, some argued that workers were less militaristic than other groups in society. An analysis of six local antiwar referenda suggested that "disapproval of the war appeared to be related to working class rather than high status characteristics."[36]

A substantial number of workers did become disillusioned with Vietnam, but the sources of their dissatisfaction and the form it took nevertheless placed them in opposition to radical critics of the war. Radicals objected to the conflict primarily on moral grounds, on the grounds, that is, that the Vietcong and North Vietnamese had a just cause; they emphasized American atrocities, South Vietnamese governmental corruption, and the indiscriminate slaughter of Vietnamese peasants; they embraced militant antiwar protest as the truest form of patriotism; they favored immediate American withdrawal. Working-class disenchantment issued from an entirely different set of premises. The workers who opposed the war usually did so on pragmatic grounds, never questioning the justice, but only the consequences, of American intervention; they emphasized communist atrocities, Vietcong terrorism, and the terrible loss of American lives; they abhorred all forms of protest as bordering on the treasonous; they sometimes preferred escalation to a pullout, so long as the war would end soon.

All these attitudes, if far removed from a radical perspective, nevertheless attested to an antiwar position. In interviews with workers the same themes were expressed repeatedly: a distrust of high-ranking decision makers; a belief that the war was not worth the cost; a conviction that the cost was being unfairly shared; a hatred of what one woman called the "peace people." A construction worker, viewing a coffin carrying an American soldier as it went by: "For Christ's sake, how long are they going to let that slaughter go on over there? The whole goddamn country of South Vietnam is not worth the life of one American boy, no matter what the hell our politicians tell us. I'm damn sick and tired of watching those funerals go by."[37] A man who had lost a son in Vietnam: "I'm bitter. You bet your goddam dollar I'm bitter. It's people like us who give up our sons for the country. The business people, they run the country and make money from it. The college types, the professors, they go to Washington and tell the government what to do. Do this, they say; do that. But their sons, they don't end up in the swamps over there, in Vietnam. No sir. . . . I think we ought to win that war or pull out. . . . I hate those peace demonstrators. . . . The sooner we get the hell out of there the better." And his wife: "I'm against this war, too—the way a mother is, whose sons are in the army, who has lost a son fighting in it. The world hears those demonstrators making their noise. The world doesn't hear me."[38]

A striking aspect of this response is the clear sense of class aggrievement. The war in Vietnam victimized blue-collar workers and the lower middle class, and they knew it. As another working-class woman put it: "We can't understand how all those rich kids—the kids with beads from the suburbs—how they get off when my son had to go over there and maybe get his head shot off."[39] Class inequities respecting who was drafted and who deferred, who was sent into combat and who sat behind a desk, who lived and who died were not only rampant but widely recognized. The most recent study of the subject concludes: "The discriminatory social, economic, and racial impact of Vietnam cannot be fairly measured against other wars in American history, but the American people were never before as conscious of how unevenly the obligation to serve was distributed."[40]

Class bias of an intentional and accidental nature pervaded the Selective Service System. The military required all registrants to pass an Armed Forces Qualification Test as well as a physical examination. Both eliminated many of the poor and the black. More than two-thirds of all black youths, compared with less than one-fifth of the whites, failed the AFQT. If these tests disqualified many of the poor, special deferments and exemptions spared the more privileged. For much of the war, millions of college students received 2-S deferments, which, according to the *Harvard Crimson,* provided "one of the clearest examples of class-privilege legislation in American history." Parlaying student deferments into occupational exemptions became a national pastime of the well-to-do. Mathematicians, scientists, teachers, linguists, and others whose jobs were considered to be in the national interest escaped the draft. Local draft boards, composed predominantly of upper-middle-class members, may have used their authority to assign conscientious objector status or to grant medical exemptions in such a way as to benefit certain social strata, or so some scholars have claimed.[41]

Although the armed forces never released a breakdown

of casualties by social class, the war appears to have "hit hardest at the center of the class structure." In 1969 a reporter for a Long Island, New York, newspaper analyzed the backgrounds of 400 men killed in battle. Five of every six were high school graduates, and no more than one in eight had ever taken a college course. "As a group, Long Island's war dead have been overwhelmingly white, working-class young men. Their parents were typically blue collar or clerical workers, mailmen, factory workers, building tradesmen, and so on."[42] A more comprehensive survey of 1,300 Illinois casualties classified the census tracts in which the deceased had lived by median income, rent, and value of homes; the author discovered that the risks of dying in Vietnam "were inversely related to the social status of these men." The casualty rate (per 10,000 males aged eighteen or over) was twice as high in census tracts with median incomes under $5,000 as in tracts with median incomes from $5,000 to $12,500 and twice as high in the latter tracts as in tracts with median incomes over $15,000. Inasmuch as induction rates from the poorest areas were substantially lower than from the middle category, the high casualty rate among lower-class youths seems to have resulted from their volunteering for, or being assigned to, dangerous combat action more frequently.[43]

In all, 56,000 Americans died in Vietnam and 270,000 were wounded in battle. That "middle America" bore the brunt of the nation's casualties helps explain why "opposition to the war and opposition to active protest against it go together for a significant part of the population." The dual response, in turn, helps explain why George Wallace and Richard Nixon could so successfully exploit a politics of resentment, why stereotypical views of workers as "overfed slobs named Joe and Archie" could make inroads even on the New Left, and why the Ford Foundation, in January 1970, thought it necessary to sponsor a Conference on Blue-Collar Alienation. After considerable discussion, a panel of experts concluded somberly that "disaffection does exist within a large segment of the white working class."[44] This estrangement was, in fact, a two-edged sword, cutting workers off not only from political leaders who seemed remote and unresponsive but also from radical antiwar activists who, from a class perspective, appeared as much a part of the establishment as the President himself. In that sense, the war in Vietnam served to foster class suspicion.

3.

At the height of the civil rights movement in 1963 some members of the Student Nonviolent Coordinating Committee began to express doubts about the prominent role whites had assumed in the organization. One of SNCC's leaders, Robert Moses, argued strongly, and for the moment successfully, against the drawing of such racial distinctions. "I always thought," he said, "that the one thing that we can do for the country that no one else can do is to be above the race issue." Two years later, however, having decided that "this black-white thing doesn't work," Moses left the United States for Tanzania.[45] His expatriation, although an extreme reaction, symbolized a growing sense of alienation in the black community. During the war in Vietnam, and largely as a result of that war, a belief in integration and assimilation gave way, for many, to a belief in separatism and nationalism. In some ways the government encouraged the tendency toward racial self-identification by adopting policies, most notably in the area of education, that emphasized group rather than individual traits.

Black nationalism, a doctrine deeply rooted in the black community, came to the public's attention largely through the efforts of Malcolm X, who, in the years before his assassination in February 1965, attracted a substantial following, particularly among young people in northern ghettos. At first a follower of Elijah Muhammad, the Black Muslim leader, Malcolm preached the orthodox message of total partition: the United States, as compensation for having enslaved blacks, should finance their repatriation to Africa or, alternatively, "set aside some separated territory right here in the Western Hemisphere where the two races can live apart from each other, since we certainly don't get along peacefully while we are together."[46] After his break with the Nation of Islam early in 1964, Malcolm attached increasing importance to black control over community institutions and politicians. Yet certain themes never changed: appeals to racial pride; opposition to integration; advocacy of self-defense rather than nonviolence; a belief that the world is a jungle with the races pitted against each other like predatory animals. In that feral world, like sought out like, or, in Malcolm's words, "lions love lions. They hate leopards." Angry, eloquent, and implacable, Malcolm insisted, as one biographer has noted, that "the Negro was really in exile in America." He made the terms of the exile agonizingly clear: "No, I'm not an American. I'm one of the 22 million black people who are the victims of Americanism. . . . And I see America through the eyes of the victim. I don't see any American dream; I see an American nightmare."[47]

For Malcolm X to reject nonviolence and integration was one thing; for many who had fought in the front ranks of the civil rights movement to do so was quite another. Yet that is what happened after 1966, when Stokely Carmichael's cry of "Black Power" spread like a firestorm through black ghettos. Both CORE and SNCC quickly adopted variants of the nationalist position, which, as Carmichael explained it, called for retaliation instead of nonviolence, autonomy instead of alliances with white liberals, "liberation" instead of integration, and the raising of racial consciousness rather than its eradication. Advocates of Black Power looked toward the mobilization of voters to elect black candidates, the development of self-sufficient business enterprises and cooperatives, and the creation of community-controlled schools and cultural organizations. Underlying Carmichael's version of nationalism, no less than Malcolm's, was a wish to dissolve the bonds linking blacks to a white society that was, at bottom, racist, materialistic, and inhumane. The Black Power manifesto declared: "The goal of black people must *not* be to assimilate into middle-class America, for that class—as a whole—is without a viable conscience as regards humanity."[48]

Even the harshest black critics of the new nationalism, those who, like Kenneth Clark, denounced "its programmatic emptiness and its pragmatic futility," conceded that Black Power held a "tremendous psychological appeal" for the black masses.[49] This appeal produced few tangible changes in political or economic institutions, but it revolutionized cultural and intellectual perspectives. The Black Power movement, broadly conceived, legitimized Afro-American values and life-styles, food and fashions, poetry and prose, theater and dance, dialect and music. The repercussions were felt in diverse ways: the spread of a black nationalist theology which presented Jesus as a Black Messiah preaching black liberation; the demand for black studies programs at universities; the willingness of Maulana Ron Karenga's followers to learn Swahili, take African surnames, wear dashikis, and observe Kawaida, the seven principles of blackness. Whatever form it took, Black Power implied the repudiation of a purely American identity and the affirmation of a broadly racial one. The poet June Jordan expressed this when she described the slave-owning Virginian whom whites revered as the father of their country: "George the father hypocrite/ his life some other bit/ than freedom down to every man."[50]

This mood was related to the eruption of ghetto riots. To be sure, scholars disagree about who rioted and why; they even disagree about what constitutes a riot and how many riots there were. Yet certain things can be said with certainty about the wave of disorders that began in New York City in 1964, that reached a peak in Los Angeles in 1965, in Detroit in 1967, and in hundreds of cities following the assassination of Martin Luther King in April 1968, and that continued sporadically until 1972. Hundreds of thousands of ghetto residents took part in these riots; 60,000 people were arrested for arson, looting, or resisting arrest; 10,000 people were seriously injured; about 250 people were killed. Plunging entire communities into fear and turmoil for days at a time, the riots were finally suppressed by massive shows of military strength; 32,000 soldiers and national guardsmen were called out in 1967, and 60,000 in 1968. All these statistics, however, may be less dramatic than the report of a single incident. A National Guard machine gunner riding a tank in Detroit spotted a man at a window, lighting a cigarette: "The assistant gunner pointed toward a flash in the window of an apartment house from which there had been earlier reports of sniping. The machine gunner opened fire. As the slugs ripped through the window and walls of the apartment, they nearly severed the arm of 21-year-old Valerie Hood. Her 4-year-old niece, Tonya Banding, toppled dead, a .50 calibre bullet hole in her chest."[51]

Although the early rioting erupted before the Black Power slogan was adopted, and there is little evidence to show that later outbursts were directly incited by "extremists . . . preaching a doctrine of black power and violence," a connection between riotous behavior and black nationalism did exist.[52] The typical rioter was not a deviant member of the community, not the most economically disadvantaged and poorly educated, but rather a "new ghetto man," more intensely sensitive to his deprivation relative to other blacks and more keenly conscious of his racial identity. When ghetto residents in Newark and Detroit were placed in three categories—those who rioted, those who remained uninvolved, and those who tried to quell the disturbances—"the rioters were highest and counter-rioters were lowest on several measures of racial pride." Various studies concluded that riots occurred because blacks had developed "a sense of black consciousness and a desire for a way of life with which they can feel the same pride and sense of potency they now derive from being black." Riots developed, that is, out of the "self-discovery of the American Negro and his attempt to recreate himself socially in ways that are commensurate with this new image."[53] If the conditions facing blacks in 1967 were no worse (but were in many ways better) than they had been ten or twenty years before, the discrepancy between these conditions and blacks' self-perception was infinitely worse.

To attribute the impulse toward black nationalism to the war in Vietnam would be to claim too much, but as in the case of ghetto riots, the two were in many respects complementary. Opinion polls revealed that blacks were among the most dovish of groups, and while many blacks opposed the war on the practical grounds that it diverted resources from solving domestic problems, others did so in the belief that American intervention was a racist manifestation. For both CORE and SNCC the adoption of a nationalist position coincided with the assumption of an antiwar stance. In 1966 SNCC stated: "Vietnamese are being murdered because the United States is pursuing an aggressive policy in violation of international law." The war appeared to confirm two theories advanced by Black Power adherents: that racism at home produced imperialism abroad and that national liberation movements in urban ghettos were as justifiable as in the third world. As "alienation from the flag and other conventional symbols of the nation [became] acute," an accent on racial rather than national identification seemed natural.[54]

That sense of dissociation was captured by the poet Nikki Giovanni: "We kill in Vietnam/ for them/ We kill for UN & NATO & SEATO & US/ And everywhere for all alphabet but BLACK."[55] Her sentiments were echoed, to a remarkable degree, by black soldiers stationed in Vietnam, or so a 1970 survey indicated. Black servicemen expressed a decidedly more unfavorable view of the war than they had a few years earlier. The poll showed that "more than half of the enlisted men objected to taking part in the war because they believe it is a race war pitting whites against nonwhites or because they flatly don't want to fight against dark skin people." Sanctioning race riots "to gain Black demands," three times as many soldiers said they would join in as said they would suppress such rebellions if ordered to do so. Most black soldiers insisted on being called "black" or "Afro-American" rather than "Negro," and most preferred to live in all-black barracks and serve in all-black units. One marine sergeant explained that it might be necessary to use weapons in the fight for equality at home: "I ain't coming back playing 'Oh, Say, Can You See.' I'm whistlin' 'Sweet Georgia Brown,' and I got the band."[56] For many, then, Vietnam served as a crucible in which racial nationalism hardened and congealed.

If it was ironic that black nationalism flourished just when the civil rights movement had finally succeeded in winning the legislation it had sought for decades, it was doubly ironic that the same legislation, the intent of which was to achieve equality by the elimination of racial considerations in public life, was construed in a way that elevated these considerations to new levels. Of course, those who defended this construction acted from a belief that only if racial distinctions were made could social and economic equality be ensured. This belief helps explain the development of government policies regarding school busing, affirmative action, and, to a much lesser extent, open housing. Whatever the intent, the effect of those policies was to make the Constitution the very opposite of color-blind. Law was rendered as sensitive to color as a spectroscope and as capable as that instrument of splitting what came within its range into its component parts.

Federal policy took this direction in the late 1960s and early 1970s not so much because the President and Congress wanted it to as because the Supreme Court and the federal bureaucracy decided it should. Although Great Society laws providing for aid to education, equal employment opportunity, and fair housing served as the legal foundation for what happened, the interpretation of those laws rested with the Supreme Court and their implementation with the Equal Employment Opportunity Commission, the Office of Federal Contract Compliance, the Department of Housing and Urban Development, and other agencies. Lyndon Johnson, shocked by the ghetto riots (which he regarded as a repudiation of his civil rights leadership) and preoccupied with the war in Vietnam, did little to guide federal policy into these channels. Richard Nixon tried, on occasion, to redirect that policy. Recognizing that the election results in 1968 pointed unmistakably toward the importance of the white backlash vote, Nixon set out to win George Wallace's constituency with the ardor of a Don Juan. Yet despite Johnson's indifference and Nixon's predilections, the government sought to promote equality by defining rights largely on the basis of race.

The most conspicuous example of this was provided by Supreme Court decisions that required the busing of schoolchildren to promote racial integration. In *Green* v. *County School Board of New Kent County* (1968), the justices had to determine whether a school district in Virginia that had once been segregated could adopt a freedom-of-choice policy, under which black and white parents could send their children to either of two schools, when the result was that one school remained all-black and the other predominantly white (with 550 white and 115 black pupils). Lower courts had ruled that the Constitution did not require "compulsive assignments to achieve greater intermixture of the races," but the Supreme Court disagreed. Observing that the pattern of separate racial schools persisted to a considerable degree despite freedom of choice, the justices held unanimously that the school district had the "affirmative duty to take whatever steps might be necessary to convert to a unitary system in which racial discrimination would be eliminated root and branch."[57] In effect the Court ordered the school board to assign pupils on the basis of race in order to achieve integration.

Over the next three years the Supreme Court extended the *Green* ruling, and it did so unanimously despite the appointments of Chief Justice Warren Burger in 1969 and Associate Justice Harry Blackmun in 1970. In *Alexander* v. *Holmes County Board of Education* (1969) the Court ruled that Mississippi school districts had to terminate dual systems "at once" even if this meant assigning blacks and whites to certain schools regardless of parental preference. In April 1971 the Court went a step further in *Swann* v. *Charlotte-Mecklenburg Board of Education.* The case involved a large district—one thirty-six miles long and twenty-two miles wide, with 107 schools and 84,000 pupils—in North Carolina. Blacks made up 29 percent of the district's population, but most lived in one section of Charlotte, so although they could attend schools of their choice, a largely segregated system remained. The Court thought this intolerable. Proposing a "very limited use of mathematical ratios" to help determine an appropriate racial balance, the justices turned to busing as the only solution. Sending a child from one end of the district to the other might be expensive and inconvenient, but busing was a "normal and accepted tool of educational policy" and, as such, an acceptable remedial technique. If desegregation was not to be "limited to the walk-in school," districts had to do more than allow a child of either race to attend any school; they had, in fact, to do the very opposite.[58]

In October 1971 a Gallup poll showed that three out of every four whites opposed busing for the purposes of integration and that the practice was nearly as unpopular in the North as in the South and among Democrats as among Republicans. Blacks themselves, by a margin of 47 to 45 percent, opposed busing. The Nixon administration aligned itself on the popular side of the issue by urging the postponement of busing plans, by politically exploiting the Senate's rejection of two southerners nominated for the Supreme Court, and, finally, by asking Congress in 1972 to impose a moratorium on busing orders while legislation (or a constitutional amendment) could be devised to restrict the practice. This stand earned Nixon the distrust of civil rights spokesmen, but if some antibusing sentiment was undoubtedly motivated by hostility toward blacks, all of it was not. Christopher Jencks, in a study of class inequality and the public schools written from a radical perspective, criticized busing on both empirical and philosophical grounds. Jencks and his associates found that the compulsory busing of black children had no significant impact on their educational achievement. Instead, it implied that "all black schools are *by definition* inferior. This position strikes us as both racist and politically unworkable over the long haul."[59]

Federal policies designed to guarantee fair employment practices underwent a transmutation no less dramatic than those in the area of education. The point of departure was Title VII of the Civil Rights Act of 1964, which, while barring discrimination in hiring on the basis of race, religion, sex, or national origin, added: "Nothing contained in this title shall be interpreted to require any employer . . . to grant preferential treatment to any individual or to any group . . . on account of an imbalance which may exist." Responding to fears that employers might have to meet racial quotas, Joseph Clark, the bill's floor manager in the Senate, said that "quotas are themselves discriminatory."[60] But prohibiting discriminatory hiring was no more successful in the integration of the work force than prohibiting segregated schools was in the integration of the classroom. In 1968 the Department of Labor requested each major federal contractor to submit a "written affirmative action compliance program." In 1969 the Nixon administration backed the "Philadelphia Plan," which required construction workers' unions employed on federally funded projects to accept a quota of black apprentices with the promise of union membership when their training was completed. By 1971 the Office of Federal Contract Compliance called for "goals and timetables to which the contractor's good faith efforts must be directed" to correct imbalances.[61]

In 1971 the Supreme Court gave its imprimatur to this approach in *Griggs* v. *Duke Power Company,* a case Chief Justice Burger considered the most important in his two years as Chief Justice. At issue was the constitutionality of an employer's use (among other expedients) of scores on an intelligence test to determine an employee's eligibility for a certain position when the test results differentiated between blacks and whites in such a way as to prevent blacks from obtaining higher-level jobs. The justices ruled unanimously that in such instances the burden of proof fell on the employer to demonstrate that such tests were essential, irreplaceable, and directly related to job performance. In the absence of such evidence, their use constituted a prima facie case of discrimination. Burger explained: "The Act proscribes not only overt discrimination but also practices that are fair in form but discriminatory in operation." Even apparently neutral tests "cannot be maintained if they operate to 'freeze' the status quo of prior discriminatory employment practices."[62] By 1972, as the government extended affirmative-action requirements to colleges and universities, it had moved far toward assuming that an employer could demonstrate an absence of discrimination in one way and only one way: by showing a statistical parity between the racial composition of his work force and that of the population at large.

The government made an effort, less sustained and less successful, to treat housing as it treated education and employment. The Housing and Urban Development Act of 1968, which envisaged the construction of 6 million subsidized units over a ten-year period, sought to ban discrimination in the sale or rental of housing by eliminating unfair practices on the part of real estate agents, bankers, and landlords. The government then required builders who obtained federal subsidies or mortgage guarantees to develop affirmative-action marketing plans, a requirement carrying considerable force, since by 1971 one in every four new housing units was built with government financing (compared with one in every twenty a decade earlier). Further impetus came from George Romney, Secretary of HUD, who detected an "ominous trend toward stratification of our society by race and income." In 1969 he launched Operation Breakthrough in an attempt to open the suburbs to low-income groups in general and to blacks in particular. When Warren, a suburb of Detroit, applied for federal funds for renewal projects, Romney indicated that the community's willingness to accept a low-income project would determine his response. "You can try to hermetically seal Warren off from the surrounding areas if you want to," he commented, "but you won't do it with federal money."[63]

The government, however, discovered it had little actual leverage in the field of housing largely, as Nathan Glazer has noted, because "people are not assigned to housing by central bureaucratic institutions, as they are assigned to schools."[64] Whereas building contractors, large corporations, and universities depended on federal largess, suburban communities did not. The government could threaten to cut off funds for building sewer and water lines, but the threat scared no one. As a HUD official wryly explained: "We talk a lot about carrots and sticks, but looked at closely all we have are carrots." The Supreme Court never took a stand on residential discrimination comparable to its position on busing and affirmative action. Indeed, in 1971 the Court upheld California's requirement that public housing projects win approval in a referendum before construction could begin. Local opposition to Romney's initiatives reached so intense a level that the Nixon administration publicly repudiated policies designed to integrate the suburbs. Romney himself beat a quick retreat, assuring the residents of Warren that "our role is not to prescribe quotas or numerical standards which a community must meet."[65]

Yet that was exactly the role the government had assumed when it decreed school busing and affirmative action, and Romney's disavowal may have reflected only a resigned realization that the attempt to prescribe housing quotas was destined to fail. Public officials who devised the new policies thought that racial equality could eventually be achieved only by making, at least for a time, the color of a person's skin the basis of certain rights. This required these officials to make a 180-degree turn in the enforcement of civil rights law. But in an age when blacks, to the extent they subscribed to the tenets of nationalism, were swerving no less sharply, federal policy seemed to make eminent good sense. Defining themselves primarily in racial terms, blacks found the government was defining them that way, too. During the Vietnam era it was increasingly difficult for anyone, white or black, to remain, in Robert Moses's phrase, "above the race issue."

4.

In November 1969 the Census Bureau did something it had never done before: it asked Americans, or rather a representative sample of them, to identify themselves by ethnic origin. Until then the composition of the population had to be inferred from information about a person's place of birth, parentage, mother tongue, or surname. Now interviewers asked, "Is ———'s origin or descent ———?" and offered seven choices: German, English, Irish, Spanish, Italian, Polish, and Russian. People of either a mixed or a different origin were placed in an "other" category. Of 198.2 million people, 75 million put themselves in one of the seven categories. In March 1972, the Census Bureau conducted another survey, but modified it subtly. Interviewers phrased their question differently: "What is ——'s origin or descent?" The choices were somewhat more inclusive. "English" was expanded to include people of Scottish and Welsh ancestry, and a new category, French, was added for a total of eight. Finally, "interviewers were instructed to probe for a more specific and earlier origin if the respondent reported 'American' as his origin." The results were notably different. Of 204.8 million people, 102 million said they belonged in one of the eight categories.

The increase—amounting to 27 million "new" ethnics—can be explained only in part by the general population growth, by additional immigration, by the inclusion of the French, Scottish, and Welsh, and by the new instructions given to the census takers. By 1972 people were, it appears, more conscious of their national origins or at least more willing to claim affiliation with an ethnic group. Providing, as the Census Bureau noted, "a study in what people perceive their origins to be," the second poll turned up 5.5 million additional German Americans, 3.1 million additional Irish Americans, 1.6 million additional Italian Americans, and 1.1 million additional Polish Americans. People who identified with these four groups seemed to make up 22.5 percent of the population in 1969 but 27.3 percent in 1972. If the bureau's decision to ask directly about national origins was proof of a revived interest in ethnicity, the responses offered proof of a yet more convincing sort.[66]

Evidence of a new ethnic awareness could be found everywhere in the late 1960s and early 1970s: in the stream of books offering step-by-step instructions in how to trace one's ethnic roots; in the popularity of visits to ancestral homelands; in the tendency to give children ethnically derived names. It could be found, too, in the activities of organizations formed to advance ethnic interests. The Italian American Civil Rights League, for example, denounced motion pictures and television programs which, by their portrayal of the Mafia, gave the impression that all gangsters were Italians. Sensitive to the adverse influence of Madison Avenue commercial stereotypes, especially on children, Mexican American groups induced a potato chip manufacturer to replace Frito Bandito, a cartoon creature who stole corn chips, with the less objectionable Frito Amigo, who gave them away to children. A Polish American group launched "Project: Pole," a series of newspaper advertisements providing information about Copernicus, Chopin, and other Polish notables. To encourage scholarly research into ethnicity, the Center for Urban Ethnic Affairs and the Center for the Study of American Pluralism were created. To mobilize voters, spokesmen for the new ethnicity organized the Ethnic Millions for Political Action Committee and the National Coalition for Cultural Pluralism. The title of a *Newsweek* article in December 1970 captured the mood precisely: "A Rising Cry: 'Ethnic Power.' "[67]

The new ethnicity also produced an appropriate literature. Written largely, if not exclusively, by third-generation immigrants of Southern and Eastern European origin, the books, often autobiographical in approach, examined the ethnic experience from a fundamentally sympathetic perspective. There was an emphasis on the way in which second-generation immigrants, with the best of intentions but with unfortunate results, had sought to eradicate ethnic consciousness in their children so that they might more easily win acceptance. What parents could not accomplish, the public schools often did. Michael Novak, for example, recalled his educational experiences in a largely Slovak community in Johnstown, Pennsylvania: "The strategy was clearly to make an American of me. English literature, American literature, and even the history books, as I recall them, were peopled mainly by Anglo-Saxons from Boston (where most historians seemed to live)."[68] Expressing an appreciation for ethnic values, family loyalty, and neighborhood solidarity, the new ethnic literature suggested that only when people were comfortable with their own backgrounds would they be socially and psychologically whole. The goals of public policy followed logically enough: "A genuinely pluralistic society is one of creative ethnicities. . . . It is not a melting pot."[69]

Congress expressly sanctioned the ethnic revival. The Ethnic Heritage Studies Act of 1972, designed, its proponents said, to launch "a new federal effort to legitimize ethnicity and pluralism in America," authorized the U.S. Office of Education to provide grants to promote ethnic studies. Congress allocated $15 million for the first year and, to ensure that the funds were used for the intended purposes, proposed guidelines defining ethnic groups in the broadest terms. Groups eligible for grants were those "whose members define themselves as a people claiming historical peoplehood" or those that were "distinctive as subcultural groups within the national society by virtue of race, religion, language, or national origin." Limited in financial scope, the act was not limited in symbolic importance. It gave, as one of its sponsors claimed, "official recognition to ethnicity as a positive constructive force in our society today."[70] It repudiated an older assimilationist ideology as surely as the Immigration Act of 1965 had repudiated a still older racist mentality.

The new ethnicity drew nourishment from several sources. The Black Power movement, which "legitimized definitively the idea of cultural pluralism," provided an attractive model for Puerto Ricans, Chicanos, Native Americans, and, indeed, the descendants of nearly every immigrant group.[71] Ethnic consciousness, particularly among German, Irish, and Italian Americans, was also rooted in economic improvement. "Education and middle-class status," one writer observed, "have enabled white ethnic Americans to strip away the scar tissue which their grandparents first acquired when they were physically and psychologically assaulted by native bigots decades ago."[72] It was precisely among the grandchildren of immigrants that the new awareness seemed to blossom most fully, thereby demonstrating a common tendency for the third generation to rediscover a heritage that the second generation had done its best to forget. Finally, hovering over everything, was the war in Vietnam. As the war called into question national values, symbols, and purposes, many people turned with relief to the values, symbols, and purposes associated with the ethnic group.

Those who believed that "ethnic differences provide richness and structure to a society" denied that an acceptance of such differences would have socially regressive consequences. The new ethnicity seemed entirely compatible with various shades of left-of-center opinion. Liberals, affirming that ethnic voters were "an asset to liberalism," and radicals, asserting that "the new ethnic politics, in a word, is a radical politics," argued along several lines.[73] They cited public opinion polls which indicated that white ethnics, on the whole, were more dovish on Vietnam and more prointegrationist than native Americans. Although the data were far too fragmentary to support the more extravagant of these claims, they at least suggested that widely held stereotypes were misconceived. Conceding that some white ethnics certainly did fear blacks, observers nevertheless held that this did not reflect an intrinsic racism but a commonsense view of blacks as "territorial aggressors on their residential and employment turfs." Various writers stressed the substantial community of interest between white ethnic and black workers, pointing to interracial friendships that often developed on the job.

Spokesmen for the new ethnicity also applauded the political style of white ethnics, which, disdaining pious talk about morality and conscience, preferred "straight talk about power and economics."[74]

These arguments did not persuade all commentators. Critics charged that the ethnic revival was either largely spurious, with affluent suburbanites returning to the old neighborhoods on weekends to stock up on their favorite ethnic foods, or largely anachronistic, with people exhibiting an interest in antiquated cultural forms. In South Chicago, a sociologist noted, "musicians in some of the Serbian and Croatian taverns perform tamburitza music. The fine wooden instruments they use have been replaced in Yugoslavia by accordions and electric guitars." Some argued that the new ethnicity was essentially a form of chauvinism with inevitably harmful implications for the nation and the individual. Not only did it weaken society's consensual basis, but it also pressured individuals, even those who preferred not to acknowledge the primacy of ethnic allegiances, to conform to group norms, since an ethnic group's influence depended heavily on its claim to speak for a united ethnic community.[75]

Politicians of both parties fished for ethnic votes in 1972, but where Richard Nixon proved as compleat an angler as Izaac Walton, George McGovern could hardly get a nibble. On the assumption that white ethnics, like workers and lower-middle-class Americans in general, were acutely sensitive to the social issue, Nixon used an assortment of baits and lures. He appealed to Catholics, for instance, by condemning abortion and defending federal aid to parochial schools. In an ambitious effort to capture the ethnic vote, the Republican party formed a National Republican Heritage Groups Council, allocating $2 million for its war chest. Nixon's strategists, sensing the restlessness of "millions of traditionally Democratic ethnic voters," moved in for the kill. The Democratic party had once welcomed ethnic voters, Senator Robert Dole of Kansas reminded a Republican gathering, but "now some of the more radical members of its youth wing seem more interested in 'pot' than in melting pots, and the solid mass of religious, patriotic, hard-working ethnic Americans who once identified with the Democratic Party find themselves in search of a new political base."[76]

To retain their support among ethnic voters, the Democrats spent a puny $12,000. Yet had they spent more they might not have achieved much more success. Two problems plagued the Democrats throughout the campaign. First, there was a lingering resentment over the party's decision in 1969 to establish delegate quotas at the 1972 convention for blacks, women, and persons under thirty years of age. That decision offended white ethnics, who felt themselves unwelcome and who, in fact, were egregiously underrepresented at the convention. Second, many ethnic voters, however unjustly, perceived George McGovern as the darling of affluent intellectuals or, worse still, a captive of the counterculture. Since his opposition to the war in Vietnam was voiced in stern, moralistic tones, some voters shrugged it off as easily as they did his allegations that the Watergate break-in and cover-up were matters of national concern. As one observer of the ethnic scene commented: "Many white ethnic voters in New York are turned off by McGovern's self-righteousness."[77] The outcome was predictable. Nixon cut deeply into the Democratic party's constituency and most incisively into its ethnic constituency. From 1968 to 1972 Nixon improved his showing among Irish, Italian, and Jewish voters by nearly 20 percent. He emerged with 61 percent of the popular vote and an easy triumph.

By the time of Nixon's second inauguration the United

States had passed through a period of sharp internal division along ethnic, racial, and class lines. If the fragmentation had many sources, one was surely the strain of fighting a war that was unnecessary, unpopular, and, in the end, unsuccessful. Nixon, however, seemed to thrive on the polarization, believing it to be in his partisan interest and not much caring whether it served a national purpose. But on March 28, 1973, when the last American soldiers left Vietnam, an era came to a close. A harbinger of things to come had appeared a few days earlier, when the President, discussing the complicity of his closest aides in the Watergate scandal, commented that "you've got to keep the cap on the bottle."[78] Once released, however, the genie of Watergate could never again be made to disappear.

[7]
A Segmented Society

Travelers crossing the United States by automobile in the late 1970s could hardly fail to be impressed by the evidence of regional homogeneity. Driving along highways commonly known by numbers rather than by names—Interstate 80, for example, stretched from New York City to San Francisco—they could stop to eat almost anywhere at a Kentucky Fried Chicken franchise or a McDonald's outlet and would discover, wherever they were, that one drumstick or hamburger tasted exactly like another. From Maine to Oregon a tourist could spend a night at a Holiday Inn, a Quality Court, or a Howard Johnson's Motor Lodge, and, as historian Daniel Boorstin has remarked, in any one of them "he would know where to find the ice maker, the luggage rack, the TV set; he would recognize the cellophane wrapping on the drinking glass, the paper festoon on the toilet seat. . . . Wherever he travelled across the continent, he felt a new assurance that he would be at home, and somehow in the same place." To cross the Mississippi River on Interstate 20, one traveler commented, was to encounter "an almost imperceptible interruption."[1] Behind the appearance of uniformity, however, differences along class, racial, and ethnic lines persisted. While they had changed dramatically over a forty-year period, these distinctions continued to shape the lives of most Americans.

1.

In the early morning hours of June 18, 1972, five agents of President Nixon's reelection committee were arrested while burglarizing Democratic National Committee headquarters in the Watergate Hotel. Although undertaken to obtain political intelligence and to install wiretaps, the break-in was airily dismissed by the President as a "very bizarre incident." This disavowal of White House involvement was at first widely accepted, but in 1973, as a result of persistent inquiries by newspaper reporters and by Judge John J. Sirica, before whom the Watergate defendants were being tried, it became evident that the administration was telling anything but the whole truth. The Senate appointed a special investigating committee, headed by Sam Ervin of North Carolina, which held hearings from May to August 1973 and unearthed further evidence of wrongdoing. In February 1974 the House of Representatives authorized the Judiciary Committee to determine whether sufficient grounds existed for impeachment of the President. In July the committee voted three articles of impeachment, charging him with obstruction of justice, abuse of executive powers, and defiance of congressional subpoenas. In August, faced with the certainty of an impeachment vote in the Senate, Nixon resigned, relinquishing his office to Vice President Gerald Ford. Yet the political ramifications of Watergate were not at an end. In 1976 Jimmy Carter won the Democratic nomination and defeated Ford in the presidential election largely as "the candidate of the Watergate backlash."[2]

"Watergate" became a generic term for a range of illegal and immoral governmental activities. Investigators not only proved that Nixon's campaign manager, former Attorney General John N. Mitchell, had sanctioned the break-in but also revealed that the administration had taken punitive action against its political opponents, had ordered unwarranted Internal Revenue Service audits of their tax returns, had tapped the telephones of government officials and newspaper reporters without court approval, and had hired agents to break into a psychiatrist's office and ransack his files in an effort to embarrass Daniel Ellsberg, a critic of the Vietnam War who had consulted the doctor professionally. The public learned that the administration had dropped antitrust suits against certain corporations in return for campaign contributions and that the President, after directing Deputy Attorney General Richard Kleindienst to discontinue an antitrust suit against International Telephone and Telegraph, had offered no rebuttal when Kleindienst, under oath, denied having received such an order. In October 1973 Vice President Spiro Agnew resigned when a grand jury investigation revealed that as governor of Maryland he had accepted payoffs from building contractors and engineering firms. In April 1974 President Nixon, who, by claiming dubious deductions and failing to report capital gains on the sale of property, had paid federal taxes of $800 on a salary of $200,000 in 1971 and 1972, agreed to pay $432,000 in back taxes. By the time Nixon left office public confidence in the presidency had, with good reason, slipped to a low point.

What finally undid Nixon, however, were not these transgressions so much as the existence of tape recordings which proved his culpability. The President, perhaps, as one aide later suggested, because "he wanted to write memoirs better than Churchill's," had ordered the installation of an elaborate taping system in February 1971.[3] Whirring away in the Oval Office, the Executive Office Building, the Cabinet Room, the Lincoln Sitting Room, and Aspen Lodge at Camp David, the SONY

800B instruments were, in most of the locations, triggered automatically by the sound of voices and were engineered to record conversations (as well as telephone calls) as the President moved from one room to another. "I don't think it should ever get out that we taped this office, Bob," Nixon said to Haldeman in April 1973, but three months later a White House appointments secretary, Alexander P. Butterfield, told investigators for the Ervin committee about the system, whose existence until then had been known only to an inner circle. The disclosure was a bombshell. Asked whether "the device would pick up any and all conversations no matter where the conversations took place in the room and no matter how soft the conversations might have been?" Butterfield replied: "Yes, sir." Asked "what would be the best way to reconstruct those conversations?" Butterfield answered: "Well, in the obvious manner . . . to obtain the tape and play it."[4]

From July 1973 to July 1974 the Watergate controversy centered on efforts to do just that. Demands for the tapes came from every direction: from the Ervin committee, from the House Judiciary Committee, and from the special Watergate prosecutors—first Archibald Cox and, after he was fired, Leon Jaworski—whom Nixon had appointed under the pressure of public opinion. As quickly as subpoenas were served on the President, his lawyers discovered reasons why they should not be honored. To turn the tapes over to a congressional committee, the White House asserted, would violate the principle of separation of powers, would compromise national security, would undermine executive privilege, and "would unquestionably destroy any vestige of confidentiality of Presidential communications." To turn them over to the special prosecutors for use by a grand jury would set a disastrous precedent. Unless presidential communications were "beyond the process of any court," any one of 400 federal district judges could call for transcripts of presidential conversations. If that happened, "the damage to the institution of the Presidency will be severe and irreparable. . . . The issue here is starkly simple: Will the Presidency be allowed to continue to function."[5]

Despite these arguments, pressure to release the tapes grew so insistent that in April 1974 Nixon made public 1,250 pages of transcripts, although not before editing and censoring them. In addition, he provided copies of some tapes to the House Judiciary Committee and the special prosecutor's office. But the President's adamant refusal to provide Jaworski with key recordings led, in May, to an appeal to the Supreme Court. In July the Court ruled, by an 8–0 margin, that Nixon must turn over sixty-four tapes to Judge Sirica, who would then make the relevant portions available to Jaworski. Conceding that a constitutional basis for executive privilege existed, Chief Justic Burger nevertheless held that it must be weighed against an interest in "the fair administration of criminal justice." He found that "the generalized assertion of privilege must yield to the demonstrated, specific need for evidence in a pending criminal trial."[6] Nixon, who might have refused to abide by a less-than-unanimous decision, was told by an aide that there was "no air" in Burger's ruling and that defiance would ensure his impeachment. He then released the transcripts of several June 23, 1972, conversations which proved beyond any doubt his complicity in the cover-up. Whatever Republican support Nixon had maintained swiftly evaporated, and August 9 he resigned the presidency.

The White House tapes, both the bowdlerized and unexpurgated versions, revealed what Senator Hugh Scott, the Republican minority leader, called a "deplorable, shabby, disgusting and immoral performance."[7]

They exposed a President addicted to the use of profanity, absorbed with the banal and trivial, mesmerized by a belief that public relations could make the bad seem good, and prone to making vicious remarks about his supposed friends. The tapes revealed a man who, secretly transcribing virtually everything that visitors said, lived in mortal fear that they were doing the same to him. Realizing that his counsel, John Dean, might testify against him before the Ervin committee, Nixon had a hunch that Dean might have secretly recorded their conversations. "Does he, does he, does he tape-record everything . . . ?" the President stammered aloud, and he then asked Haldeman if it would be possible to determine "even surreptitiously or discreetly or otherwise . . . whether Dean might have walked in there with a recorder on him? . . . That's what may be his bomb. . . . Where do you carry them, in your hip pocket or your breast pocket?" Haldeman explained: "Oh, under your arm, you know, where they carry a pistol holster or something. . . . It's so remote as to be almost beyond the realm of possibility." Nixon replied soberly: "In this nothing is beyond the realm of possibility."[8]

Beyond demonstrating that nothing, indeed, was beyond that realm in a White House that had come to resemble, in columnist Joseph Alsop's words, "the back room of a second-rate advertising agency in a suburb of hell,"[9] the tapes revealed at least three sinister traits, the first of which was deceit. A week after the Watergate entry Nixon learned his aides were the perpetrators, and he then and there decided to hide the truth. He instructed Haldeman to have the Central Intelligence Agency tell the Federal Bureau of Investigation to discontinue its investigation on the grounds that a covert CIA operation might be exposed. In Nixon's words: "Call the F.B.I. in and [unintelligible] don't go any further into this case period!" Once having approved the cover-up, the President thwarted the investigatory process, sanctioned the destruction of evidence, agreed to pay $450,000 in hush money, discussed with aides the possibility of granting the Watergate defendants executive clemency, and counseled potential witnesses to lie under oath. "I don't give a shit what happens," Nixon told John Mitchell, "I want you all to stonewall it, let them plead the Fifth Amendment, cover-up, or anything else, if it'll save it—save the plan."[10]

If deceitfulness could largely be explained by Nixon's desire to save his political skin, a second trait could not. Running like a skein through the transcripts was a quality best described as that of rage. It surfaced in the drafting of "enemies lists," in outbursts against the eastern liberal establishment, in the chilling assertion that in the curbing of domestic dissent "everything is valid, everything is possible," and in a contemptuous disregard for restraint in the exercise of power. The administration's "Opponents List, Political Enemies Project," updated periodically, eventually contained several hundred names, including those of prominent Democratic politicians, newsmen and reporters, actors and actresses, and the presidents of Yale, the Harvard Law School, the Massachusetts Institute of Technology, the Ford Foundation, and the World Bank. Imagining himself beset on all sides by enemies, regarding each step as the one that might expose him to ambush, Nixon viewed politics as a fight to the finish. "This is a war," he told John Dean during the 1972 presidential campaign. "I wouldn't want to be on the other side right now. Would you? . . . I want the most comprehensive notes on all those who tried to do us in. . . . They are asking for it and they are going to get it." It was only natural that given this outlook, Dean would himself have wanted to "use the available federal machinery to screw our political enemies."[11]

Although publicly Nixon spoke of a desire to "bring the American people together," privately he maneuvered to drive them apart. As his aides later conceded, Nixon intended to unite only "the like-minded, the forgotten Americans, the 'good, decent, taxpaying, lawabiding people,'" and to unite them by offering a calculated choice of scapegoats: antiwar demonstrators, welfare recipients, and the media.[12] With "planned polarization" their goal, members of the White House staff recommended a strong stand against school busing on the grounds that it "would really tear up the pea patch," urged the President to "take the side of the Far Left" in order to cause general havoc, and exclaimed "great" when informed that antiwar groups were planning violent demonstrations. A calculated attempt to foster division, no less than a deliberate dishonesty and a barely suppressed rage, characterized Oval Office conversations. The Nixon administration's strategy was, as Jonathan Schell explained, "to embitter American life and destroy national unity in the hope of consolidating itself in power."[13]

The excesses of Watergate explain, perhaps as well as anything else, Jimmy Carter's stunning success first in capturing the Democratic nomination and then in defeating Gerald Ford in the 1976 election. Virtually unknown outside his native Georgia, where he had served a single term as governor, Carter shrewdly turned his standing as an outsider into a political virtue. "We know from bitter experience," he said in the spring of 1976, "that we're not going to get the changes we need simply by shifting around the same group of Washington insiders."[14] Once he had won the nomination, Carter did more than exploit a generalized resentment at politics-as-usual. Three of his chief slogans—"I will never lie to you," "The Golden Rule [should] be applied in all public matters," and "It is now a time for healing"—specifically repudiated the deception, rancor, and divisiveness associated with Watergate.[15] The election of 1976 hinged not only on substantive differences between the two candidates but, to an extraordinary degree, on what Carter's campaign manager called "personal honesty and integrity and confidence."[16]

Carter, receiving 40.8 million votes to Ford's 39.1 million, obtained a narrow 297–241 victory in the electoral college. The class, racial, and ethnic dimensions of the vote were notable. With the ending of the war in Vietnam and the declining importance of the social issue, class distinctions reasserted themselves in the polling booth. Whites earning under $5,000 a year were sixteen points more pro-Carter than whites earning over $15,000, a differential that, if not overwhelming, was substantial enough to permit one pollster to conclude: "The affluent, the well-educated, the suburbanites largely went for Ford; the socially and economically disadvantaged for Carter."[17] Carter's appeal to blacks, however, provided the key to his triumph. Although Ford won more than 51 percent of the white vote, Carter garnered more than 90 percent of the black vote. It provided his margin of victory in Ohio, Pennsylvania, and seven of the ten states he carried in the Deep South. Ethnic voting patterns were more complex. Ford did better than expected among some groups, winning 55 percent of the Italian and 45 percent of the Jewish vote. On the other hand, Carter captured about 55 percent of the vote among Catholics of Irish and Eastern European origin.

The 1976 election did not witness a reincarnation of Franklin Roosevelt's New Deal coalition. Carter won support from the poor, but not to the same degree as Roosevelt had. He won support from blacks, but that support now enabled him to carry Texas, Louisiana, and Mississippi, states which had excluded blacks from the polls in the 1930s. Carter made a respectable showing among Jews and Catholics, but massive Democratic pluralities in ethnic wards were things of the past. Although sounding vaguely Rooseveltian when he attacked a ruling "political and economic elite," called for "an end to discrimination because of race or sex," and remarked that the Democrats had "welcomed generations of immigrants—the Jews, the Irish, the Italians, the Poles and all the others," Carter in the late 1970s faced a task of governing a nation that, in its class, racial, and ethnic composition, had changed markedly since the late 1930s.[18]

2.

In December 1977 the Office of Federal Statistical Policy and Standards of the Department of Commerce published *Social Indicators, 1976*. Consisting of lavishly prepared graphs, charts, and maps, the 550-page work provided detailed information about population, the family, housing, Social Security and welfare, health and nutrition, public safety, education, work, income and expenditures, culture and leisure, and social mobility. The volume contained, as well, "indicators of well-being" which purportedly measured the degree of satisfaction Americans received from their jobs, their friendships, even their marriages. A poll on "Marital Happiness: 1973–1975," for example, divided people into three categories: "very happy," "pretty happy," and "not too happy." The statistics in *Social Indicators, 1976* were broken down—or, as social scientists prefer saying, "disaggregated"—by race, age, sex, and, to a lesser extent, income and occupation. While the editors, in their introduction, warned against "inferring the reasons for the differences which are apparent among these population groups," the differences were indeed striking. The government was, in part, depicting the American class structure, and the portrait was no less sharply defined for being painted in cool, statistical colors.[19]

The picture that emerged showed levels of income rising dramatically since World War II but the degree of inequality remaining about the same. Real personal income, after being adjusted for a fourfold increase in consumer prices, doubled from the late 1930s to the late 1970s. By 1977 median family income had reached $15,000. Of the nation's 56.7 million families, 10 percent had incomes under $5,000, 20 percent had incomes between $5,000 and $10,000, 20 percent had incomes between $10,000 and $15,000, 32 percent had incomes between $15,000 and $25,000, and 18 percent had incomes over $25,000. The proportion of its weekly budget that the average family spent on food and clothing had declined sharply, while the amount it spent on transportation and medical care had risen appreciably. Yet personal income, while dwarfing the total of forty years before, was distributed only slightly less unequally: the wealthiest fifth of American families received about 40 percent of all income, while the poorest fifth received about 5 percent.

An income of $6,000, which would have enabled a family to live in moderate luxury in 1938, placed an urban family of four just below the poverty line in 1978. By this standard, nearly 26 million Americans, or 12 percent of the population, lived in poverty. One-third were children under the age of fourteen. Single men and women made up a disproportionate number of those in poverty. Poor families were, preponderantly, headed by the aged, nonwhites, and women. Poor people received wide-ranging forms of direct federal assistance. Fully one-third of their income came from Social Security payments, Aid to Families with Dependent Children, and other such programs. Without such assistance, more than twice as many people—about one-fourth of all Americans—would have been below the poverty line. In addition, the government spent $30 billion a year on "in-kind" transfers, such as food stamps, housing subsidies, and medical care premiums. The aggregate income deficit of those in poverty—that is, the amount of money required to lift every American to the line dividing the poor from the nonpoor—came to less than $15 billion, or 1 percent of the gross national product.

At the opposite extreme were the 1.1 million families, or 2 percent of the total, with annual incomes in excess of $50,000. Those families were usually headed by white males, in their prime earning years, who held executive or managerial positions. They still lived preponderantly in the Northeast, although, since 1970, per capita income had increased most rapidly in the South and regional differentials had narrowed sharply. Yet at a time when fully one-fourth of all workers were employed as professionals, managers, officials, and proprietors, only a small fraction scaled the upper reaches of the income ladder. Those who did found it possible to earn as much in forty-eight hours as an unskilled worker did in a year, as the title of one article ingeniously explained: "Another Day, Another $3,000." In 1976 the president of the Ford Motor Company earned $970,000 in salary and bonuses, and his counterpart at General Motors, at $950,000, did not trail far behind. Harold S. Geneen, the president of International Telephone and Telegraph, whose combined 1976 income amounted to a mere $846,000, still had miles to go, since he was on record as having said, "Maybe I'm worth $5 million a year."[20] None of these figures included substantial payments under deferred compensation plans, profit-sharing arrangements, and stock purchase options.

Sociologists in the 1970s devised elaborate statistical

techniques for measuring social mobility. One of them, the "OCG Scale," described occupational changes in a generation by cross-tabulating sons' jobs (or incomes, or educational attainment) with their fathers' (at appropriate points in the fathers' lives). Applied to a population sample in 1973, and reported in *Social Indicators, 1976,* the scale revealed "a marked tendency toward occupational status inheritance for the total male civilian labor force."[21] Despite a general trend away from manual and toward white-collar work, "sons in a given occupational status category were more likely to have been recruited from their father's occupational category than from any other occupational category."[22] Mobility, both upward and downward, occurred within that framework: 60 to 70 percent of the sons of white-collar workers had remained in that category, while 30 to 40 percent had become manual workers; 60 to 70 percent of the sons of manual workers had remained in that category, while 30 to 40 percent had become white-collar workers. A more intensive study of the inheritance of economic status among families in Cleveland confirmed these findings. A son whose parents' income ranked 10 percent from the top had a 51 percent chance of having a 1976 income of more than $25,000; a son whose parents' income ranked 10 percent from the bottom, however, had a 2 percent chance of earning that much. Since marriages almost always occurred along class lines, "parents' economic status was transferred to daughters almost to the same extent as it would have been if they had married their brothers."[23]

With its unquenchable thirst for measuring anything that appeared amenable to measurement, *Social Indicators, 1976* made clear the imprint of social class on people's behavior and attitudes. One chart, "Participation in Outdoor Recreation Activities," provided statistical evidence to show that in the summertime people earning under $8,000 most liked hunting, driving four-wheel vehicles off the road, and fishing; that people earning $8,000 to $15,000 preferred camping, hiking, and visiting zoos and fairs; and that people earning over $15,000 favored sailing, golf, and tennis. Another survey asked people to describe their "Satisfaction with Selected Life Concerns" on a scale ranging from "terrible" to "delightful." People of "high socio-economic status" generally expressed greater satisfaction than did those of "low socio-economic status," not only when questioned about their incomes and standards of living but also when queried about their marriages and opportunities for "fun and enjoyment." The pervasive impact of class, however, was more strikingly illuminated in three other areas: health, housing, and education.

Most Americans lived longer and healthier lives in the 1970s than they had in the 1930s. In that period, average life expectancy increased from sixty-three to seventy-two years, the death rate (per 100,000) fell from 1,076 to 666, and the infant and neonatal mortality rates (per 1,000 live births) declined from 47 to 17. By 1975 per capita health expenditures amounted to $476, two-thirds of which was paid by public funds and private insurance plans. But prosperous people on the whole lived even longer and healthier lives than poor people, for mortality and illness were inversely related to income level. Poor people were bedridden twice as much as upper-income individuals and were eight times as likely to have limited mobility; their teenaged children, moreover, had four times as many decayed teeth as more privileged youngsters had. According to *Social Indicators, 1976*, a perfect correlation existed between perceptions of health and family income: of those earning under $5,000, 32 percent reported themselves in excellent health, compared with 45 percent of those earning $5,000–$10,000, 53 percent of those earning $10,000–

$15,000, and 61 percent of those earning over $15,000. While the percentages declined perceptibly with advancing age, the class differential remained constant at all age levels.

Before World War II class distinctions in housing could be gauged by the presence of such fundamental necessities as indoor plumbing or central heating. But upgrading and modernization—resulting from the surge of new construction since the 1950s, steady migration from rural areas to cities and suburbs, and the advance in real income—meant that by the 1970s this was no long true. In 1940, 45 percent of all homes were without some plumbing facilities, but in 1976 only 3 percent were; in 1940 one household in five had more than one person per room, but in 1976 that figure had declined to one in twenty. The persistence of class distinctions could, however, still be measured by the spaciousness of the home, the elegance of the furnishings, the desirability of the neighborhood, and the availability of certain conveniences. *Social Indicators, 1976* provided information about the number of households at different income levels that owned television sets, washing machines, clothes dryers, refrigerators, freezers, dishwashers, and air conditioners. Of the households earning $3,000–$5,000, 55 percent owned washing machines, 25 percent clothes dryers, and 7 percent dishwashers; among households earning $15,000–$25,000, the figures were 84 percent, 72 percent, and 42 percent. The one statistic that did not vary by income was ownership of a black-and-white television set. Sociologists noted that class distinctions revolved not around the ownership of a television set but rather around its location in the home: poorer families placed it in their living rooms; well-to-do-families, somewhere else.[24]

Just as Americans had longer life expectancies and lived in more comfortable dwellings, so they received more years of formal schooling. By 1974, among people aged twenty-five to thirty-four, fully 20 percent had completed four years of college while only 20 percent had not completed high school; by contrast, in the forty-five to fifty-four age-group, 12 percent held bachelor's degrees while 37 percent had not received high school diplomas. In 1976 colleges and universities awarded more than 900,000 bachelor's degrees, 300,000 master's degrees, 35,000 doctorates, and 60,000 professional degrees. Yet educational opportunity, while more widespread than in the past, remained in many respects a function of social position. More than intellectual capacity, more than academic motivation, class determined whether or not a young person would attend college. As *Social Indicators, 1976* made clear, the proportion of high school graduates who enrolled in four-year colleges varied directly with family income: in families earning more than $18,000, one in two; in families earning $13,500 to $18,000, one in three; in families earning $7,500 to $13,500, one in four or five; in families earning under $7,500, one in six.

In the 1970s, as in the 1930s, political controversies centered largely on such class-related issues of housing, health insurance, and education. Moreover, most of the unsolved problems of the 1970s—how to restrain inflation while controlling unemployment, how to safeguard the environment while encouraging economic growth, how to obtain adequate supplies of energy while holding down the price of fuel—had equally clear class implications. This was also true of perhaps the paradigmatic issue of the 1970s: women's liberation and, more particularly, the Equal Rights Amendment. The amendment, stating that "equality of rights under the law shall not be denied or abridged by the United States or by any State on account of sex," empowered Congress to pass laws enforcing that provision. The House of Representatives passed the ERA by a vote of 354–23 in October 1971, the Senate by a vote of 84–8 in March 1972. Congress also stipulated that the amendment would have to be approved by the necessary thirty-eight states within seven years. The conflict over the ERA, like the women's rights movement itself, illustrated the importance of class divisions.

The women's liberation movement was instrumental in achieving victories that aided virtually all working-women, regardless of their position in society. Title VII of the Civil Rights Act of 1964, which outlawed discrimination in hiring and employment on account of sex as well as race and national origin, served as the cornerstone of the drive for economic equality. In 1970, under heavy pressure from women's groups, the Office of Federal Contract Compliance issued guidelines banning sex discrimination by federal contractors. A triple breakthrough came in 1972, when Congress passed the Equal Pay Act, prohibited sexual discrimination in federally supported education programs, and expanded the jurisdiction of the Equal Employment Opportunity Commission to include local government agencies and educational institutions. By the mid-1970s affirmative-action programs were helping women even more than members of racial minorities. These federal efforts were associated with a dramatic increase in the number of women workers. From 1965 to 1975 about 10 million women entered the labor force, compared with 7 million men. By then nearly half of all American women held jobs.

As a movement, however, women's liberation drew its support largely from the upper middle class. Admittedly, some feminists argued that all women constituted an "oppressed class," maintaining that the relationship between a wife and husband was "a *class* relationship" and marital disputes "*political* conflicts which can only be solved collectively."[25] But other feminists spoke frankly about "the reality of how class separates women." *Women: A Journal of Liberation,* for example, printed an article by several working-women who asserted that "many of the values of Women's Liberation Movement are not the values of working class women but the values of upper middle class women" and proceeded to list thirteen ways in which privileged women betrayed their class bias (by "never remembering your waitress's face because you don't consider her on your own level" or by insisting that "a working class person speak in your own way without realizing that she has not had access to those speech patterns").[26] Jo Freeman's analysis of the "general social base of the women's liberation movement," based on a sample of the 200,000 subscribers to *Ms.* magazine in 1973, tended to support this interpretation of the movement's class composition: nine out of ten subscribers were college-educated, and two out of three who worked full time held professional, technical, managerial, or official positions.[27]

From the start the debate over the ERA revealed a division along the lines of social class. That division was best exemplified by the dispute over existing laws that protected workingwomen by establishing minimum wages, limiting overtime, mandating special sanitary facilities, prescribing rest periods, and restricting the weights that had to be lifted. Conceding that the ERA would render such laws unconstitutional, advocates insisted that such forms of protection were unnecessary and discriminatory, for they prevented women from competing for certain desirable jobs. As Representative Shirley Chisholm of New York City put it: "Women need no protection that men do not need. What we need are laws to protect working people, to guarantee them fair pay, safe working conditions, protection against sickness and layoffs. Men and women need these things equally. That one sex needs protection more than the other is male supremacism."[28] The opposing view, advanced by a spokeswoman for hotel and restaurant employees, held that women "working as maids, laundry workers, hospital cleaners, or dishwashers" benefited from protective legislation in a way professional women did not. But then, she added, "the feminists' movement in the main is middle class, professional women, college girl oriented."[29]

The issue of protective labor legislation, while never becoming entirely moot, eventually lost some of its bite. By 1972 the courts had construed the 1964 Civil Rights Act so as to strike down many statutes which, although designed to protect women, effectively deprived them of equal job opportunities. The feminist argument that useful forms of protection would, under the ERA, not be taken away from female employees but would be extended to males then became persuasive, so much so that the AFL-CIO, in October 1973, reversed its historic stand and supported the amendment. Yet the debate over ratification continued to strike sparks along class lines. In 1975, after voters in New York and New Jersey had rejected state equal rights amendments (although both states had ratified the federal amendment), *Ms.* magazine interviewed several women who had opposed the measure. One, who "resented what she perceives as the middle-class bias of the Women's Movement," exclaimed: "Like, why are they always putting down hard hats? I've gone out with guys in the construction trades. They're human too." By July 1978 the New York *Times* could note that waning support for the amendment "may also reflect a growing impression that the E.R.A. is some kind of elite measure designed mainly to improve the lives of highly educated women who want full-time jobs outside the home. In this view, it seems to have little to offer to poor women in routine jobs or women who intend to devote themselves fully to children and home."[30]

Six years earlier the ratification of the ERA had seemed a certainty, not only because it had won lopsided majorities in the House and Senate but because it had drawn support from people who could agree on little else—Strom Thurmond and Jane Fonda, for example, or Richard Nixon and George McGovern. By mid-1973, a year after Congress passed the amendment, twenty-eight states had rushed to ratify it. Then groups opposing the measure, most of them of a strong conservative inclination, swung into action, their acronyms —such as HOME (Happiness of Women Eternal) or HOTDOG (Humanitarians Opposed to Degrading Our Girls)—reflecting the grim attempts at humor that marked their efforts. By mid-1975 only six more states had ratified the ERA, and in January 1977 Indiana became the thirty-fifth state to do so. In the meanwhile, the amendment had gone down to defeat in a number of states, and several others had rescinded their approval (an unprecedented action, the constitutionality of which remained in doubt). As the March 1979 deadline approached, feminists obtained from Congress an extension of the ratification period to June 30, 1982. Opponents immediately challenged the legality of the extension and, in the winter of 1978–79, defeated the ERA in Oklahoma, North Carolina, and Illinois. The continuing battle reflected, above all, what one scholar termed "the class antagonisms that haunt the New Feminism as a political movement and women as a group."[31]

3.

Most observers had expected that the Supreme Court would ultimately determine the constitutionality of affirmative-action programs. In 1974 the Court had barely avoided ruling in the case of Marco DeFunis, a white applicant who had been turned down by the University of Washington Law School in 1971, at a time when preferential admission was granted to blacks, Chicanos, Native Americans, and Filipinos. Since DeFunis had then gained admission under a temporary restraining order and was, in fact, completing his studies, a majority of the justices concluded that the case was moot. The instance confronting the Court, therefore, involved Allan Bakke, who had been denied admission to the medical school of the University of California at Davis in 1973 and 1974. Since the school reserved 16 of the 100 places in its entering class for "disadvantaged students"—that is, for blacks, Chicanos, Native Americans, and Asian Americans—and since Bakke had a better academic record than some of the 16 minority students, he claimed that he had been denied the equal protection of the law. When the California Supreme Court ruled in his favor in 1976, the university appealed to the Supreme Court, which heard arguments in 1977 and handed down its decision on June 28, 1978.

By a 5–4 margin the Court ruled that the use of an "explicit racial classification," in situations where no former discriminatory behavior had been demonstrated, violated the equal protection clause of the Fourteenth Amendment. The University of California was therefore ordered to admit Bakke to the medical school. At the same time, also by a 5–4 margin, the Court found that affirmative-action programs that made race "simply one element" in the admissions process did not violate the equal protection clause, since universities had a legitimate interest in seeking diversity in their student populations. Although some criticized the ruling, most observers hailed it as "very civilized," as an "act of judicial statesmanship, a brilliant compromise that gives both sides what they want," and, in the most frequently applied phrase, as "a Solomonic decision."[32]

The justices, however, had faced a choice quite unlike that facing King Solomon, who, when he said, "Divide the living child in two, and give half to the one and half to the other," knew that the real mother would not permit the infant to be slain. The Supreme Court, attempting, as it were, to divide the equal protection clause in two, found that both advocates and opponents of affirmative action were only too eager to accept whatever part they were given.

Justice Lewis Powell, who wrote the Court's decision and provided the swing vote, accepted nearly every argument advanced by those who condemned affirmative action as reverse discrimination. Powell reasoned that it was impossible to determine which groups in society deserved special consideration. Since the white majority was itself made up of various minorities "most of which can lay claim to a history of prior discrimination," there could be "no principled basis for deciding which groups would merit 'heightened judicial solicitude' and which would not." Powell also believed that preferential admissions policies were not necessarily benign, for they might reinforce stereotypes "holding that certain groups are unable to achieve success without special protection based on a factor having no relationship to individual worth" and they might exacerbate "racial and ethnic antagonisms," since "there is a measure of inequity in forcing innocent persons . . . to bear the burdens of redressing grievances not of their making." In Powell's view, a "consistent application of the Constitution from one generation to the next" was possible only if rights were accorded to individuals rather than to racial groups. Nor were the stated goals of the Davis program —with the exception of seeking a diverse student body —acceptable. Davis wanted to increase the number of minority doctors in order to rectify, for its own sake, a historic deficit, but "preferring members of any one group for no other reason than race or ethnic origin is discrimination for its own sake." Davis wanted to counteract the general effects of societal discrimination, but, Powell concluded, doing so placed an unfair burden on white applicants "who bear no responsibility" for that discrimination. Davis wanted to improve health care in poverty-stricken communities but conceded it had no way of knowing whether minority students would later decide to practice in ghettos.[33]

Four justices—William Brennan, Byron White, Thurgood Marshall, and Harry Blackmun—disagreed fundamentally with these premises. The Constitution, Brennan asserted, had not been color-blind in the past, and the nation could not afford to "let color blindness become myopia which masks the reality that many 'created equal' have been treated within our lifetimes as inferior both by the law and by their fellow citizens." Legitimate statutory purposes "could be found that would justify racial classifications," and Congress, in passing the 1964 Civil Rights Act, had not intended to bar "all race-conscious efforts to extend the benefits of federally financed programs to minorities who have been historically excluded from the full benefits of American life." Since the inability of many minority students to meet the usual admission standards at Davis "was due principally to the effects of past discrimination," it followed that "race-conscious programs" were permissible, and, indeed, indispensable. Brennan conceded that a white applicant who was thereby denied admission suffered an injury, but one that was "not distinguishable from disadvantages caused by a wide range of government programs." Since such an applicant was not branded as inferior, rejection would not "affect him throughout his life in the same way as the segregation of the Negro school children in *Brown I* would have affected them." Justice Marshall made the case forcefully: "It is unnecessary in 20th century America to have individual Negroes demonstrate that they have been victims of racial discrimination; the racism of our society has been so pervasive that none, regardless of wealth or position, has managed to escape its impact." Justice Blackmun put it more succinctly: "In order to get beyond racism, we must first take account of race."[34]

Blackmun's argument, his very choice of words, closely followed an article by McGeorge Bundy, head of the Ford Foundation, in the November 1977 *Atlantic Monthly*. Insisting that no racially neutral admissions process would "produce more than a handful of minority students," Bundy wrote: "To get past racism, we must here take account of race." The question Bundy posed in his title was equally instructive: "Who Gets Ahead in America?"[35] Alluding to the same point, Justice Marshall stated: "It is because of a legacy of unequal treatment that we now must permit the institutions of this society to give consideration to race in making decisions about who will hold the positions of influence, affluence and prestige in America."[36] The debate over affirmative action—a debate that, given the disagreements on the Court, gave no indication of ending with *Bakke*—came down precisely to the question of the distribution of social rewards. Affirmative-action programs could be justified only on the grounds that blacks and other minorities continued to suffer from "a legacy of unequal treatment." If it could be shown they no longer did, racially preferential programs would, in Justice Blackmun's words, become "only a relic of the past."[37] Consequently, evaluations of the social and economic status of blacks in the late 1970s assumed critical implications for the making of public policy.

Such evaluations, however, were rendered difficult by a number of developments—most importantly, the deepening of class divisions within the black community.

Those divisions had always existed, but never to the same extent as in the 1970s, when the black middle class became larger, wealthier, and more dispersed geographically, while the black "underclass," also growing larger, became relatively poorer and more isolated residentially. Expanded opportunities for the one were more than matched by diminished opportunities for the other. Observing that the distribution of income among blacks was more unequal than among whites and that the disparity was widening, William Julius Wilson, a sociologist at the University of Chicago, pointed to the development of "a deepening economic schism . . . in the black community, with the black poor falling further and further behind middle- and upper-income blacks." Wilson concluded that "class has become more important than race in determining black life-chances."[38]

Of the nation's 25 million black people, 7.5 million had incomes below the poverty line. That is, of every ten blacks, three lived in poverty, while of every ten whites, one did. Black workers found it harder to get jobs in the late 1970s than at any time since the Great Depression, as manufacturers abandoned northern cities for the Sun Belt and the suburbs, as automation eliminated many positions, as a rising federal minimum wage made employers reluctant to hire unskilled workers, and as young people proved "less willing to accept the kinds of low-paying and menial jobs that their grandfathers or fathers readily accepted."[39] The unemployment rate among blacks, 13 to 14 percent, was twice that among whites; the rate among black teenagers, a staggering 40 percent, was two and one-half times that among white teenagers. Constituting 11 percent of the population, blacks received 27 percent of all welfare payments and made up 44 percent of the enrollees in the Aid to Families with Dependent Children program. One in every twenty-five white households purchased food stamps; one in every five black households did. "Nobody starved," a survey noted, "but many people are malnourished on a diet of hot dogs, Twinkies, Fritos, soda pop and, in rare cases, whatever can be fished out of the garbage can." To an unemployed black worker in Kansas City things seemed no better in 1978 than they might have seemed in 1938: "The truth is that black people ain't no closer to catching up with whites than they were before."[40]

Across town, the black dean of student affairs at a community college expressed a radically different view: "I think most of the racial barriers have fallen." For him, and many like him, they undoubtedly had. In 1976 a substantial number of black families had incomes that placed them solidly in the upper middle or middle class: 7 percent earned more than $25,000, 21 percent earned $15,000–$25,000, and 11 percent earned $12,000–$15,000. Occupation was closely tied to income. By the late 1970s one-third of all black workers (twice the 1960 rate) held white-collar jobs as professionals, managers, officials, and clerical workers. As Wilson explained: "Talented and educated blacks are experiencing unprecedented job opportunities in the growing government and corporate sectors, opportunities that are at least comparable to those of whites with equivalent qualifications."[41] Before World War II, the black middle class had consisted either of workers whose jobs and incomes most nearly resembled those of the white working class, or of salaried professionals—doctors, lawyers, teachers, ministers—who served a clientele predominantly or exclusively black. In the 1970s the occupational structure and earnings of the black middle class were comparable to those of the white middle class, and blacks made their way in the world of banks, corporations, government agencies, and universities.

Increasingly, middle-class black families seemed able

to transmit their status to their children. That at least was the conclusion drawn by sociologists who used the "Occupational Changes in a Generation Scale" to measure mobility among black men.[42] In 1962, 10 percent of the sons of "upper white collar" blacks themselves held upper white-collar jobs, and another 10 percent held lower white-collar jobs; in 1973 the corresponding figures were 33 percent and 22 percent. (The sons of "upper white collar" whites, however, were somewhat less likely to hold white-collar jobs in 1973 than in 1962.) Upward mobility among blacks depended on the opportunity to attend college. By 1977 about 1.1 million blacks were enrolled on a part-time or full-time basis. Since 1970 the number of black students had more than doubled, while the number of whites had increased by about one-third. With "education serving as an effective mechanism of allocating persons to jobs," a bachelor's degree served a crucial economic function, especially, as Wilson said, since "affirmative action programs have benefited those blacks who are able to qualify for the expanding white-collar salaried positions."[43]

Blacks who prospered often became estranged from those who had not, an estrangement tinged with feelings of guilt. "Rich and poor blacks have fallen out of touch," one black journalist commented. " 'They' suddenly has the same meaning to well-off blacks as it does to the white middle class."[44] Public opinion surveys, turning up unexpectedly sharp differences among blacks, concluded: "Gone was anything approaching black solidarity on basic issues or even on assessments of social, economic and political progress."[45] These assessments, not surprisingly, were largely determined by social class, as were feelings of alienation, beliefs about separatism, and attitudes toward racial violence. One study found that "the more disaffected urban blacks are likely to be those who reside in the North, are male, are under age 30, and are of low socioeconomic status." Such an individual—an unemployed teenager in Harlem, for example—would surely have responded differently from a black woman, working as a broker for a prominent Wall Street house, who, when asked about racial discrimination, remarked that "the way you cope with it is by not making it an issue."[46]

Many blacks who made good began to do what whites had been doing for years, but what blacks had often been prevented from doing: they moved to the suburbs. They were seeking the same things city dwellers had always sought: safe streets; good public schools; more comfortable homes. Governmental efforts to relocate the poor in suburban communities continued to stir up local opposition, but now resistance came from black as well as white homeowners. From 1970 to 1976 the number of whites living in the suburbs of metropolitan areas increased by 9 percent, while the number of blacks, starting from a much smaller base, increased by 36 percent. In 1978 the New York *Times* reported that "one of the most striking developments in American society in the last decade has been the abandonment of the ghetto by millions of upwardly mobile blacks."[47] In writing about the rising black middle class, *Time* did a cover story, appropriately enough, on a suburban family. The husband was a lawyer, businessman, and politician, the wife a school psychologist; they lived in a $35,000 three-bedroom ranch home, with a Cadillac and a Buick parked in their two-car garage.[48]

The family lived not only in a suburb but in a suburb of Birmingham, Alabama. The 1970s saw a reversal of a historic pattern of migration: for the first time, a substantial number of blacks began leaving the North for the South. In the past the stream of migrants from the South was comprised mainly of rural blacks seeking industrial jobs; in the 1970s the stream of migrants from the North was made up in some measure of college-educated blacks seeking white-collar positions. By 1978, when *Ebony* magazine listed the "ten best cities for Blacks" in the United States, five of them turned out to be Atlanta, Dallas, Houston, Baltimore, and Washington—all cities that had once been rigidly segregated. The magazine's comment on Atlanta was typical: "The fact that Blacks control Atlanta's government, its police and fire departments and the city's school system is a strong recommendation for Blacks who are planning to move to this clean, fast-growing and young city. In particular, professional advancement opportunities make the city attractive."[49]

Blacks who moved South as well as those who never left faced radically changed conditions. "They can eat in any restaurant and sleep in any motel. They can register and vote. They can go to school with whites. They can sit in front of the bus." In many respects, the South had become the most truly integrated region of the country. About half the black children in the South, but only one-third of those in the North and West, attended integrated public schools. The civil rights movement had become enshrined as a part of southern tradition. In Birmingham the public library devoted a newly created archive to the movement, and in Selma a street was named after Martin Luther King. The media had once purveyed crudely bigoted stereotypes. Now, on a Jackson, Mississippi, television station "owned by whites who were once leaders of massive resistance, a black newscaster interviewed a white candidate for Governor who apologized for having belonged to a citizens' council that stood for white supremacy."[50] There were signs that the ultimate taboo, that against interracial marriage, was weakening. Interracial couples in the South reported that they were generally accepted in their communities. The black mayor of Tuskegee and his white wife noted that they had "encountered no problems" in traveling through Alabama.[51]

Perhaps nothing better exemplified the new order in the South than the black's role in politics. Gradually closing the registration gap, black voters began to flex their political muscles. In the 1976 election 46 percent of the southern blacks, compared to 57 percent of southern whites, went to the polls. (In the North and West the black turnout rate was 52 percent, and the white rate 63 percent). By 1978 more than 2,200 blacks held elective office in the South, a tenfold increase in a decade. Both Atlanta and New Orleans had black mayors. White politicians who had once favored segregation acted like repentant sinners. Senator Strom Thurmond of South Carolina decided to send his child to an integrated school, and James Eastland of Mississippi, who had fought civil rights legislation in the Senate ever since 1942, appealed to local NAACP officials for help in obtaining black support. When the organization's president told him, "You have a master-servant philosophy with regard to blacks," Eastland, according to the official, "just burst into tears. He said, 'Son, you criticize me for not being involved in the black community. Did you realize you never did invite me?' " In 1978 Eastland announced his retirement.[52] "Whites are appealing to blacks for votes in a respectable manner now," said the black sheriff of Greene County, Alabama. "Ain't nobody in Alabama trying to out-nigger the other one. Ain't nobody in the South playing those nigger games anymore."[53]

The right to vote and the opportunity to hold office, equality before the law and free access to public facilities, the chance to live in the neighborhood of one's choice and send one's children to integrated schools—all represented major advances. Yet the limited nature of those advances was apparent. Although blacks constituted 20 percent of the population in the South, they accounted for only 3 percent of the elected officials. Of 100 counties with black majorities, two-thirds did not elect a single black to office. Atlanta and New Orleans were the exceptions; as a rule, black mayors were elected in small towns with dwindling populations and severely depressed local economies. The granting of political and legal rights hardly made a dent in certain chronic problems: rural poverty; unemployment; dilapidated housing; inadequate health care. Those problems were equally intractable under a black mayor and city council. An NAACP official in McComb, Mississippi, provided needed perspective: "There has been progress, certainly, but you have to measure that progress against how bad it was."[54]

4.

By the late 1970s patterns of ethnicity were undergoing a transformation no less startling than patterns of class and race. The roots of the transformation could be traced to a legislative source: the Immigration Reform Act of 1965. Advocates of that measure had contended that Congress, by abolishing national origins quotas, could effect a major symbolic change in policy without changing very much. The act, its sponsors had claimed, would merely bring the law into harmony with existing practice. As oracles, however, they proved inferior even to Cassandra, who was at least blessed with the gift of prophecy even if it was ordained that her predictions would never be believed. The reform of 1965 promoted sweeping, if unforeseen, changes in the composition of the immigrant population. It produced, in addition, an influx of illegal aliens whose presence created a jarring discrepancy between the law and existing practice. Because illegal aliens constituted a "new urban poverty class," class divisions within the immigrant community, like those among blacks, intensified sharply.[55]

The 1965 act had provided for the admission each year of 170,000 immigrants from Europe, Asia, and Africa (with a maximum of 20,000 from any one nation) and for the entry of 120,000 people from the Western Hemisphere (with no maximum assigned to any country). These numerical limitations, however, did not apply to relatives of American citizens, and with the reunion of families a stated priority of the law, about 100,000 such people were admitted each year. In the decade after 1965, therefore, 390,000 immigrants entered the United States, on the average, each year. In the late 1970s the figure was closer to 400,000. Although that represented less than one-quarter of 1 percent in a population of 218 million, as the national birthrate fell, immigration accounted for an ever-larger proportion of total population growth. In 1940 immigration had accounted for only 6 percent of that increase, but in 1976 it accounted for nearly 25 percent.

Not only were more people coming to the United States, but they were coming from different places and bringing with them different skills. The number of immigrants from Europe declined steadily until, by 1976, more than half of all immigrants came from seven Asian and Latin American nations: Mexico, the Philippines, Korea, Cuba, Taiwan, India, and the Dominican Republic. In 1969 three immigrants had arrived from Europe for every two from Asia; by 1976 two arrived from Asia for every one from Europe. By then the United States was receiving fewer immigrants from Italy and Greece combined than from India alone, fewer from Germany than from Thailand, fewer from Ireland than from Egypt, and fewer from Poland than from Trinidad and Tobago. This was accompanied by a shift in occupational patterns. In the 1930s perhaps one of every five immigrants had held a white-collar position. By 1976 one of every two had, and one of every four had acquired professional skills or technical expertise that qualified them, in most instances, for places at the top of the middle-class world.

The narrowing of the European stream of immigration and the widening of the Asian and Latin American streams modified the nature of ethnic culture in the United States. Before World War II that culture, European in linguistic origin, Catholic and Jewish in religion, flourished most fully in older cities of the North and West. In the 1970s all this changed. Although foreign languages were less widely used—the Census Bureau reported in 1975 that "as a Nation, few Americans are bilingual. Nine out of every ten persons reported that they had no second language"—more people whose usual language was not English spoke Spanish than all other foreign languages combined.[56] There were more homes in which Chinese, Japanese, Korean, or Filipino was the usual language than homes in which people ordinarily used Italian, and nearly as many as homes in which people ordinarily used French, German, and Greek. Many immigrants, particularly from Mexico and the Philippines, were Roman Catholics, but Asian immigrants were usually Buddhists, Sikhs, or Hindus, and immigrants from Turkey, Egypt, and Pakistan were mostly Moslems. Settling, as always, near ports of debarkation, immigrants in the 1970s were more likely to be found in California, Texas, or Florida than in New York or Massachusetts.

The new immigration sometimes rejuvenated declining ethnic communities. In 1965, for example, it had seemed that San Francisco's Chinatown might not survive. "There is some evidence that this ethnic enclave is breaking up," an official report concluded. "Many younger Chinese are choosing to live away from Chinatown." Then a steadily accelerating flow of Chinese immigrants, averaging 2,000 to 4,000 a year, reinvigorated Chinatown "as a place of residence, a business center, and a community." For the most part, the immigrants settling there were unskilled or semiskilled laborers, many of whom came from Hong Kong and most of whom could not speak English. As Chinatown's population exploded to more than 50,000, unemployment became severe. Suicide and tuberculosis rates were among the highest in the nation. Housing conditions deteriorated to a point where they resembled those in immigrant quarters at the turn of the century: "Communal cooking and communal bathrooms are a way of life in these buildings, where families arrange cooking hours in shifts and where tenants line up with washing items in hand to await the use of bathroom facilities in the morning."[57]

Yet Chinatown was no longer the home of all, or even most, of San Francisco's Chinese American population. As "the number of Chinese who work and move freely in all areas of American society increases," two scholars observed, "Chinatown is slowly losing its significance as the center of American Chinese life."[58] Never had opportunities to work and move freely been greater than in the 1970s. A very high proportion of Chinese immigrants, well over half, had professional, scientific, or technical backgrounds. They, along with the children of earlier generations of immigrants, "have found satisfying positions in universities, laboratories, hospitals, or architectural and engineering firms and have settled in suburban homes and good residential districts."[59] The median income of Chinese American families was higher than the national average, and the median number of years of school completed higher still. No longer the subjects of malicious stereotypes, Chinese Americans came to be viewed in the 1970s as a "model minority," clean, unobtrusive, and hard-working.[60]

Unlike the Chinese, relatively few Japanese sought to emigrate to the United States. The absence of any substantial number of new, unassimilated immigrants helps explain, although only partially, the remarkable success of Japanese Americans. Once restricted mainly to farming, gardening, and small ethnically related enterprises, Japanese Americans by the 1970s ranked considerably higher than average on the scales of income and education. Those who made good, following a trail carved by members of other ethnic groups, often discarded ethnic appurtenances as quickly as they could. Studies found that "high status Japanese Americans tend to live in mostly Caucasian neighborhoods, tend not to belong to Japanese American organizations, are less likely to be Buddhists, and are less likely to speak Japanese well. They have been mobile not only *up* in the status hierarchy but also *out* of the ethnic community."[61] Intermarriage provided the most striking evidence of assimilation. Forbidden in California until 1948, intermarriage remained uncommon until the 1960s. By the 1970s, in San Francisco and Fresno, about half of all Japanese Americans were marrying Caucasians. The researchers who discovered this (by examining surnames on marriage licenses) concluded that "the boundary that historically set the Japanese Americans off from the rest of American society is disappearing."[62] The highest rates of intermarriage occurred in the third generation, among the children of the Japanese Americans who, when children themselves, had been interned during World War II.

If Asian Americans, on the whole, enjoyed better-than-average living standards, the reverse was true of the other major group of new immigrants; Spanish-speaking Americans. In 1979 the Census Bureau estimated that more than 12 million persons of Hispanic descent were living in the United States: 7.2 million from Mexico, 1.8 million from Puerto Rico, 700,000 from Cuba, 900,000 from Central and South America, and 1.4 million from other lands. The Spanish-origin population was overwhelmingly urban; one out of every two people resided in central cities, and one out of every three lived in the suburbs. It was, moreover, a youthful population: the median age was twenty-two years as compared with thirty years for Americans of other than Spanish ancestry. It was, finally, a relatively deprived population, with low levels of educational attainment, a high proportion of blue-collar as compared with white-collar workers, and a 1977 median family income ($10,300) about two-thirds that of other families. Nearly one out of four Spanish-speaking families subsisted below the poverty line, but some groups were distinctly worse off than others. While 17 percent of Cuban families lived in poverty, 22 percent of Mexican families and 39 percent of Puerto Rican families did.[63]

The trouble with these statistics is that they did not take into account millions of recent immigrants, the vast majority from Mexico and Latin America, who had entered the United States illegally. By the late 1970s the problem of illegal aliens had reached acute proportions. The problem was spawned by the Immigration Reform Act of 1965, which, for the first time, imposed a limit on immigration from the Western Hemisphere. The number selected—120,000 a year—while not entirely arbitrary, was based on little more than a wishful expectation that about as many people from Western Hemisphere nations would want to emigrate in the future as had wanted to in the past. "If you look at the present immigration figures from Western Hemisphere countries there is not much pressure to come to the United States from these countries," an official in the Johnson administration said. "There are in a relative sense not many people who want to come."[64] But as the rates of population growth in Mexico and South America soared, and as industrialization in those areas displaced millions of agricultural workers, a wave of illegal immigrants entered the United States.

No one knew for sure just how many illegal aliens there were. Some estimates were based on the number of apprehensions made by the Immigration and Naturalization Service: 110,000 in 1965; 335,000 in 1970; 756,000 in 1975; and more than 1 million in 1977. It was, however, not at all certain whether the agency's rule of thumb—that it captured one in three or four illegal aliens—was accurate. As INS Commissioner Leonel J. Castillo admitted: "I know that we've apprehended some people 20 times. We apprehended one man five times in one day. . . . He came back five times in one day, and we picked him up five times. For all we know, he's here now."[65] Other estimates were based on a commonsense attempt to strike an average. Figuring the number of illegal aliens to be 4 to 5 million in 1974, an official said: "It is just a midpoint between the two extremes. I have heard one or two million at one end of the scale and eight or 10 million at the other. So I am selecting a midpoint. . . . Just a guess, that is all. Nobody knows."[66] By the late 1970s it was commonly assumed that at least 1 million illegal aliens succeeded in entering each year and that no fewer than 7 million were residing in the United States.

The smuggling of illegal aliens blossomed into a big and lucrative business. As Castillo remarked: "There are great, big operations almost like travel agencies. They have an office in New York, and they can find you 50 workers—complete with phony documents—to work in carwashes in Philadelphia. They'll get them in from Brownsville, Tex., for example, with stops in different places."[67] Smugglers perfected their techniques—using a small group of decoys, for example, to divert guards' attention while a larger group was crossing the border—and employed increasingly sophisticated equipment. "Scout cars with two-way radios warn vehicles smuggling aliens of the location of Border Patrol agents," an official report noted. "Some vehicles are custom designed. They have special springs so you can't tell that there are 20 people in the back of a pickup truck."[68] A wide assortment of supporting industries was needed. Not only did taxi companies transport aliens from border points to Los Angeles, Chicago, or New York, but in addition, there were "guides, drivers, innkeepers, labor agencies, job foremen, fabricators of false documents, and the like; and certain predatory lawyers, immigrant consultants, and public notaries, who work immigrant hardship cases."[69] Smugglers had little to lose and much to gain: fewer than half who were caught were prosecuted, and those convicted paid only a light fine.

The task of law enforcement was virtually impossible. With only 1,700 agents in the Southwest, and only a few hundred of them working on an average shift, the INS could not have effectively patrolled the 2,000-mile-long border with Mexico even if every agent had been able to be in two places at the same time. An alien who was not apprehended at or near the border (where 80 percent of the apprehensions were made) was not likely to be apprehended at all. The INS maintained only a skeleton staff outside the Southwest, employing, for example, twenty-eight agents in the New York–New Jersey region, where there were surely more than 1 million illegal aliens. Moreover, attempts to round up illegal aliens raised thorny civil liberties questions. For a time the INS utilized "residential enforcement tactics" in Hispanic communities by "surrounding an entire city block and questioning persons at bus stops on their way to work."[70] It abandoned these dragnet raids in 1975 after Americans of Spanish origin protested and an injunction against the raids was obtained in Illinois. Finally, several Supreme Court decisions restricted the right of INS agents, at points removed from the border, to stop and search vehicles without probable cause. The INS thereafter eliminated its roving patrols.

Illegal aliens dwelt in a Stygian realm, in "an invisible subculture outside the boundaries of law and legitimate institutions."[71] Those who came were, for the most part, young people, "the more ambitious, the more daring, the more active. The destitute are not coming; the elderly are not coming."[72] Seeking anonymity above all else, they were easily exploited by landlords and employers who knew that substandard dwellings and violations of the minimum wage laws would not be reported. Illegal aliens, working at the least desirable jobs for the lowest wages, still earned more than would have been possible had they not migrated. "While employment opportunities for illegal aliens in the U.S. may be poor by American standards, they are considerably better than those in the country of origin," investigators concluded.[73] Like modern indentured servants, illegal aliens might pay the smuggler's fee out of their wages and were also likely to send part of their earnings home to help relatives. Always, no matter how many years had passed since the illegal alien had entered the United States, the fear of discovery persisted. A woman who made her way to Los Angeles from Central America explained the dilemma: "I constantly live in fear I may be expelled. I try not to go out of the house. I always carry my baby for fear that they may send me back and put my baby in a home. I want to stay here. It's a better chance for me."[74]

In August 1977 President Carter offered a plan to

deal with the problem, hoping, thereby, to "avoid having a permanent 'underclass' of millions of persons who have not been and cannot practicably be deported, and who would continue living here in perpetual fear." Those who could prove they had entered the United States before 1970 (a number estimated at 765,000) would be granted status as permanent resident aliens, the same status for which they would have been eligible had they entered legally. Those who had entered between 1970 and 1977 (a number estimated at 5 million) would be offered temporary resident alien status for five years while a final determination was made. Meanwhile, although ineligible for federal welfare payments and unable to bring in their relatives, they could leave and reenter the United States legally, "and they could seek employment, under the same rules as permanent resident aliens." Those who had entered after January 1, 1977, presuming they could be located, would be expelled. To facilitate the task of identification, the President proposed making it illegal for employers knowingly to hire unauthorized aliens. To relieve future pressures, Carter urged an increase in economic aid to Mexico and Latin America.

A year after its unveiling, the plan, caught in a congressional crossfire, had made no headway. On one side were those who opposed any relaxation of the law. Arguing that illegal aliens took jobs away from citizens, depressed wages to rock-bottom levels, and utilized public services they paid no taxes to support, these critics insisted that Carter's plan would "reward this illegal conduct with special benefits. . . . It puts the government squarely behind the lawbreaker."[75] On the other side were those who favored greater leniency than Carter's plan envisioned. Pointing out that illegal aliens ordinarily took jobs no one else would do ("there is no great rush of unemployed persons on the East Coast to go pick onions in 100-degree heat for three weeks"), usually worked for wages that, while low, were at legal levels, and normally paid withholding and sales taxes even though they hesitated to use governmental services, these critics favored a general amnesty for nearly all illegal aliens. Ruefully observing the debate, INS Commissioner Castillo commented in February 1978: "We thought we had taken a middle position, struck a creative balance, but now we find ourselves crunched in the middle."[76]

By the late 1970s, then, the United States possessed a large and growing class of illegal aliens, most of whom lived at bare subsistence levels. As the *Wall Street Journal* observed: "The people who benefit the most from this situation are certainly the employers, who have access to an underground market of cheap productive labor, unencumbered by minimum wage laws, union restrictions or pension requirements."[77] One such employer, who owned a chain of restaurants which hired illegal aliens as dishwashers and paid less than the minimum wage, was equally blunt: "It feels kind of good to see these boys come and work hard for you."[78] The result was an enormous discrepancy in living standards—in levels of income, education, housing, and health—between the illegal arrivals and other immigrants, notably the Asian Americans. That discrepancy, however, rarely showed up in official statistics. In an age noted for its ability to collect data, the full extent of class differences among ethnic groups remained anybody's guess.

The controversy over the illegal alien issue, like those over the Bakke ruling and the Equal Rights Amendment, suggested that ethnicity, race, and class were no less important in the late 1970s than they had been in the late 1930s. Yet it is worth observing that these forty years were marked by change as well as by continuity. To measure that change, one need only imagine the reception that the women's rights movement, affirmative-action programs, or proposals to legalize the status of a vast number of illegal aliens might have received in 1938 or, better still, to speculate on the reception that, in 1978, would have been accorded arguments against establishing a 25-cent-an-hour minimum wage, passing an antilynching bill, or admitting 20,000 children fleeing totalitarian rule. The preacher's cry in Ecclesiastes—"There is no new thing under the sun"—should be taken not as witness to the immutability of class, racial, and ethnic patterns for as testament to their enduring influence.

Notes

1. The Eve of War

1. Zephine Humphrey, *Green Mountains to Sierras* (New York, 1936), p. 45.

2. W. Lloyd Warner and Paul S. Lunt, *The Social Life of a Modern Community* (New Haven, 1941), p. 82.

3. Allison Davis *et al.*, *Deep South: A Social Anthropological Study of Caste and Class* (Chicago, 1941), p. 238; W. Lloyd Warner, *Democracy in Jonesville* (New York, 1949), pp. 22–23.

4. "The National Health Survey," *Public Health Reports* (March 15, 1940), p. 452; "Housing and Health Relationships Re-examined," *ibid.* (March 29, 1940), pp. 550–51.

5. John M. Blum, *From the Morgenthau Diaries: Years of Crisis* (Boston, 1959), p. 288.

6. Selden Menefee and Orin C. Cassmore, *The Pecan Shellers of San Antonio* (Washington, 1940), pp. 44–45.

7. Daniel S. Hirshfield, *The Lost Reform* (Cambridge, 1970), p. 141.

8. John M. Blum, *From the Morgenthau Diaries: Years of Urgency* (Boston, 1964), pp. 41–42.

9. Hortense Powdermaker, *After Freedom: A Cultural Study in the Deep South* (New York, 1939), pp. 47–48.

10. *Ibid.*, pp. 44–46; Charles S. Johnson, *Patterns of Negro Segregation* (New York, 1943), p. 140.

11. Ralph Bunche, *The Political Status of the Negro in the Age of FDR*, Dewey Grantham, ed. (Chicago, 1973), pp. 203–04.

12. Arthur Raper, "Race and Class Pressures," research memorandum for the Carnegie-Myrdal Study (June 7, 1940), p. 105.

13. Bunche, *Political Status,* pp. 49–50.

14. Gunnar Myrdal, *An American Dilemma* (New York, 1944), p. 530.

15. *Ibid.,* p. 525.

16. Davis, *Deep South,* pp. 527–28.

17. Paul Oliver, *The Blues Tradition* (New York, 1970), p. 143.

18. Dan Carter, *Scottsboro: A Tragedy of the American South* (Baton Rouge, 1969), pp. 392–98.

19. Robert W. Dubay, "Mississippi and the Proposed Federal Anti-Lynching Bills of 1937–1938," *The Southern Quarterly* (October 1968), pp. 73–87.

20. Sidney Baldwin, *Poverty and Politics: The Rise and Decline of the Farm Security Administration* (Chapel Hill, 1968), p. 307.

21. Roosevelt to Marvin McIntyre, June 7, 1941, Roosevelt MSS, Official File 391.

22. Federal Writers' Project, *New York City Guide* (New York, 1939), p. 270.

23. Federal Writers' Project, *Massachusetts: A Guide to Its Places and People* (Boston, 1937), p. 136.

24. Jeanette Sayre Smith, "Broadcasting for Marginal Americans," *Public Opinion Quarterly* (Winter 1942), pp. 588–603.

25. Elin Anderson, *We Americans: A Study of Cleavage in an American City* (Cambridge, 1938), p. 43.

26. Maurice J. Karpf, *Jewish Community Organization in the United States* (New York, 1938), p. 20.

27. Philip Klein, *A Social Study of Pittsburgh* (New York, 1938), pp. 252–53; see also John E. Bodnar, "Steelton's Immigrants: Social Relationships in a Pennsylvania Mill Town, 1870–1940" (Ph.D. dissertation, University of Connecticut, 1975), pp. 177, 199.

28. Ellsworth Barnard, *Wendell Willkie* (Marquette, Mich., 1966), p. 251.

29. Ben Marcin, "The Truth About the Protocols," *Social Justice* (October 3, 1938), pp. 10–11; New York *Times*, June 24, 1938, p. 20; Sander A. Diamond, *The Nazi Movement in the United States, 1924–1941* (Ithaca, 1974), p. 240.

30. Saul Friedman, *No Haven for the Oppressed* (Detroit, 1973), p. 102; Henry Feingold, *The Politics of Rescue* (New Brunswick, 1970), p. 150.

31. "Treachery in the Air," *American Magazine* (September 1940), pp. 44–46; Cabell Phillips, "G-Men of the Airwaves," *New York Times Magazine* (September 14, 1941), p. 9.

32. "Our Enemies Within," *The Nation* (June 22, 1940), pp. 745–46; "Clear and Present Danger," *ibid.* (June 29, 1940), p. 772.

33. Lewis Mumford, *Faith for Living* (New York, 1940), pp. 106–07.

34. Conference on National Defense, May 30, 1940, Roosevelt Press Conferences, XV, pp. 420–21.

35. J. Woodford Howard, *Mr. Justice Murphy* (Princeton, 1968), p. 207.

36. Felix Frankfurter, "Memorandum to the Conference," February 15, 1941, Frankfurter MSS.

2. Wartime America

1. James M. Landis to Roosevelt, April 27, 1942, Roosevelt MSS, Official File 4422.

2. Edmund A. Walsh to Roosevelt, December 18, 1941, Roosevelt MSS, President's Personal File 7883; Charles A. Lindbergh, *The Wartime Journals of Charles A. Lindbergh* (New York, 1970), p. 561; Steve Early to "Pa" Watson, December 10, 1941, Roosevelt MSS, PPF 245.

3. Marvin W. Schlegel, *Virginia on Guard* (Richmond, Va., 1949), p. 66.

4. Ulric Bell and William B. Lewis to Archibald MacLeish, February 3, 1942, Henry Pringle MSS; see also Charles D. Lloyd, "American Society and Values in World War II

from the Publications of the OWI" (Ph.D. dissertation, Georgetown University, 1975).

5. Chicago *Tribune,* May 25, 1943.

6. John M. Blum, *From the Morgenthau Diaries: Years of War* (Boston, 1967), pp. 17–20.

7. Mary Watters, *Illinois in the Second World War* (Springfield, 1951), Vol. I, pp. 272, 276.

8. Petroleum Industry War Council, *Bulletin,* July 10, 1942, Roosevelt MSS, OF 4435-B.

9. Raymond Rubicam, "Advertising," in Jack Goodman, ed., *While You Were Gone* (New York, 1946), pp. 437–39; Frank W. Fox, "Advertising and the Second World War" (Ph.D. dissertation, Stanford University, 1973), p. 32.

10. Ernie Pyle, *Here Is Your War,* 1971 ed. (New York, 1943), pp. 126, 90.

11. John Hersey, *A Bell for Adano* (New York, 1944), p. vi; Harry Brown (pseud.), *A Walk in the Sun* (New York, 1944), p. 97.

12. W. Lloyd Warner, *Democracy in Jonesville* (New York, 1949), p. 287; *Life* (October 22, 1943), p. 93.

13. Richard Hasbany, "Bromidic Parables: The American Musical Theatre During the Second World War," *Journal of Popular Culture* (Spring 1973), pp. 642–65.

14. Norman Corwin, *More by Corwin* (New York, 1944), pp. 85–86.

15. Samuel M. Strong, "Observations on the Possibility of Attitude Modification: A Case of Nationality and Racial Group Inter-Relationships in Wartime," *Social Forces* (March 1944), pp. 323–31.

16. *Ibid.,* pp. 324–25; Francis J. Brown and Joseph S. Roucek, eds., *One America* (New York, 1945), p. 426.

17. Peter H. Irons, " 'The Test Is Poland': Polish Americans and the Origins of the Cold War," *Polish American Studies* (Autumn 1973), p. 44.

18. "Summary of Discussion at Conference," December 5, 1942, Frankfurter MSS.

19. *Schneiderman* v. *United States* (1943) 320 U.S. 118 at 120.

20. "Notes on the Schneiderman Case," June 16, 1943, Frankfurter MSS.

21. Alpheus Thomas Mason, *Harlan Fiske Stone: Pillar of the Law* (New York, 1956) , p. 691.

22. John L. Cable, *Loss of Citizenship; Denaturalization; The Alien in Wartime* (Washington, 1943) , p. 86.

23. Francis Biddle, *In Brief Authority* (New York, 1962) , pp. 230–31; John Diggins, *Mussolini and Fascism: The View from America* (Princeton, 1972) , p. 352.

24. Samuel I. Rosenman, ed., *The Public Papers and Addresses of Franklin D. Roosevelt* (New York, 1950) , Vol. XIII, pp. 331–32; Biddle, *In Brief Authority,* p. 207.

25. Roosevelt, *Public Papers,* XIII, pp. 352–53; Edward J. Kelly to Harry Hopkins, September 13, 1944, Roosevelt MSS, PPF 3166.

26. "The New Poor," *Wall Street Journal,* November 11–16, 1942; *ibid.,* October 31, 1942.

27. Roland Young, *Congressional Politics in the Second World War* (New York, 1956) , p. 103.

28. Buffalo, N.Y., UAW to Roosevelt, March 31, 1943, Roosevelt MSS, OF 98–A.

29. Minutes, War Labor Board Executive Meeting, February 6, 1942, Roosevelt MSS, OF 4710.

30. Thomas Amlie to James Loeb, May 12, 1942, Union for Democratic Action MSS.

31. Claude Pepper to Bernard Baruch, December 17, 1944, Baruch MSS.

32. Hadley Cantril to Samuel Rosenman, September 30, 1944, Rosenman MSS.

33. Katherine Archibald, *Wartime Shipyard: A Study in Social Disunity* (Berkeley, 1947) , pp. 183–84, 47.

34. Agnes E. Meyer, *Journey Through Chaos* (New York, 1944) , pp. 286–302; Robert J. Havighurst and H. Gerthon Morgan, *The Social History of a War-Boom Community* (New York, 1951) , pp. 108–09, 172.

35. Havighurst and Morgan, *Social History,* pp. 102, 81.

36. Pitirim A. Sorokin, *Man and Society in Calamity* (New York, 1942), p. 310.

37. Ashley Montagu, *Man's Most Dangerous Myth: The Fallacy of Race,* 2nd ed. (New York, 1945), p. 240; *ibid.,* 1st ed. (New York, 1942), pp. 179–80.

38. *Amsterdam News,* June 19, 1943; Paul Oliver, *The Meaning of the Blues* (New York, 1960), p. 283.

39. Gunnar Myrdal, *An American Dilemma* (New York, 1944), p. 1003; William D. Barnard, *Dixiecrats and Democrats: Alabama Politics, 1942–1950* (University, Ala., 1974), pp. 98–99.

40. Myrdal, *American Dilemma,* p. 1007; St. Clair Drake and Horace R. Cayton, *Black Metropolis* (New York, 1945), p. 745.

41. Charles S. Johnson, *To Stem This Tide* (Boston, 1943), p. 109.

42. Sterling A. Brown, "Count Us In," in Rayford W. Logan, ed., *What the Negro Wants* (Chapel Hill, 1944), p. 318.

43. Louis Ruchames, *Race, Jobs and Politics* (Chapel Hill, 1948), pp. 196–98.

44. Ulysses Lee, *The Employment of Negro Troops* (Washington, 1966), p. 140.

45. Edgar Brown to Roosevelt, May 20, 1942, Roosevelt MSS, OF 93–B.

46. "Memorandum by Turner Catledge," August 25, 1943, Arthur Krock MSS.

47. Alfred McClung Lee and Norman D. Humphrey, *Race Riot* (New York, 1943), pp. 61–62.

48. Stetson Conn *et al., Guarding the United States and Its Outposts* (Washington, 1964), pp. 136–37.

49. Henry L. Stimson Diary, February 3, 10, 1942, Stimson MSS.

50. Department of the Interior, *WRA: A Story of Human Conservation* (Washington, 1946), p. 181; War Department,

Chief of Staff, *Final Report: Japanese Evacuation from the West Coast, 1942* (Washington, 1943), p. 34.

51. Harold R. Isaacs, *Scratches on Our Minds* (New York, 1958), p. 175; Robert Divine, *American Immigration Policy* (New Haven, 1957), p. 150; Fred W. Riggs, *Pressure on Congress: A Study of the Repeal of Chinese Exclusion* (New York, 1950).

52. Mary Oyama, "This Isn't Japan," *Common Ground* (Autumn 1942), pp. 32–34.

53. Audrie Girdner and Anne Loftis, *The Great Betrayal* (London, 1969), pp. 257, 259.

54. Sidney Fine, "Mr. Justice Murphy and the Hirabayashi Case," *Pacific Historical Review* (May 1964), p. 201; Eugene V. Rostow, "The Japanese-American Cases—A Disaster," *The Yale Law Journal* (June 1945), p. 505; Jacobus ten Broek *et al., Prejudice, War and the Constitution* (Berkeley, 1954), p. 263.

55. J. Woodford Howard, *Mr. Justice Murphy* (Princeton, 1968), p. 335.

56. M. E. Gilfond to Lowell Mellett, July 15, 1942, Mellett MSS.

3. The Cold War

1. NSC–68, "A Report to the National Security Council," April 14, 1950, p. 7.

2. Richard M. Freeland, *The Truman Doctrine and the Origins of McCarthyism* (New York, 1972), pp. 85, 89.

3. Raymond J. Sontag and James S. Beddie, eds., *Nazi-Soviet Relations, 1939–1941* (Washington, 1948), pp. 75, 99; *Time*, February 2, 1948, p. 17.

4. John M. Blum, ed., *The Price of Vision: The Diary of Henry A. Wallace, 1942–1946* (Boston, 1973), p. 503.

5. Ronald Radosh and Leonard P. Liggio, "Henry A. Wallace and the Open Door," in Thomas G. Paterson, ed., *Cold War Critics* (Chicago, 1971), p. 99; Karl Schmidt,

Henry A. Wallace, Quixotic Crusade, 1948 (Syracuse, 1960), p. 285.

6. Clark M. Clifford to Truman, November 19, 1947, Clifford MSS; Richard J. Walton, *Henry Wallace, Harry Truman and the Cold War* (New York, 1976), p. 205.

7. Dwight Macdonald, *Henry Wallace: The Man and the Myth* (New York, 1948), pp. 109, 175.

8. "From the Court Testimony of the Communist Leaders," *Political Affairs* (September 1949), pp. 27–28.

9. Herbert A. Philbrick, *I Led 3 Lives,* 1972 ed. (New York, 1952), p. 168; Leslie Adler, "The Red Image: American Attitudes Toward Communism in the Cold War Era" (Ph.D. dissertation, University of California, 1971), p. 158.

10. Angela Calomiris, *Red Masquerade* (Philadelphia, 1950), p. 80; Adler, "The Red Image," pp. 147–48.

11. Whittaker Chambers, *Witness* (New York, 1952), pp. 25–88.

12. Stefan Kanfer, *A Journal of the Plague Years* (New York, 1973), pp. 57, 49.

13. Russell E. Shain, "Hollywood's Cold War," *Journal of Popular Film* (November 1974), p. 348.

14. George Orwell, *1984* (New York, 1949), pp. 220, 247, 17; Adler, "The Red Image," p. 473.

15. Harry S. Truman, *Memoirs,* 1965 ed. (New York, 1956), Vol. II, p. 353.

16. Carl Solberg, *Riding High: America in the Cold War* (New York, 1973), p. 140.

17. Tang Tsou, *America's Failure in China, 1941–1950* (Chicago, 1963), Vol. II, p. 508.

18. Solberg, *Riding High,* p. 149.

19. *Public Papers of the Presidents: Harry S. Truman, 1950* (Washington, 1965), pp. 234–35.

20. NSC–68, April 14, 1950, pp. 13, 6.

21. "President Truman's Conversation with George M. Elsey, June 26, 1950; Charles S. Murphy to Connelly, June 27, 1950, Elsey MSS.

22. Adler, "The Red Image," pp. 107–08.

23. Cecilia B. Stendler, *Children of Brasstown: Their Awareness of the Symbols of Social Class* (Urbana, 1949); Herman M. Case, "An Independent Test of the Interest-Group Theory of Social Class," *American Sociological Review* (December 1952), pp. 751–54.

24. Gerhard E. Lenski, "American Social Classes: Statistical Strata or Social Groups?" *American Journal of Sociology* (September 1952), pp. 139–44; Walter Goldschmidt, "Social Class in America—a Critical Review," *American Anthropologist* (October–December 1950), p. 483.

25. W. Lloyd Warner *et al., Social Class in America* (Chicago, 1949), pp. 9–10, v–vii, 31.

26. "A Sociologist Looks at an American Community," *Life* (September 12, 1949), pp. 108–18.

27. Peter Drucker, "The Myth of American Uniformity," *Harper's* (May 1952), p. 76.

28. David Riesman *et al., The Lonely Crowd,* 1971 ed. (New Haven, 1950), p. 214.

29. Reinhold Niebuhr, *The Irony of American History* (New York, 1952), pp. 1, 100–01.

30. Fortune, *USA: The Permanent Revolution* (New York, 1951), pp. 111, 90–91.

31. *Ibid.,* p. 95.

32. David M. Oshinsky, "Labor's Cold War: The CIO and the Communists," in Robert Griffith and Athan Theoharis, eds., *The Specter* (New York, 1974), pp. 132, 151; James R. Prickett, "Communists and the Communist Issue in the American Labor Movement, 1920–1950" (Ph.D. dissertation, UCLA, 1975), pp. 401–19.

33. Richard Harris, *A Sacred Trust* (New York, 1966), pp. 35–57.

34. Donald R. McCoy and Richard T. Ruetten, *Quest and Response: Minority Rights and the Truman Administration* (Lawrence, 1973), p. 264.

35. *Ibid.,* pp. 66, 120.

36. Wayne A. Clark, "An Analysis of the Relationship Between Anti-Communism and Segregationist Thought in the Deep South, 1948–1964" (Ph.D. dissertation, University of North Carolina, 1976), pp. 29–30.

37. Clement E. Vose, *Caucasians Only* (Berkeley, 1967), p. 215.

38. Ann M. McLaurin, "The Role of the Dixiecrats in the 1948 Election" (Ph.D. dissertation, University of Oklahoma, 1972), p. 104.

39. *Ibid.*, p. 233; Gary C. Ness, "The States' Rights Democratic Movement of 1948" (Ph.D. dissertation, Duke University, 1972), pp. 186–87.

40. Wilson Record, *Race and Radicalism* (Ithaca, 1964), p. 164.

41. James L. Roark, "American Black Leaders: The Response to Colonialism and the Cold War, 1945–1953," *African Historical Studies* (1971), pp. 253–70.

42. Gilbert Osofsky, ed., *The Burden of Race* (New York, 1967), p. 466.

43. Dorothy B. Gilliam, *Paul Robeson* (Washington, 1976), pp. 137–43.

44. Carl T. Rowan with Jackie Robinson, *Wait Till Next Year* (New York, 1960), pp. 201–10.

45. McCoy and Ruetten, *Quest and Response,* p. 199.

46. *Ibid.,* p. 272.

47. Fortune, *USA,* pp. 167–70.

48. *Communist Activities Among Alien and National Groups,* Hearings Before the Subcommittee on Immigration and Naturalization of the Committee on the Judiciary, U.S. Senate, 81st Congress, 1st Session (Washington, 1950), pp. 38, 116, 218.

49. *Ibid.,* p. 320.

50. Freeland, *Truman Doctrine,* p. 219.

51. Robert L. Jefferys, "The Wong Yang Sung Decision," U.S. Immigration and Naturalization Service, *Monthly Review* (April 1950), pp. 131–37.

52. *Communist Activities,* Hearings, p. 101; Theodore Huff, *Charlie Chaplin,* 1972 ed. (New York, 1951), p. 285.

53. C. Herman Pritchett, *Civil Liberties and the Vinson Court* (Chicago, 1954), pp. 113, 117.

54. Fortune, *USA,* p. 18.

55. *Permitting Admission of 400,000 Displaced Persons,* Hearings Before the Subcommittee on Immigration and Naturalization of the Committee on the Judiciary, House of Representatives, 80th Congress, 1st Session (Washington, 1947), p. 158.

56. Robert A. Divine, *American Immigration Policy, 1924–1952* (New Haven, 1957), p. 133.

57. The Final Report of the U.S. Displaced Persons Commission, *Memo to America: The DP Story* (Washington, 1952), p. 162.

58. Joseph McCarthy to Douglas MacArthur, August 29, 1950, MacArthur MSS.

59. *Congressional Record,* 81st Congress, 2nd Session (1950), p. 1954.

60. *Ibid.,* 82nd Congress, 1st Session (1951), pp. 6556–6603.

61. Seymour Martin Lipset, "The Sources of the Radical Right," in Daniel Bell, ed., *The Radical Right* (New York, 1963), p. 362.

62. Richard Rovere, *Senator Joe McCarthy* (Cleveland, 1960), p. 141.

63. Seymour Martin Lipset and Earl Raab, *The Politics of Unreason* (New York, 1970), p. 244.

64. Donald F. Crosby, "The Angry Catholics: American Catholics and Senator Joseph R. McCarthy" (Ph.D. dissertation, Brandeis University, 1973), pp. 476–91.

4. The Suburban Society

1. Eric Larrabee, "The Six Thousand Houses That Levitt Built," *Harper's* (September 1948), p. 84.

2. Kenneth T. Jackson, "The Crabgrass Frontier: 150 Years of Suburban Growth in America," in Raymond A. Mohl and James F. Richardson, eds., *The Urban Experience* (Belmont, Calif., 1973), p. 218.

3. Herbert J. Gans, *The Levittowners: Ways of Life and Politics in a New Suburban Community* (New York, 1967), pp. 39, 41.

4. Edward T. Chase, "The Hundred Billion Dollar Question," *Architectural Forum* (July 1957), p. 135.

5. William J. Levitt, "What! *Live* in a Levittown?," *Good Housekeeping* (July 1958), pp. 175–76; "Up from the Potato Fields," *Time* (July 3, 1950), pp. 67–72.

6. "4,000 Houses per Year," *Architectural Forum* (April 1949), pp. 84–85.

7. "Three Successful Shopping Centers," *Architectural Forum* (October 1957), p. 111.

8. "Big Shopping Center with No 'Mr. Big,'" *Architectural Forum* (June 1954), p. 120.

9. David Riesman, "The Suburban Sadness," in William Dobriner, ed., *The Suburban Community* (New York, 1958), pp. 375–402.

10. John Keats, *The Crack in the Picture Window* (Boston, 1957).

11. Richard E. Gordon *et al.*, *The Split-Level Trap* (New York, 1960), pp. 33, 54, 142.

12. William H. Whyte, Jr., *The Organization Man* (New York, 1956), pp. 7, 391.

13. John Cheever, *The Wapshot Chronicle* (New York, 1957), pp. 228–30, 238.

14. William M. Dobriner, *Class in Suburbia* (Englewood Cliffs, N. J., 1963), p. 17.

15. *Ibid.*, p. 13.

16. Stanley Rowland, Jr., "Suburbia Buys Religion," *The Nation* (July 28, 1956), pp. 78–80.

17. *Time* (November 17, 1952), p. 24.

18. Whyte, *Organization Man*, p. 330; Andrew M. Greeley, *The Church and the Suburbs* (New York, 1959), p. 57.

19. "4,000 Houses per Year," *Architectural Forum* (April 1949), p. 85.

20. David Riesman, "Introduction," in John R. Seeley *et al., Crestwood Heights* (New York, 1956), p. vii.

21. Dobriner, *Class in Suburbia*, p. 37.

22. Gans, *Levittowners*, p. xxiii.

23. Dobriner, *Class in Suburbia*, p. 100.

24. Bennett M. Berger, *Working-Class Suburb: A Study of Auto Workers in Suburbia* (Berkeley, 1960), p. 84.

25. Gans, *Levittowners*, p. 131.

26. Samuel Lubell, *Revolt of the Moderates* (New York, 1956), p. 246; Dobriner, *Class in Suburbia*, p. 24.

27. Gans, *Levittowners*, p. 24.

28. Edwina Austin Avery, "Veterans Day (1954) Mass Naturalizations," U.S. Immigration and Naturalization Service, *Reporter* (January 1955), p. 39.

29. Will Herberg, *Protestant-Catholic-Jew* (Garden City, N.Y., 1955), pp. 31, 59.

30. Andrew M. Greeley, *Why Can't They Be Like Us? America's White Ethnic Groups* (New York, 1975), pp. 104, 108.

31. Benjamin B. Ringer, *The Lakeville Studies: The Edge of Friendliness* (New York, 1967), pp. 267, 29; Marshall Sklare and Joseph Greenblum, *The Lakeville Studies: Jewish Identity on the Suburban Frontier* (New York, 1967), Chapter 8.

32. Albert I. Gordon, *Jews in Suburbia* (Boston, 1959), p. 16.

33. "Simeon Stylites," "Satan in the Suburbs," *Christian Century* (November 26, 1952), p. 1375.

34. Stanley Rowland, Jr., "Suburbia Buys Religion," *The Nation* (July 28, 1956), pp. 78–80.

35. Gans, *Levittowners*, p. 85.

36. John H. Denton, "Phase I Report" to the National Committee Against Discrimination in Housing, cited in Michael N. Danielson, *The Politics of Exclusion* (New York, 1976), p. 12.

37. *The National Conference and the Reports of the State Advisory Committees to the U.S. Commission on Civil Rights, 1959* (Washington, 1960), p. 308.

38. James G. Coke and Charles S. Liebman, "Political Values and Population Density Control," *Land Economics* (November 1961), p. 354.

39. Richard Kluger, *Simple Justice* (New York, 1976), pp. 779–85.

40. *Ibid.*, p. 354.

41. J.M.L., "Bench Memo," December 10, 1952, Harold Burton MSS.

42. Kluger, *Simple Justice*, pp. 646, 781.

43. Steven F. Lawson, *Black Ballots: Voting Rights in the South, 1944–1969* (New York, 1976), p. 141.

44. E. Frederic Morrow, *Black Man in the White House* (New York, 1963), p. 98.

45. Lawson, *Black Ballots*, p. 146.

46. Peter Lyon, *Eisenhower: Portrait of the Hero* (Boston, 1974), p. 789.

47. Numan V. Bartley, *The Rise of Massive Resistance: Race and Politics in the South During the 1950s* (Baton Rouge, 1969), p. 265.

48. Eisenhower to Richard Russell, September 27, 1957, in Robert L. Branyan and Lawrence H. Larsen, eds., *The Eisenhower Administration, 1953–1961*, 2 vols. (New York, 1971), Vol. II, p. 1136.

49. Marvin Bressler, "The Myers' Case: An Instance of Successful Racial Invasion," *Social Problems* (Fall 1960), pp. 126–42.

50. Gans, *The Levittowners*, pp. 371–84.

5. The Age of Reform

1. Ted Lewis, "Congress Versus Kennedy," *The Nation* (July 14, 1962), p. 4.

2. Theodore H. White, *The Making of the President, 1960* (New York, 1961), p. 426.

3. Lawrence H. Fuchs, *John F. Kennedy and American Catholicism* (New York, 1967), p. 168.

4. E. S. James to Kennedy, March 11, 1960, Theodore Sorensen MSS.

5. White, *Making of the President,* pp. 468–72.

6. John Courtney Murray, *We Hold These Truths: Catholic Reflections on the American Proposition* (New York, 1960), pp. 73–74, 70.

7. Paul Blanshard: *American Freedom and Catholic Power* (Boston, 1949), pp. 289, 267; *God and Man in Washington* (Boston, 1960), pp. 198–206.

8. Fuchs, *Kennedy and Catholicism,* p. 134.

9. Louis Harris, "Public Reaction to President Kennedy During the First 60 Days of His Administration," March 22, 1961, Kennedy MSS, President's Office Files; *Public Papers of the Presidents, John F. Kennedy, 1961* (Washington, 1962), p. 142.

10. William A. Carroll, "The Constitution, the Supreme Court, and Religion," *American Political Science Review* (September 1967), pp. 657–74.

11. The texts of both decisions may be consulted in Paul Blanshard, *Religion and the Schools: The Great Controversy* (Boston, 1963), pp. 195–244.

12. Robert Birkby, "The Supreme Court and the Bible Belt: Tennessee Reaction to the 'Schempp' Decision," *Midwest Journal of Political Science* (August 1966), p. 315.

13. Eugene Bianchi, *John XXIII and American Protestants* (Washington, 1968), p. 130; John Cogley, Oral History Memoir, Kennedy MSS, p. 52.

14. Arthur Schlesinger, Jr., *A Thousand Days* (Boston, 1965), pp. 17–18; William E. Leuchtenburg, *A Troubled Feast* (Boston, 1973), p. 142.

15. *Economic Report of the President, 1965* (Washington, 1965), pp. 61–62.

16. Daniel Patrick Moynihan, "The Professionalization of Reform," *The Public Interest* (Fall 1965), pp. 6–16.

17. Joseph Heller, *Catch-22* (New York, 1962), pp. 83, 19.

18. Paul L. Murphy, *The Constitution in Crisis Times* (New York, 1972), p. 465.

19. *Ibid.*, p. 389.

20. Richard Hofstadter, "Goldwater and Pseudo-Conservative Politics," in his *The Paranoid Style in American Politics* (New York, 1967), pp. 109, 128, 98.

21. Eric F. Goldman, *The Tragedy of Lyndon Johnson* (New York, 1969), p. 336.

22. White, *Making of the President,* p. 413; Schlesinger, *A Thousand Days,* p. 120.

23. Doris Kearns, *Lyndon Johnson and the American Dream* (New York, 1976), pp. 221, 237.

24. Goldman, *Tragedy of Lyndon Johnson,* p. 70.

25. Martin Luther King, *Why We Can't Wait* (New York, 1964), pp. 83, 87.

26. Martin Luther King, *Stride Toward Freedom* (New York, 1958), p. 84.

27. Kenneth Clark, "The Civil Rights Movement: Momentum and Organization," in Talcott Parsons and Kenneth Clark, eds., *The Negro American* (Boston, 1967), p. 604; Howard Zinn, *SNCC: The New Abolitionists* (Boston, 1965), p. 34.

28. Edward Jay Epstein, *News from Nowhere: Television and the News* (New York, 1973), pp. 219–20.

29. Benjamin Muse, *The American Negro Revolution* (New York, 1970), p. 49; Galen R. Weaver, "Radical Change and Relevant Religious Faith and Action," *Religious Education* (January 1964), pp. 91–94.

30. G. Theodore Mitau, *Decade of Decision: The Supreme Court and the Constitutional Revolution* (New York, 1967), p. 215.

31. Mathew Ahmann, *Race: Challenge to Religion* (Chicago, 1963), pp. 33, 63, 171–73.

32. "American Revolution, 1963," *Variety* (September 4, 1963), p. 31.

33. King, *Why We Can't Wait*, pp. 62–63.

34. Carl M. Brauer, *John F. Kennedy and the Second Reconstruction* (New York, 1977), pp. 238, 246.

35. *Public Papers of the Presidents, John F. Kennedy, 1963* (Washington, 1964), pp. 468–71.

36. Louis Oberdorfer to Robert Kennedy, December 27, 1963, Robert Kennedy MSS; Mike Mansfield to John F. Kennedy, June 18, 1963, Sorensen MSS.

37. Kearns, *Lyndon Johnson*, p. 191.

38. Mitau, *Decade of Decision*, p. 230.

39. *Public Papers of the Presidents, Lyndon B. Johnson, 1965* (Washington, 1966), pp. 281–87.

40. *Public Papers, Johnson, 1965*, p. 840.

41. John Bibby and Roger Davidson, *On Capitol Hill: Studies in the Legislative Process* (New York, 1967), p. 239; Peter Marris and Martin Rein, *Dilemmas of Social Reform* (Chicago, 1973), p. 270.

42. Michael Harrington, *The Other America*, 1963 ed. (Baltimore, 1962), p. 163; Harry Caudill, *Night Comes to the Cumberlands* (Boston, 1963), p. xii.

43. Dwight Macdonald, "Our Invisible Poor," *The New Yorker* (January 19, 1963), p. 84; Gunnar Myrdal, *Challenge to Affluence*, 1965 ed. (New York, 1963), p. 53.

44. Homer Bigart, "Kentucky Miners: A Grim Winter," New York *Times*, October 20, 1963.

45. Robert F. Munn, "The Latest Rediscovery of Appalachia" (1965), reprinted in David S. Walls and John B. Stephenson, eds., *Appalachia in the Sixties: Decade of Reawakening* (Lexington, Ky., 1972), p. 25.

46. Oscar Lewis, *La Vida: A Puerto Rican Family in the Culture of Poverty* (New York, 1966), p. xliii.

47. Lewis, *La Vida,* pp. xlii–lii; Harrington, *Other America,* pp. 24, 135.

48. Lewis, *La Vida,* p. xlv; Harrington, *Other America,* p. 164.

49. Charles A. Valentine, "The 'Culture of Poverty': Its Scientific Significance and Its Implications for Action," in Eleanor Burke Leacock, ed., *The Culture of Poverty: A Critique* (New York, 1971), pp. 193–225.

50. Walter W. Heller, "Selected Facts on the Low-Income Population in the U.S.," December 16, 1962, Kennedy MSS, President's Office Files; Schlesinger, *A Thousand Days,* p. 1012.

51. Otis Dudley Duncan, "Inheritance of Poverty or Inheritance of Race?" in Daniel Moynihan, ed., *On Understanding Poverty: Perspectives from the Social Sciences* (New York, 1969), pp. 85–87; Stephen M. Rose, *The Betrayal of the Poor: The Transformation of Community Action* (Cambridge, 1972), p. 40; *Appalachia, A Report by the President's Appalachian Regional Commission* (Washington, 1964).

52. Bibby and Davidson, *On Capitol Hill,* p. 235.

53. Sar A. Levitan, *The Great Society's Poor Law* (Baltimore, 1969), p. 112.

54. *Ibid.*

55. Mollie Orshansky, "Counting the Poor: Another Look at the Poverty Profile," *Social Security Bulletin* (January 1965), reprinted in Louis A. Ferman *et al., Poverty in America* (Ann Arbor, 1968), p. 78. The 40 percent reduction for rural families was changed later to 30 percent and then to 15 percent.

56. William C. Selover, "The View from Capitol Hill: Harassment and Survival," in James L. Sundquist, ed., *On Fighting Poverty: Perspectives from Experience* (New York, 1969), p. 167.

57. Nathan Glazer and Daniel Moynihan, *Beyond the Melting Pot* (Cambridge, 1963), pp. 12–14.

58. John F. Kennedy, *A Nation of Immigrants,* rev. ed. (New York, 1964), p. 77. See also Abba Schwartz, *The Open Society* (New York, 1968), p. 25.

59. *Immigration,* Hearings Before the Subcommittee on Immigration and Naturalization of the Committee on the Judiciary, U.S. Senate, 89th Congress, 1st Session (Washington, 1965), p. 714.

60. Marion T. Bennett, "The Immigration and Nationality Act of 1952, as Amended to 1965," *Annals of the American Academy* (September 1966), p. 136.

61. *Immigration,* Senate Hearings, pp. 168, 240; *Congressional Digest* (May 1965), pp. 145–47.

62. John Higham, *Send These to Me* (New York, 1975), p. 66.

63. *Public Papers, Johnson, 1965,* p. 1039.

6. Vietnam

1. John McNaughton, "Draft Presidential Memorandum," May 19, 1967, *The Senator Gravel Edition: The Pentagon Papers,* 4 vols. (Boston, 1975), Vol. IV, p. 479.

2. Geoffrey Hodgson, *America in Our Time* (Garden City, N.Y., 1976), p. 364; Alexander Kendrick, *The Wound Within* (Boston, 1974), p. 16.

3. David Halberstam, *The Best and the Brightest* (New York, 1972), p. 530.

4. Herbert Y. Schandler, *The Unmaking of a President: Lyndon Johnson and Vietnam* (Princeton, 1977), pp. 225–26.

5. Lyndon Baines Johnson, *The Vantage Point* (New York, 1971), p. 118; Halberstam, *Best and Brightest,* p. 414.

6. Johnson, *Vantage Point,* p. 126.

7. Halberstam, *Best and Brightest,* p. 533.

8. *Pentagon Papers,* Vol. III, p. 446.

9. Schandler, *Unmaking of a President,* p. 30.

10. *Public Papers of the Presidents, Lyndon B. Johnson, 1965* (Washington, 1966), p. 801.

11. *Pentagon Papers,* Vol. IV, pp. 314, 507.

12. Doris Kearns, *Lyndon Johnson and the American Dream* (New York, 1976), p. 300.

13. Schandler, *Unmaking of a President,* p. 213.

14. Edward Jay Epstein, *News from Nowhere* (New York, 1973), p. 250.

15. George A. Bailey and Lawrence W. Lichty, "Rough Justice on a Saigon Street: A Gatekeeper Study of NBC's Tet Execution Film," *Journalism Quarterly* (Summer 1972), pp. 221–29, 238.

16. Schandler, *Unmaking of a President,* p. 197; Peter Braestrup, *Big Story: How the American Press and Television Reported and Interpreted the Crisis of Tet 1968 in Vietnam and Washington* (Garden City, N.Y., 1978), pp. 348–52.

17. Townsend Hoopes, *The Limits of Intervention* (New York, 1969), pp. 219, 216.

18. Epstein, *News from Nowhere,* p. 17.

19. *Public Papers of the Presidents, Richard M. Nixon, 1970* (Washington, 1971), p. 409.

20. Jonathan Schell, *The Time of Illusion* (New York, 1976), p. 34.

21. Morton H. Halperin *et al., The Lawless State* (New York, 1976), p. 141; *Village Voice,* February 16, 1976, p. 90.

22. Daniel Bell, *The Cultural Contradictions of Capitalism* (New York, 1976), p. 190.

23. Norman Mailer, *The Armies of the Night* (New York, 1968), pp. 260–61, 287.

24. Lewis Chester *et al., An American Melodrama: The Presidential Campaign of 1968* (New York, 1969), p. 695; Seymour Martin Lipset and Earl Raab, *The Politics of Unreason* (New York, 1970), pp. 350, 347.

25. Lipset and Raab, *Politics of Unreason,* p. 349.

26. Richard M. Scammon and Ben J. Wattenberg, *The Real Majority* (New York, 1971), p. 43; Schell, *Time of Illusion*, p. 87.

27. Schell, *Time of Illusion*, p. 62.

28. Kevin Phillips, *The Emerging Republican Majority* (New Rochelle, 1969), p. 464.

29. Fred J. Cook, "Hard-Hats: The Rampaging Patriots," *The Nation* (June 15, 1970), pp. 712–19.

30. Robert E. Lane and Michael Lerner, "Why Hard-Hats Hate Hairs," *Psychology Today* (November 1970), pp. 45–48; Andrew Levison, *The Working-Class Majority* (New York, 1974), p. 136.

31. "Jonah in a Hard Hat," *Time* (July 27, 1970), p. 68.

32. John Leonard, "Bigotry as a Dirty Joke," *Life* (March 19, 1971), p. 10; Marshall Frady, "It's All in This Family, Too," *Life* (November 19, 1971), pp. 61–62.

33. John P. Diggins, *The American Left in the Twentieth Century* (New York, 1973), pp. 192, 194.

34. Marvin Garson, "When the Workers Start to Move," *Berkeley Barb*, May 19–25, 1967, p. 12; Harold Jacobs, ed., *Weatherman* (Ramparts Press, 1970), pp. 66–67.

35. Paul A. Baran and Paul M. Sweezey, *Monopoly Capital* (New York, 1966), p. 363; Jacobs, *Weatherman*, p. 72.

36. Irving Howe, ed., *The World of the Blue-Collar Worker* (New York, 1972), p. 4; Levison, *Working-Class Majority*, pp. 159, 160.

37. E. E. LeMasters, *Blue-Collar Aristocrats: Life-Styles at a Working-Class Tavern* (Madison, 1975), p. 173.

38. Robert Coles and Jan Erikson, *The Middle Americans* (Boston, 1971), pp. 130–34.

39. Patricia Cayo Sexton and Brendan Sexton, *Blue Collars and Hard Hats* (New York, 1971), pp. 52–53.

40. Lawrence M. Baskir and William A. Strauss, *Chance and Circumstance: The Draft, the War and the Vietnam Generation* (New York, 1978), pp. 7–8.

41. Dean Carper, *Bitter Greetings* (New York, 1967), p. 88; Michael Useem, *Conscription, Protest, and Social Conflict* (New York, 1973), pp. 81–91.

42. Useem, *Conscription,* pp. 83–84.

43. John Martin Willis, "Who Died in Vietnam: An Analysis of the Social Background of Vietnam War Casualties (Ph.D. dissertation, Purdue University, 1975), pp. 38, 64.

44. Milton J. Rosenberg *et al., Vietnam and the Silent Majority* (New York, 1970), p. 45; Sar A. Levitan, ed., *Blue-Collar Workers: A Symposium on Middle America* (New York, 1971), p. 19.

45. Howard Zinn, *SNCC* (Boston, 1965), p. 189; Hodgson, *America in Our Time,* p. 217.

46. Thomas L. Blair, *Retreat to the Ghetto* (New York, 1977), p. 34.

47. Archie Epps, *Malcolm X and the American Negro Revolution* (London, 1969) pp. 16, 56; George Breitman, ed., *Malcolm X Speaks* (New York, 1966), p. 26.

48. Stokely Carmichael and Charles V. Hamilton, *Black Power* (New York, 1967), p. 40.

49. Kenneth Clark, "The Present Dilemma of the Negro," in August Meier *et al.,* eds., *Black Protest Thought in the Twentieth Century* (Indianapolis, 1971), p. 618.

50. June Jordan, "Cameo No. II," in Dudley Randall, ed., *The Black Poets* (New York, 1971), p. 244.

51. *The Report of the National Advisory Commission on Civil Disorders* (New York, 1968), p. 102.

52. *Ibid.,* p. 205.

53. Nathan Caplan, "The New Ghetto Man: A Review of Recent Empirical Studies," *Journal of Social Issues* (Winter 1970), pp. 59–73; Joe R. Feagin and Harlan Hahn, *Ghetto Revolts: The Politics of Violence in American Cities* (New York, 1973), pp. 300–04.

54. Benjamin Muse, *The American Negro Revolution* (New York, 1970), p. 231; Rosenberg, *Vietnam and the Silent Majority,* p. 75.

55. Nikki Giovanni, "The True Import of Present Dialogue: Black vs. Negro," in Randall, *Black Poets,* p. 319.

56. Wallace Terry II, "Bringing the War Home," *The Black Scholar* (November 1970), pp. 6–18.

57. Lino A. Graglia, *Disaster by Decree* (Ithaca, 1976), pp. 68, 72.

58. *Ibid.,* pp. 121–26.

59. Christopher Jencks et al., *Inequality* (New York, 1972), p. 41.

60. Nathan Glazer, *Affirmative Discrimination* (New York, 1975), p. 45.

61. *Ibid.,* pp. 46, 48.

62. William B. Gould, *Black Workers in White Unions: Job Discrimination in the United States* (Ithaca, 1977), p. 92.

63. Michael N. Danielson, *The Politics of Exclusion* (New York, 1976), pp. 222–23.

64. Glazer, *Affirmative Discrimination,* p. 158.

65. Danielson, *Politics of Exclusion,* pp. 221, 224.

66. U.S. Bureau of the Census, Current Population Reports, P–20, Nos. 221, 249, *Characteristics of the Population by Ethnic Origin* (Washington, 1971, 1973).

67. "A Rising Cry: 'Ethnic Power,'" *Newsweek* (December 21, 1970), pp. 32–33.

68. Michael Novak, *The Rise of the Unmeltable Ethnics* (New York, 1973), p. 65.

69. Richard Gambino, *Blood of My Blood* (New York, 1974), p. 373.

70. Michael Wenk, S. M. Tomasi, and Geno Baroni, eds., *Pieces of a Dream: The Ethnic Worker's Crisis with America* (New York, 1972), pp. 9, 68–71, 176; see also *Ethnic Heritage Studies Centers,* Hearings Before the General Subcommittee on Education of the Committee on Education and Labor, House of Representatives, 91st Congress, 2nd Session (Washington, 1970).

71. Andrew M. Greeley, "The Rediscovery of Diversity," *Antioch Review* (Fall 1971), p. 359.

72. Richard Krickus, *Pursuing the American Dream: White Ethnics and the New Populism* (New York, 1976), p. 362.

73. Greeley, "Rediscovery of Diversity," *loc. cit.*, p. 355; Michael Novak, "New Ethnic Politics vs. Old Ethnic Politics," in Wenk *et al., Pieces of a Dream,* p. 140.

74. Peter Binzen, *Whitetown, U.S.A.* (New York, 1970), p. 29; Novak, "New Ethnic Politics," *loc. cit.*, p. 136.

75. William Kornblum, *Blue Collar Community* (Chicago, 1974), pp. 77–79; Orlando Patterson, *Ethnic Chauvinism: The Reactionary Impulse* (New York, 1977), Chapter 6.

76. Perry L. Weed, *The White Ethnic Movement and Ethnic Politics* (New York, 1973), pp. 174, 177–79.

77. Krickus, *Pursuing the American Dream,* p. 248.

78. New York *Times, The End of a Presidency* (New York, 1974), p. 179.

7. A Segmented Society

1. Daniel J. Boorstin, *The Americans: The Democratic Experience* (New York, 1973), p. 433; Leon Mandel, "Travelin' On: America Through a Windshield," *Car and Driver* (July 1975), p. 62.

2. New York *Times,* July 12, 1976.

3. William Safire, *Before the Fall* (Garden City, N.Y., 1975), p. 664.

4. J. Anthony Lukas, *Nightmare: The Underside of the Nixon Years* (New York, 1976), p. 379; New York *Times,* ed., *The Watergate Hearings: Break-in and Cover-up* (New York, 1973), pp. 437, 439.

5. Lukas, *Nightmare,* pp. 389, 393.

6. The text of the decision may be found in New York *Times,* ed., *The End of a Presidency* (New York, 1974), pp. 293–317.

7. *Ibid.*, p. 251.

8. Lukas, *Nightmare,* pp. 380–81.

9. *Ibid.*, p. 491.

10. New York *Times,* ed., *End of a Presidency,* p. 336; Theodore H. White, *Breach of Faith* (New York, 1975), p. 204.

11. New York *Times,* ed., *The White House Transcripts* (New York, 1974), p. 63.

12. Safire, *Before the Fall,* p. 309.

13. Jonathan Schell, *The Time of Illusion* (New York, 1975), pp. 180–85.

14. Jules Witcover, *Marathon: The Pursuit of the Presidency, 1972–1976* (New York, 1977), p. 357.

15. Jimmy Carter, *Why Not the Best?* (New York, 1976), p. 157; New York *Times,* July 16, 1976; Walter Dean Burnham, "Jimmy Carter and the Democratic Crisis," *New Republic* (July 3 and 10, 1976), pp. 17–19.

16. New York *Times,* June 10, 1976.

17. "Marching North from Georgia," *Time* (November 15, 1976), p. 20.

18. New York *Times,* July 16, 1976; see also Everett Carll Ladd, Jr., "Liberalism Upside Down: The Inversion of the New Deal Order," *Political Science Quarterly* (Winter 1976–77), pp. 597–600.

19. U.S. Department of Commerce, *Social Indicators, 1976* (Washington, 1977), p. xxv. The January 1978 issue of the *Annals of the American Academy of Political and Social Science* was devoted to an analysis of the volume.

20. Paul Blumberg, "Another Day, Another $3,000: Executive Salaries in America," *Dissent* (Spring 1978), pp. 157–68.

21. William H. Sewell, "Social Mobility and Social Participation," *The Annals* (January 1978), p. 230; see also Robert M. Hauser and David Featherman, *The Process of Stratification: Trends and Analyses* (New York, 1977).

22. Sewell, "Social Mobility," *loc. cit.*, p. 230; see also Richard F. Curtis and Elton F. Jackson, *Inequality in American Communities* (New York, 1977).

23. John A. Brittain, *The Inheritance of Economic Status* (Washington, 1977), p. 24.

24. Edward O. Laumann and James S. House, "Living Room Styles and Social Attributes: The Pattern of Material Artifacts in a Modern Urban Community," *Sociology and Social Research* (April 1970), pp. 321–42.

25. "Redstockings Manifesto," in Leslie B. Tanner, ed., *Voices from Women's Liberation* (New York, 1970), p. 109.

26. "Perspectives on Class," *Women: A Journal of Liberation* (1971), pp. 48–50.

27. Jo Freeman, *The Politics of Women's Liberation* (New York, 1975), pp. 36–37.

28. Catherine Stimpson, ed., *Women and the "Equal Rights" Amendment: Senate Hearings* (New York, 1972), p. 25.

29. *Ibid.*, p. 92.

30. Lindsy Van Gelder, "The 400,000 Vote Misunderstanding," *Ms.* (March 1976), p. 68; New York *Times*, July 4, 1978.

31. Stimpson, *Women and the "Equal Rights" Amendment*, p. xvi.

32. New York *Times*, June 29–30, 1978; "Bakke Wins, Quotas Lose," *Time* (July 10, 1978), p. 9; "The Landmark Bakke Ruling," *Newsweek* (July 10, 1978), p. 20.

33. *Regents of the University of California* v. *Allan Bakke, The United States Law Review* (June 27, 1978), pp. 4902–10.

34. *Ibid.*, pp. 4912–25, 4931, 4933.

35. McGeorge Bundy, "The Issue Before the Court: Who Gets Ahead in America," *Atlantic Monthly* (November 1977), pp. 41–54.

36. *California* v. *Bakke, loc. cit.*, p. 4931.

37. *Ibid.*, p. 4932.

38. William Julius Wilson, *The Declining Significance of Race: Blacks and Changing American Institutions* (Chicago, 1978), pp. 152, 150. For an opposing view see Sar A. Levitan *et al.*, *Still a Dream* (Cambridge, 1975), Chapter 9.

39. Wilson, *Declining Significance of Race*, pp. 107–08.

40. "The American Underclass," *Time* (August 29, 1977), pp. 14–27; New York *Times*, February 27, 1978.

41. Wilson, *Declining Significance of Race*, p. 151.

42. David L. Featherman and Robert M. Hauser, "Changes in the Socioeconomic Stratification of the Races, 1962–1973," *American Journal of Sociology* (1976–1977), pp. 621–51.

43. Wilson, *Declining Significance of Race*, p. 100.

44. Joel Dreyfuss, " 'Black Progress' Myth and Ghetto Reality," *The Progressive* (November 1977), pp. 21–25.

45. New York *Times*, February 27, 1978.

46. Castellano B. Turner and William J. Wilson, "Dimensions of Racial Ideology: A Study of Urban Black Attitudes," *Journal of Social Issues* (1976), p. 147; "Careers for the Future," *Ebony* (March, 1978), p. 140.

47. New York *Times*, February 28, 1978.

48. "America's Rising Black Middle Class," *Time* (June 17, 1974), pp. 19–28.

49. "The Ten Best Cities for Blacks," *Ebony* (February 1978), pp. 95–102.

50. New York *Times*, April 2–3, 1978.

51. Bill Berry, "Interracial Marriages in the South," *Ebony* (June 1978), pp. 65–72.

52. New York *Times*, April 3, 1978.

53. *Ibid.*

54. *Ibid.*, April 2, 1978.

55. Washington *Post*, February 2, 1975.

56. U.S. Census Bureau, Current Population Reports, P-23, *Language Usage in the United States: July, 1975* (Washington, 1976), p. 1.

57. Victor G. and Brett de Bary Nee, *Longtime Californ': A Documentary Study of an American Chinatown* (New York, 1973), p. 253.

58. *Ibid.*, p. 256.

59. *Ibid.*

60. Stanley Sue and Harry H. L. Kitano, "Stereotypes as a Measure of Success," *Journal of Social Issues* (April–June 1973), pp. 83–98.

61. John N. Tinker, "Intermarriage and Ethnic Boundaries: The Japanese American Case," *Journal of Social Issues* (April–June 1973), p. 64.

62. *Ibid.;* see also Darrell Martin Montero, "The Japanese American Community: A Study of Generational Changes in Ethnic Affiliation" (Ph.D. dissertation, UCLA, 1975).

63. U.S. Census Bureau, Current Population Reports, Series P-20, *Persons of Spanish Origin in the United States: March, 1977* (Washington, 1977).

64. Elliott Abrams and Franklin S. Abrams, "Immigration Policy—Who Gets In and Why?" *The Public Interest* (Winter 1975), p. 8.

65. "Why the Tide of Illegal Aliens Keeps Rising," an interview with Leonel J. Castillo, *U.S. News and World Report* (February 20, 1978), pp. 33–35.

66. Abrams and Abrams, "Immigration Policy," *loc. cit.*, p. 21.

67. "Tide of Illegal Aliens," *U.S. News*, pp. 33–35.

68. *Smugglers, Illicit Documents, and Schemes Are Undermining U.S. Controls Over Immigration,* Report to the Congress by the Comptroller General (Washington, 1976), p. 5; "Tide of Illegal Aliens," *U.S. News*, pp. 33–35.

69. Domestic Council Committee on Illegal Aliens, *Preliminary Report* (Washington, 1976), p. 73.

70. *Ibid.*, p. 206.

71. *Ibid.*, p. 2.

72. "Tide of Illegal Aliens," *U.S. News*, pp. 33–35.

73. *Preliminary Report,* p. 141.

74. New York *Times,* December 30, 1974.

75. "The Carter Amnesty Proposal," *Congressional Digest* (November 1977), pp. 232, 235.

76. "Tide of Illegal Aliens," *U.S. News*, pp. 33–35.

77. *Congressional Digest* (November 1977), pp. 251–52. The editorial appeared on June 18, 1976.

78. Washington *Post,* February 2, 1975.

Essay on Sources

The Eve of War

The most influential work on class stratification during the Depression is the five-volume "Yankee City" study, especially W. Lloyd Warner and Paul S. Lunt, *The Social Life of a Modern Community* (New Haven, 1941), and *The Status System of a Modern Community* (New Haven, 1942). Warner's methodology strongly influenced Allison Davis *et al., Deep South* (Chicago, 1941), an account of caste and class in Natchez, Mississippi; August Hollingshead, *Elmtown's Youth* (New York, 1949; rev. ed., 1975), a study of adolescents in Morris, Illinois; St. Clair Drake and Horace R. Clayton, *Black Metropolis* (New York, 1945; rev. ed., 1962), an examination of Negro life in Chicago; and William Foot Whyte, *Street Corner Society,* 1945; rev. ed., 1955), an account of Italian immigrants in Boston. For the class structure of an Ozark Mountain community, see James West (pseudonym for Carl Withers), *Plainville, USA* (New York, 1945), and a sequel, Art Gallaher, Jr., *Plainville Fifteen Years After* (New York, 1961). Also useful are Robert and Helen Lynd, *Middletown in Transition* (New York, 1937), on Muncie, Indiana; Walter Goldschmidt, *As You Sow* (Glencoe, Ill., 1947), on Wasco, California; Alfred Winslow Jones, *Life, Liberty, and Property* (Philadelphia, 1941), on Akron, Ohio; and Elin L. Anderson, *We Americans* (Cambridge, 1938), on Burlington, Vermont.

Scathing criticisms of Warner's study of Newburyport, Massachusetts, can be found in three articles in the *American Sociological Review:* C. Wright Mills's review (VII, October 1942) denounced the book for confusing class with status; Stephan Thernstrom, "'Yankee City' Revisited: The Perils of Historical Naïveté" (XXX, April 1965), attacked Warner's "historical ignorance"; and Harold W. Pfautz and

Otis Dudley Duncan, "A Critical Evaluation of Warner's Work in Community Stratification" (XV, April 1950), condemned the conceptual inadequacies of "Yankee City." For more balanced assessments, see Ruth Rosner Kornhauser, "The Warner Approach to Social Stratification," in Reinhard Bendix and Seymour M. Lipset, eds., *Class, Status and Power* (Glencoe, Ill., 1953) and Maurice R. Stein, *The Eclipse of Community* (Princeton, 1960; rev. ed., 1972).

The political context within which the Roosevelt administration addressed social problems in the late 1930s is evaluated in James Patterson, *Congressional Conservatism and the New Deal* (Lexington, Ky., 1967), and Richard Polenberg, "The Decline of the New Deal," in John Braeman *et al.*, eds., *The New Deal* (Columbus, Ohio, 1975). For the fate of New Deal programs in four vital areas—rural relief, minimum wages, housing, and medical care—see Sidney Baldwin, *Poverty and Politics: The Rise and Decline of the Farm Security Administration* (Chapel Hill, 1967); J. Joseph Huthmacher, *Senator Robert F. Wagner and the Rise of Urban Liberalism* (New York, 1968); Timothy L. McConnell, *The Wagner Housing Act* (Chicago, 1957); and Daniel S. Hirshfield, *The Lost Reform: The Campaign for Compulsory Health Insurance* (Cambridge, 1970).

In 1938, at the invitation of the Carnegie Corporation, the Swedish economist Gunnar Myrdal undertook a study of race relations in America. Not only is Myrdal's *An American Dilemma* (New York, 1944) invaluable; many of the studies he commissioned are equally important, especially Ralph Bunche, *The Political Status of the Negro in the Age of FDR,* Dewey Grantham, ed. (Chicago, 1973), and Charles S. Johnson, *Patterns of Negro Segregation* (New York, 1943). Other Carnegie-Myrdal research memoranda, although unpublished, are available on microfilm, including Edward A. Shils, "The Bases of Social Stratification in Negro Society"; Paul H. Norgren, "Negro Labor and Its Problems"; and Arthur Raper, "Race and Class Pressures." John Dollard, *Caste and Class in a Southern Town* (New Haven, 1937), and Hortense Powdermaker, *After Freedom* (New York, 1939) are important sociological studies, each prepared independently, of Indianola, Mississippi.

The Roosevelt administration's response to racial discrimination is explored in Harvard Sitkoff, *A New Deal for Blacks: The Emergence of Civil Rights as a National Issue* (New York, 1979), and Raymond Wolters, *Negroes and the Great Depression* (Westport, Conn., 1970). The use of the legal system to uphold segregation is examined in Dan T. Carter, *Scottsboro: A Tragedy of the American South* (Baton Rouge, 1969), and Charles H. Martin, *The Angelo Herndon Case and Southern Justice* (Baton Rouge, 1976). For the most important civil rights organization, see Robert L. Zangrando, "The NAACP and a Federal Antilynching Bill, 1934–1940," *Journal of Negro History,* L (April 1965); for A. Philip Randolph's March on Washington Movement, see Herbert Garfinkel, *When Negroes March* (Glencoe, Ill., 1957). Southern white liberals are discussed in Morton Sosna, *In Search of the Silent South* (New York, 1977).

Information about ethnic communities in prewar America can be found in most of the city and state guides compiled by the Federal Writers Project of the Works Progress Administration. Many have chapters on "racial and national groups," "foreign groups," or "ethnic elements." In addition, the Federal Writers Project published studies of particular ethnic groups: *The Italians of New York* (New York, 1938); *The Swedes and Finns in New Jersey* (Bayonne, 1938); *The Armenians in Massachusetts* (Boston, 1937). Other useful works include a volume in the "Yankee City" study, W. Lloyd Warner and Leo Srole, *The Social Systems of American Ethnic Groups* (New Haven, 1945); Philip Klein, *A Social Study of Pittsburgh* (New York, 1938); and Samuel Koenig's account of Stamford, Connecticut, "The Socioeconomic Structure of an American Jewish Community," in Isacque Graeber and Steuart Henderson Britt, eds., *Jews in a Gentile World* (New York, 1942). Ronald H. Bayor, *Neighbors in Conflict: The Irish, Germans, Jews, and Italians of New York City, 1929–1941* (Baltimore, 1978) is an important work.

The growth of nativist sentiment after 1939 is described in Geoffrey S. Smith, *To Save a Nation: American Countersubversives, the New Deal, and the Coming of World War II* (New York, 1973); Carmen A. Notaro, "Franklin D. Roosevelt and the American Communists" (Ph.D. dissertation, SUNY–Buffalo, 1969); and Zechariah Chafee, Jr., *Free Speech in the United States* (Cambridge, 1941). For the relationship between isolationism and anti-Semitism, consult Myron Israel Scholnick, "The New Deal and Anti-Semitism in America" (Ph.D. dissertation, University of Maryland, 1971); Sander A. Diamond, *The Nazi Movement in the United States, 1928–1941* (Ithaca, 1974); Sheldon Marcus, *Father Coughlin* (New York, 1973); and Wayne S. Cole, *Charles A. Lindbergh and the Battle Against American Intervention in World War II* (New York, 1974). American policy toward Jewish refugees is explained in David Wyman, *Paper Walls* (Amherst, Mass., 1968); Henry Feingold, *The Politics of Rescue* (New Brunswick, 1970); and Saul S. Friedman, *No Haven for the Oppressed* (Detroit, 1973).

Wartime America

The role of war as a unifying force in society is discussed in James M. Burns, *Roosevelt: The Soldier of Freedom* (New York, 1970); Richard Polenberg, *War and Society: The United States, 1941–1945* (Philadelphia, 1972); Geoffrey Perrett, *Days of Sadness, Years of Triumph* (New York, 1973); and John M. Blum, *V Was for Victory: Politics and American Culture during World War II* (New York, 1976). The Office of War Information, which spearheaded the government's efforts to foster an official version of war aims, is treated in Allan M. Winkler, *The Politics of Propaganda* (New Haven, 1978); Charles David Lloyd, "American Society and Values in World War II from the Publications of the Office of War Information" (Ph.D. dissertation, Georgetown University, 1975); and Clayton R. Koppes and Gregory D. Black, "What to Show the World: The Office of War Information and Hollywood, 1942–1945," *Journal of American History,* LXIV (June 1977). See, in addition, Robert K. Merton, *Mass Persuasion: The Social Psychology of a War Bond Drive* (New York, 1946). For the way in which Madison Avenue and Broadway reflected and shaped mass perceptions of the war, consult Frank W. Fox, "Advertising and the Second World War: A Study in Private Propaganda"

(Ph.D. dissertation, Stanford University, 1973); and two articles in *The Journal of Popular Culture:* Richard Hasbany, "Bromidic Parables: The American Musical Theatre During the Second World War," VI (Spring 1973); and Timothy B. Donovan, "Oh, What a Beautiful Mornin': The Musical *Oklahoma!* and the Popular Mind in 1943," VIII (Winter 1974).

In *One America: The History, Contributions, and Present Problems of Our Racial and National Minorities* (New York, 1945) Francis J. Brown and Joseph S. Roucek provide a useful overview of immigrant groups; and Louis Adamic, *A Nation of Nations* (New York, 1945) captures the wartime emphasis on the loyalty of those groups. Ethnic-group responses to the war are discussed in Jeannette Sayre Smith, "Broadcasting for Marginal Americans," *Public Opinion Quarterly,* VI (Winter 1942); Samuel M. Strong, "Observations on the Possibility of Attitude Modification: A Case of Nationality and Racial Group Inter-Relationships in Wartime," *Social Forces,* III (March 1944); and Joseph S. Roucek, "Foreign Language Press in World War II," *Sociology and Social Research,* XXVII (July–August 1943). On civilian migration, two articles by Henry S. Shryock, Jr., are especially helpful: "Wartime Shifts of the Civilian Population," *Milbank Memorial Fund Quarterly,* XXV (July 1947), and "Redistribution of Population, 1940–1950," *Journal of the American Statistical Association,* XLVI (December 1951). Works dealing with the treatment of German and Italian aliens include John L. Cable, *Loss of Citizenship; Denaturalization; The Alien in Wartime* (Washington, 1943); Ernest W. Puttkammer, ed., *War and the Law* (Chicago, 1944); John W. Hastie, "Control of Enemy Aliens in the United States in World War II," (M.A. thesis, Cornell University, 1951); Francis Biddle, *In Brief Authority* (New York, 1962); and John Diggins, *Mussolini and Fascism: The View from America* (Princeton, 1972). The Supreme Court's role in cases involving citizenship rights is discussed in Alpheus T. Mason, *Harlan Fiske Stone: Pillar of the Law* (New York, 1956); Milton Konvitz, *The Alien and the Asiatic in American Law* (Ithaca, 1956); and Joseph P. Lash, ed., *From the Diaries of Felix Frankfurter* (New York, 1975).

For divisions within one immigrant group, see Peter H. Irons, "'The Test Is Poland': Polish Americans and the Origins of the Cold War," *Polish American Studies,* XXX (Autumn 1973).

The impact of the war on class relations is examined in Robert J. Havighurst and H. Gerthon Morgan, *The Social History of a War-Boom Community* (New York, 1951), a study of Seneca, Illinois; Lowell J. Carr and James E. Stermer, *Willow Run: A Study of Industrialization and Cultural Inadequacy* (New York, 1952); and Katherine Archibald, *Wartime Shipyard: A Study in Social Disunity* (Berkeley, 1947), which focuses on workers in Oakland, California. W. Lloyd Warner and Associates, *Democracy in Jonesville* (New York, 1949; rev. ed., 1964), examines Morris, Illinois, in the early 1940s from much the same perspective as was used in the earlier study of Yankee City. Patterns of income distribution are measured in Robert J. Lampman, *The Share of Top Wealth Holders in National Wealth, 1922–1956* (Princeton, 1956); and Simon Kuznets, *Shares of Income Groups in Income and Savings* (New York, 1953). For a critique of Kuznets, see Gabriel Kolko, *Wealth and Power in America* (London, 1962). Useful studies of the war economy include Seymour E. Harris, *Price and Related Controls in the United States* (New York, 1945); Harvey C. Mansfield *et al., A Short History of the OPA* (Washington, 1947); George Q. Flynn, *The Mess in Washington: Manpower Mobilization in World War II* (Westport, Conn., 1979); and Marshall B. Clinard, *The Black Market* (New York, 1952). For the role of labor in politics, see Matthew Josephson, *Sidney Hillman* (New York, 1952), and Melvyn Dubofsky and Warren Van Tine, *John L. Lewis: A Biography* (New York, 1977).

In *The Races of Mankind* (New York, 1943) the anthropologist Ruth Benedict noted that "Racism is an *ism* to which everyone in the world is exposed; for or against, we must take sides." A similar outlook informed Ashley Montagu, *Man's Most Dangerous Myth: The Fallacy of Race* (New York, 1942), and Gunnar Dahlberg, *Race, Reason and Rubbish: A Primer of Race Biology* (New York, 1942). The cultural and psychological effects of the war, as well as the economic and demographic ones, are examined in Neil A. Wynn, *The Afro-American and the Second World War* (London, 1976). For blacks in trade unions, see Robert Weaver, *Negro Labor* (New York, 1946); Herbert R. Northrup, *Organized Labor and the Negro* (New York, 1944); and Louis Ruchames, *Race, Jobs and Politics: The Story of FEPC* (Chapel Hill, N.C., 1948). Studies of blacks in the armed services include Richard M. Dalfiume, *Desegregation of the U.S. Armed Forces, 1939–1953* (Columbia, Mo., 1969), and Ulysses Lee, *The Employment of Negro Troops* (Washington, 1966). Racial tensions are analyzed in Charles S. Johnson, *To Stem This Tide* (Boston, 1943); Howard W. Odum, *Race and Rumors of Race* (Chapel Hill, 1943); Robert Shogan and Tom Craig, *The Detroit Race Riot* (Philadelphia, 1964); and Dominic J. Capeci, Jr., *The Harlem Riot of 1943* (Philadelphia, 1977). On the development of black militancy, see Harvard Sitkoff, "Racial Militancy and Interracial Violence in the Second World War," *The Journal of American History,* LVIII (December 1971), and Lee Finkle, *Forum for Protest: The Black Press during World War II* (Rutherford, N.J., 1975).

The internment of Japanese Americans is discussed in Roger Daniels, *Concentration Camps USA: Japanese Americans and World War II* (New York, 1971) and Audrie Girdner and Anne Loftis, *The Great Betrayal* (London, 1969). For the decision to issue the relocation order, see Stetson Conn *et al., Guarding the United States and Its Outposts* (Washington, 1964), and Martin Grodzins, *Americans Betrayed: Politics and the Japanese Evacuation* (Chicago, 1949); for the constitutional implications, consult Jacobus ten Broek *et al., Prejudice, War and the Constitution* (Berkeley, 1954), and Sidney Fine, "Mr. Justice Murphy and the Hirabayashi Case," *Pacific Historical Review,* XXXIII (May, 1964). The impact of evacuation on the Japanese American community is analyzed in Bill Hosokawa, *Nisei: The Quiet Americans* (New York, 1969); Harry H. L. Kitano, *Japanese Americans: Evolution of a Subculture* (Englewood Cliffs, N.J., 1969); Dorothy S. Thomas and Richard S. Nishimoto, *The Spoilage* (Berkeley, 1946); and Dorothy S. Thomas, *The Salvage* (Berkeley, 1952). Wartime attitudes leading to the repeal of Chinese exclusion are considered in Harold R. Isaacs, *Scratches on Our Minds* (New York, 1958), and Fred W. Riggs, *Pressure on Congress* (New York, 1950).

The Cold War

The more historians write about the causes and consequences of the Cold War, the wider grow their differences. The Truman administration is treated sympathetically in Alonzo L. Hamby, *Beyond the New Deal: Harry S. Truman and American Liberalism* (New York, 1973), and John L. Gaddis, *The United States and the Origins of the Cold War, 1941–1947* (New York, 1972). For more critical interpretations, see Barton J. Bernstein, ed., *Politics and Policies of the Truman Administration* (Chicago, 1970), and Richard M. Freeland, *The Truman Doctrine and the Origins of McCarthyism* (New York, 1972). American reactions to Mao Tse-tung's victory in China, Russia's acquisition of the atomic bomb, and the outbreak of the Korean War are examined in Carl Solberg, *Riding High: America in the Cold War* (New York, 1973); Joyce and Gabriel Kolko, *The Limits of Power: The World and United States Foreign Policy, 1945–1954* (New York, 1972); and Tang Tsou, *America's Failure in China, 1941–1950* (Chicago, 1963). The best account of the relationship between domestic and foreign policy is Walter LaFeber, *America, Russia, and the Cold War, 1945–1975* (New York, 1976).

The wide-ranging impact of anticommunism on American life is assessed in David Caute, *The Great Fear: The Anti-Communist Purge Under Truman and Eisenhower* (New York, 1978), and Leslie Adler, "The Red Image: American Attitudes Toward Communism in the Cold War Era" (Ph.D. dissertation, University of California, 1971). Contrasting appraisals of the federal loyalty program are offered in Alan D. Harper, *The Policies of Loyalty: The White House and the Communist Issue, 1946–1952* (Westport, Conn., 1969), and Athan Theoharis, *Seeds of Repression: Harry S. Truman and the Origins of McCarthyism* (Chicago, 1970). For accounts of the prosecution of communist leaders, consult Michal R. Belknap, *Cold War Politi-*

cal Justice: The Smith Act, The Communist Party, and American Civil Liberties (Westport, Conn., 1977), and Kevin J. O'Brien, "*Dennis* v. *U.S.:* The Cold War, The Communist Conspiracy and the F.B.I. (Ph.D. dissertation, Cornell University, 1979). Herbert L. Packer, *Ex-Communist Witnesses* (Stanford, 1962), assesses the testimony of Louis Budenz, Elizabeth Bentley, John Lautner, and Whittaker Chambers; Joseph R. Starobin, *American Communism in Crisis, 1943–1957* (Cambridge, 1972), evaluates the trial's effect. A more famous trial of the period is discussed in Allen Weinstein, *Perjury: The Hiss-Chambers Case* (New York, 1978). The film industry's capitulation to anticommunist fears is the subject of Russel E. Shain, "Hollywood's Cold War," *Journal of Popular Film,* III (November 1974), and Stefan Kanfer, *A Journal of the Plague Years* (New York, 1973).

Interest in social class during the Cold War era is demonstrated by the extraordinary number of references in Harold W. Pfautz, "The Current Literature on Social Stratification: Critique and Bibliography," *American Journal of Sociology,* LVIII (January 1953). Richard Centers, *The Psychology of Social Classes: A Study of Class Consciousness* (Princeton, 1949), and Cecilia B. Stendler, *Children of Brasstown: Their Awareness of the Symbols of Social Class* (Urbana, Ill., 1949), emphasize the continued significance of class differences. Other studies, however, stress the fluidity characteristic of a pluralist system. See, for example, W. Lloyd Warner, *Social Class in America* (Chicago, 1949); Walter R. Goldschmidt, "Social Class in America—A Critical Review," *American Anthropologist,* LII (October–December 1950); Herman M. Case, "An Independent Test of the Interest-Group Theory of Social Class," *American Sociological Review,* XVII (December 1952); and Gerhard E. Lenski, "American Social Classes: Statistical Strata or Social Groups?" *American Journal of Sociology,* LVIII (September 1952). In "The Decline and Fall of Social Class," *Pacific Sociological Review,* II (Spring 1959), Robert Nisbet argued that American society was governed by status rather than class values. Two doctoral dissertations explore the relationship between labor and radicalism: Frank Emspak, "The Break-Up of the

Congress of Industrial Organizations (CIO), 1945–1950" (University of Wisconsin, 1972), and James R. Prickett, "Communists and the Communist Issue in the American Labor Movement, 1920–1950" (UCLA, 1975).

Class differences within two black communities in the late 1940s are examined in Hylan Lewis, *Blackways of Kent* (Chapel Hill, 1955), a study of a North Carolina community, and Mozell C. Hill and Bevode C. McCall, "Social Stratification in 'Georgia Town,'" *American Sociological Review,* XV (December 1950). For Truman's civil rights policies, see Donald R. McCoy and Richard T. Ruetten, *Quest and Response: Minority Rights and the Truman Administration* (Lawrence, Kan., 1973), and William Berman, *The Politics of Civil Rights in the Truman Administration* (Columbus, Ohio, 1970); for the Supreme Court's restrictive-covenant decision, consult Clement Vose, *Caucasians Only* (Berkeley, 1967). The effect of anticommunism on the civil rights movement is treated in August Meier and Eliott Rudwick, *CORE: A Study in the Civil Rights Movement, 1942–1968* (New York, 1973); Wilson Record, *Race and Radicalism* (Ithaca, 1964), a study of the NAACP; and James L. Roark, "American Black Leaders: The Response to Colonialism and the Cold War, 1945–1953," *African Historical Studies,* IV (1973). Several works emphasize the efforts of segregationists to exploit Cold War fears, including William Barnard, *Dixiecrats and Democrats: Alabama Politics, 1942–1950* (University, Ala., 1974); Robert A. Garson, *The Democratic Party and the Politics of Sectionalism, 1941–1948* (Baton Rouge, 1974); Ann M. McLaurin, "The Role of the Dixiecrats in the 1940 Election" (Ph.D. dissertation, University of Oklahoma, 1972); and Wayne A. Clark, "An Analysis of the Relationship Between Anti-Communism and Segregationist Thought in the Deep South, 1948–1964" (Ph.D. dissertation, University of North Carolina, 1976). Three useful biographies are Jervis Anderson, *A. Philip Randolph: A Biographical Portrait* (New York, 1973); Dorothy B. Gilliam, *Paul Robeson* (Washington, 1976); and Carl T. Rowan with Jackie Robinson, *Wait Till Next Year* (New York, 1960).

The nativist strain in Cold War anticommunism is discussed in Robert A. Divine, *American Immigration Policy, 1924–1952* (New Haven, 1957); C. Herman Pritchett, *Civil Liberties and the Vinson Court* (Chicago, 1954); William R. Tanner, "The Passage of the Internal Security Act of 1950" (Ph.D. dissertation, University of Kansas, 1971); and Final Report of the U.S. Displaced Persons Commission, *Memo to America: The DP Story* (Washington, 1952). Two controversial figures are treated in Charles P. Larrowe, *Harry Bridges: The Rise and Fall of Radical Labor in the United States* (New York, 1972), and Theodore Huff, *Charles Chaplin* (New York, 1951). Louise Pettibone Smith, *Torch of Liberty* (New York, 1959) is an account by a militant defender of radical immigrants, and Jiri Kojala, "A Sociological Note on the Czechoslovak Anti-Communist Refugee," *American Journal of Sociology,* LVIII (November 1952) discusses a highly conservative group of immigrants.

The relationship between McCarthyism and ethnicity is considered in Donald F. Crosby, "The Angry Catholics: American Catholics and Senator Joseph R. McCarthy, 1950–1957" (Ph.D. dissertation, Brandeis University, 1973); Seymour Martin Lipset and Earl Raab, *The Politics of Unreason* (New York, 1970); Robert Griffith and Athan Theoharis, eds., *The Specter: Original Essays on the Cold War and the Origins of McCarthyism* (New York, 1974); and Richard M. Fried, *Men Against McCarthy* (New York, 1976). The essays in Daniel Bell, ed., *The Radical Right* (Garden City, N.Y., 1955, 1963 ed.) attempt to use a pluralist model to explain McCarthyism, an attempt that is harshly criticized in Michael P. Rogin, *McCarthy and the Intellectuals: The Radical Specter* (Cambridge, 1967).

The Suburban Nation

The literature on suburbia has, in a sense, come full circle. The earliest studies, echoing the critique implicit in the title of David Riesman's essay "The Suburban Sadness," included William H. Whyte, *The Organization Man* (Garden City, N.Y., 1965); A. C. Spectorsky, *The Exurbanites* (Philadelphia, 1955); John Keats, *The Crack in the Picture Window* (Boston, 1957); and Richard E. Gordon *et al., The*

Split-Level Trap (New York, 1960). Several works then took issue with this highly critical image of the suburbs, including Bennett M. Berger, *Working-Class Suburb: A Study of Auto Workers in Suburbia* (Berkeley, 1960), which dealt with Milpitas, California; Harold L. Wattel, "Levittown: A Suburban Community," in William M. Dobriner, ed., *The Suburban Community* (New York, 1958); William M. Dobriner, *Class in Suburbia* (Englewood Cliffs, N.J., 1963); and Herbert Gans, *The Levittowners* (New York, 1967). The rehabilitation was taken furthest by Scott Donaldson, *The Suburban Myth* (New York, 1969), which asserted that the onslaught against the suburbs was "composed of whopping irrelevancies, galloping overstatements, and poorly concealed animosities." Recently some scholars have decided that the older critique "seemed to have a ring of truth about it." See, for example, Barry Schwartz, ed., *The Changing Face of the Suburbs* (Chicago, 1976). Shifting perceptions can be followed in several anthologies, including Charles M. Haar, *The End of Innocence: A Suburban Reader* (Glenview, Ill., 1972); John Kramer, ed., *North American Suburbs: Politics, Diversity, and Change* (Berkeley, 1972); Philip C. Dolce, ed., *Suburbia: The American Dream and Dilemma* (Garden City, N.Y. 1976); and Louis H. Masotti and Jeffrey K. Hadden, *The Urbanization of the Suburbs* (Beverly Hills, Cal., 1973).

For the development of postwar suburbs, see Kenneth T. Jackson, "The Crabgrass Frontier: 150 Years of Suburban Growth in America," in Raymond A. Mohl and James R. Richardson, *The Urban Experience* (Belmont, Cal., 1973); Reynolds Farley, "Suburban Persistence," *American Sociological Review,* XXIX (February 1964); and Leo F. Schnore, "Municipal Annexations and the Growth of Metropolitan Suburbs, 1950–1960," *American Journal of Sociology,* LXVII (January 1962). The role of the automobile is evaluated in two books by John B. Rae: *The American Automobile* (Chicago, 1965), and *The Road and the Car in American Life* (Cambridge, 1971). Federal mortgage policies are considered in Henry J. Aaron, *Shelter and Subsidies* (Washington, 1972). On politics in suburbia, consult Frederick Wirt *et al., On the City's Rim: Politics and Policy in Suburbia*

(Lexington, Mass., 1972); Robert C. Wood, *Suburbia: Its People and Their Politics* (Boston, 1958); David J. Schnall, *Ethnicity and Suburban Local Politics* (New York, 1975); and a firsthand account of Port Washington, New York, Samuel Kaplan, *The Dream Deferred: People, Politics, and Planning in Suburbia* (New York, 1976).

Will Herberg, *Protestant-Catholic Jew* (Garden City, N.Y., 1955; rev. ed., 1960) remains a valuable study of religion and ethnicity. It should be supplemented with the work of Andrew M. Greeley, particularly *The Church and the Suburbs* (New York, 1959); *The Denominational Society: A Sociological Approach to Religion in America* (Glenview, Ill., 1972); and the chapter entitled "One Neighborhood" in *Why Can't They Be Like Us? America's White Ethnic Groups* (New York, 1975). Studies that focus on particular religious groups include Frederick A. Shippey, *Protestantism in Suburban Life* (New York, 1964); Albert I. Gordon, *Jews in Suburbia* (Boston, 1959); Herbert Gans, "The Origin and Growth of a Jewish Community in the Suburbs: A Study of the Jews of Park Forest," in Marshall Sklare, ed., *The Jews: Social Patterns of an American Minority Group* (Glencoe, Ill., 1958); and Benjamin B. Ringer, *The Lakeville Studies: The Edge of Friendliness* (New York, 1967). Stanley Lieberson, *Ethnic Patterns in American Cities* (New York, 1963) is a statistical survey of ten immigrant groups in ten cities over the period 1910–1950.

For an understanding of why so few blacks moved to the suburbs in the 1950s, and an analysis of the social characteristics of those who did, consult Michael N. Danielson, *The Politics of Exclusion* (New York, 1976); Karl E. Taeuber and Alma F. Taeuber, *Negroes in Cities: Residential Segregation and Neighborhood Change* (New York, 1969); Leo F. Schnore, *Class and Race in Cities and Suburbs* (Chicago, 1972); U.S. Housing and Home Finance Agency, *Our Nonwhite Population and Its Housing: The Changes Between 1950 and 1960* (Washington, 1963); Lynn B. Sagalyn and George Sternlieb, *Zoning and Housing Costs* (Center for Urban Policy Research, Rutgers University, 1973); and Charles M. Haar and Demetrius S. Iatridis, *Housing the*

Poor in Suburbia (Cambridge, 1974). Several articles are also useful, especially Leonard Blumberg and Michael Lalli, "Little Ghettos: A Study of Negroes in the Suburbs," *Phylon*, XXVII (Summer 1966), based on interviews conducted in racially segregated residential areas in suburban Philadelphia; and Harold M. Rose, "The All-Negro Town: Its Evolution and Function," *Geographical Review*, LV (July 1965), a study of twelve such communities. Reynolds Farley, "The Changing Distribution of Negroes within Metropolitan Areas: The Emergence of Black Suburbs," *American Journal of Sociology*, LXXV (January 1970) discusses developments after 1960.

The Supreme Court's school-desegregation decision is examined sympathetically in Richard Kluger, *Simple Justice* (New York, 1976), and the Court's later construction of its decision is criticized sharply in Lino S. Graglia, *Disaster by Decree: The Supreme Court Decisions on Race and the Schools* (Ithaca, 1976). The civil rights policies of the Eisenhower administration are evaluated in Steven F. Lawson, *Black Ballots: Voting Rights in the South, 1944–1969* (New York, 1976); J. W. Anderson, *Eisenhower, Brownell, and the Congress* (University, Ala., 1964); Foster Rhea Dulles, *The Civil Rights Commission, 1957–1965* (Lansing, Mich., 1968); and Peter Lyon, *Eisenhower: Portrait of the Hero* (Boston, 1974). The Montgomery bus boycott is described in David L. Lewis, *King: A Critical Biography* (New York, 1970). For the response of Southern whites to the demand for racial equality, consult Numan V. Bartley, *The Rise of Massive Resistance: Race and Politics in the South during the 1950s* (Baton Rouge, 1969); for the response of northern whites, see Marvin Bressler, "The Myers' Case: An Instance of Successful Racial Invasion," *Social Problems* VIII (Fall 1960).

The Age of Reform

The context for understanding the significance of the election of the first Catholic president is provided in David J. O'Brien, *The Renewal of American Catholicism* (New York, 1972); John Cogley, *Catholic America* (New York, 1973); and Andrew M. Greeley, *The Catholic Experience*

(New York, 1967). A sympathetic view of Kennedy's impact on Catholic assimilation is presented in Lawrence H. Fuchs, *John F. Kennedy and American Catholicism* (New York, 1967), and a more critical view of Kennedy as a "secular Catholic, celebrant of intellect and power" is offered in Garry Wills, *Bare Ruined Choirs: Doubt, Prophecy, and Radical Religion* (Garden City, N.Y., 1972). In *We Hold These Truths: Catholic Reflections on the American Proposition* (New York, 1960) John Courtney Murray explains the theological basis of liberal Catholicism. The school-prayer decisions are analyzed in William A. Carroll, "The Constitution, the Supreme Court, and Religion," *American Political Science Review,* LXI (September 1967). For the effect of the religious issue on the campaign of 1960, see Philip E. Converse, "Religion and Politics: The 1960 Election," in Angus Campbell *et al., Elections and the Political Order* (New York, 1966); Paul T. David, ed., *The Presidential Election and Transition, 1960–1961* (Washington, 1961); Lucy S. Dawidowicz and Leon J. Goldstein, *Politics in a Pluralist Democracy: Studies of Voting in the 1960 Election* (New York, 1963); and Lawrence H. Fuchs, *American Ethnic Politics* (New York, 1968). The views of Paul Blanshard, the foremost critic of Catholicism, can be found in *American Freedom and Catholic Power* (Boston, 1949), and *God and Man in Washington* (Boston, 1960), and in his autobiography, *Personal and Confidential* (Boston, 1973).

Social reform during the Kennedy administration is examined in Arthur Schlesinger, Jr., *A Thousand Days* (Boston, 1965), and Lewis J. Paper, *The Promise and the Performance* (New York, 1975). Two bitterly critical accounts, the first from a radical perspective and the second from a conservative one, are Bruce Miroff, *Pragmatic Illusions: The Presidential Politics of John F. Kennedy* (New York, 1976), and Henry Fairlie, *The Kennedy Promise* (Garden City, N.Y., 1973). Eric F. Goldman, *The Tragedy of Lyndon Johnson* (New York, 1969) is an account by a historian who served in the Johnson administration, and Doris Kearns, *Lyndon Johnson and the American Dream* (New York, 1976) is a work by a political scientist who became the president's confidante. In *The Promise of Greatness* (Cambridge, 1976) Sar A. Levitan and Robert Taggart challenge the "erroneous conclusion that the Great Society failed," and in *The Politics of Medicare* (Chicago, 1973) Theodore R. Marmer discusses the enactment of a key measure. Judicial activism is considered in Paul L. Murphy, *The Constitution in Crisis Times, 1918–1969* (New York, 1972), and G. Theodore Mitau, *Decade of Decision: The Supreme Court and the Constitutional Revolution, 1954–1964* (New York, 1967); an important figure is appraised in Gerald T. Dunne, *Hugo Black and the Judicial Revolution* (New York, 1977); and a crucial decision of the Warren Court is explained in Richard C. Cortner, *The Apportionment Cases* (New York, 1970). For the Republican debacle in 1964, consult the essay on Barry Goldwater in Richard Hofstadter, *The Paranoid Style in American Politics* (New York, 1967), and Theodore White, *The Making of the President, 1964* (New York, 1965).

The legal, political, social, and economic status of blacks in the 1960s is described in Talcott Parsons and Kenneth Clark, ed., *The Negro American* (Boston, 1967); Thomas F. Pettigrew, *A Profile of the Negro American* (Princeton, 1964); and Benjamin Muse, *The American Negro Revolution* (New York, 1970). In *Kennedy Justice* (New York, 1971) Victor Navasky argues that the Justice Department under Robert F. Kennedy adhered to the "code of the Ivy League Gentleman," which held that the solution to racial problems could be reached through patience, negotiation, and mediation. A more favorable evaluation of Kennedy is provided by Carl M. Brauer, *John F. Kennedy and the Second Reconstruction* (New York, 1977). Books by participants in the civil rights movement remain an excellent source. The movement's goals and tactics are explained in James Peck, *Freedom Ride* (New York, 1962); Sally Belfrage, *Freedom Summer* (New York, 1965); Martin Luther King, *Why We Can't Wait* (New York, 1964); and James Forman, *The Making of Black Revolutionaries* (New York, 1972). Howard Zinn, *SNCC: The New Abolitionists* (Boston, 1965) spoke for many when it called for "a permanent, cool, firm federal presence using a combination of persuasion and threat of prison to make clear that all citizens are equal before the law."

The increasing awareness of poverty in the 1960s is evident in Michael Harrington, *The Other America* (New York, 1962); Harry Caudill, *Night Comes to the Cumberlands* (Boston, 1963); Gunner Myrdal, *Challenge to Affluence* (New York, 1963); and Oscar Lewis, *La Vida: A Puerto Rican Family in the Culture of Poverty* (New York, 1966). The origins of the war on poverty are explained in David Knapp and Kenneth Polk, *Scouting the War on Poverty: Social Reform Politics in the Kennedy Administration* (Lexington, Mass., 1971), and Sar A. Levitan, *The Great Society's Poor Law* (Baltimore, 1969). The antipoverty crusade has received more scholarly attention than any other Great Society domestic policy, much of it from former officials in the Office of Economic Opportunity. Useful studies include John Bibby and Roger Davidson, *On Capitol Hill: Studies in the Legislative Process* (New York, 1967); Peter Marris and Martin Rein, *Dilemmas of Social Reform* (Chicago, 1973); James L. Sundquist, ed., *On Fighting Poverty: Perspectives from Experience* (New York, 1969); John C. Donovan, *The Politics of Poverty* (New York, 1967); Robert A. Levine, *The Poor Ye Need Not Have with You: Lessons from the War on Poverty* (Cambridge, 1970); and Joseph A. Kershaw, *Government Against Poverty* (Washington, 1970).

The use of a poverty line is justified in Mollie Orshansky, "Counting the Poor: Another Look at the Poverty Profile," in Louis A. Ferman *et al., Poverty in America: A Book of Readings* (Ann Arbor, Mich., 1968), and attacked in Walter Miller, "The Elimination of the American Labor Class as National Policy: A Critique of the Ideology of the Poverty Movement of the 1960s," in Daniel P. Moynihan, ed., *On Understanding Poverty: Perspectives from the Social Sciences* (New York, 1969). Harsh condemnations of the culture-of-poverty concept can be found in Charles A. Valentine, *Culture and Poverty: Critique and Counter-Proposals* (Chicago, 1968), and Eleanor Burke Leacock, ed., *The Culture of Poverty: A Critique* (New York, 1971). For equally harsh treatments of the community action programs, see Daniel P. Moynihan, *Maximum Feasible Misunderstanding: Community Action in the War on Poverty* (New York, 1970), and Stephen M. Rose, *The Betrayal of the Poor: The Transforma-*

tion of Community Action (Cambridge, 1972). David S. Walls and John B. Stephenson, eds., *Appalachia in the Sixties: Decade of Reawakening* (Lexington, Ky., 1972), is a useful anthology. The effect of antipoverty expenditures on patterns of income distribution is assessed in Robert Lampman, "Public and Private Transfers as Social Process," in Kenneth E. Boulding and Martin Pfaff, eds., *Redistribution to the Rich and the Poor: The Grants Economics of Income Distribution* (Belmont, Cal., 1972).

Information on immigration reform can be found in John F. Kennedy, *A Nation of Immigrants* (New York, 1958; rev. ed., 1964); John Higham, "The Politics of Immigration Restriction," in *Send These to Me* (New York, 1975); and Nathan Glazer and Daniel Moynihan, *Beyond the Melting Pot* (Cambridge, 1963). Three journals devoted entire issues to ethnicity or immigration: *Daedalus,* XC (Spring 1961); *Congressional Digest,* XLIV (May 1965), and *Annals of the American Academy of Political and Social Science,* CCCLXVII (September 1966). Abba Schwartz, *The Open Society* (New York, 1968) is a useful account, although one strongly biased in favor of Kennedy and against Johnson and Dean Rusk, by an official who served in the State Department from 1962 to 1966.

Vietnam

The most important sources for understanding American intervention in Vietnam are the documents in the Senator Gravel edition of *The Pentagon Papers,* 4 vols. (Boston, 1975). Those documents provide some basis for weighing the conflicting claims of David Halberstam, *The Best and The Brightest* (New York, 1972), and Frances Fitzgerald, *Fire in the Lake: The Vietnamese and the Americans in Vietnam* (Boston, 1972), both of whom consider intervention a disaster, and Guenter Lewy, *America in Vietnam* (New York, 1978), who believes that "the sense of guilt created by the Vietnam war in the minds of many Americans is not warranted." Two useful accounts that center on policy shifts resulting from the Tet offensive are Herbert Y. Schandler, *The Unmaking of a President: Lyndon Johnson and Vietnam* (Princeton, 1977), and Townsend Hoopes, *The Limits of Intervention* (New York, 1969). Some broader cultural implications of the war are analyzed in Morris Dickstein, *Gates of Eden: American Culture in the Sixties* (New York, 1977); Daniel Bell, *The Cultural Contradictions of Capitalism* (New York, 1976); Gloria Emerson, *Winners and Losers* (New York, 1976); Alexander Kendrick, *The Wound Within* (Boston, 1974); and Godfrey Hodgson, *America in Our Time* (Garden City, N.Y., 1976).

The role of the media in shaping perceptions of the war is examined in Edward Jay Epstein, *News from Nowhere* (New York, 1973), and David Halberstam, *The Powers That Be* (New York, 1979); for treatment of the Tet offensive, see Peter Braestrup, *Big Story* (Garden City, N.Y., 1978), and George A. Bailey and Lawrence W. Lichty, "Rough Justice on a Saigon Street: A Gatekeeper Study of NBC's Tet Execution Film," *Journalism Quarterly*, XLIX (Summer 1972). The economic impact of the war is discussed in Charles E. McClure, Jr., "Fiscal Failure: Lessons of the Sixties," in Phillip Cagan *et al.*, eds., *Economic Policy and Inflation in the Sixties* (Washington, 1972), and "The War and Its Impact on the Economy," by the editors of *Review of Radical Political Economics*, II (August 1970). The erosion of civil liberties is documented in Morton H. Halperin *et al.*, *The Lawless State* (New York, 1976), and David Wise, *The American Police State* (New York, 1976). In *Test of Loyalty* (New York, 1974) Peter Schrag discusses the trial of Daniel Ellsberg. The Peers Commission Report, *The My Lai Massacre and Its Cover-Up* (New York, 1976), is a balanced account of a volatile issue.

Class bias in the military draft is explored in Lawrence M. Baskir and William A. Strauss, *Chance and Circumstance: The Draft, the War and the Vietnam Generation* (New York, 1978); John Martin Willis, "Who Died in Vietnam: An Analysis of the Social Background of Vietnam War Casualties" (Ph.D. dissertation, Purdue University, 1975); Michael Useem, *Conscription, Protest, and Social Conflict: The Life and Death of a Draft Resistance Movement* (New York, 1973); and James M. Gerhardt, *The Draft and Public Policy: Issues in Military Manpower Recruitment, 1945–*

1970 (Columbus, Ohio, 1971). The resentment such bias produced is evident in the interviews found in Robert Coles and Jan Erikson, *The Middle Americans* (Boston, 1973), and in E. E. LeMasters, *Blue-Collar Aristocrats: Life-Styles at a Working-Class Tavern* (Madison, Wisc., 1975), which reports the views of construction workers in a Wisconsin town.

Effective critiques of the "hard hat" stereotype can be found in Andrew Levison, *The Working-Class Majority* (New York, 1974), and Richard F. Hamilton, *Class and Politics in the United States* (New York, 1972). For confirmation of the critique, see Sar A. Levitan, ed., *Blue-Collar Workers: A Symposium on Middle America* (New York, 1971); Irving Howe, ed., *The World of the Blue-Collar Worker* (New York, 1972); Louise K. Howe, ed., *The White Majority: Between Poverty and Affluence* (New York, 1970); Milton J. Rosenberg *et al.*, *Vietnam and the Silent Majority* (New York, 1970); and Patricia Cayo Sexton and Brendan Sexton, *Blue-Collars and Hard-Hats* (New York, 1971). New Left views of working-class authoritarianism can be consulted in Harold Jacobs, ed., *Weatherman* (Ramparts Press, 1970), and J. Kirkpatrick Sale, *SDS* (New York, 1973). Working-class attitudes toward racism and Vietnam, and how those attitudes affected George Wallace's electoral support, are explored in J. Michael Ross *et al.*, "Patterns of Support for George Wallace: Implications for Racial Change," *Journal of Social Issues*, XXXVI (Spring 1976); Philip E. Converse *et al.*, "Continuity and Change in American Politics: Parties and Issues in the 1968 Election," *American Political Science Review* LXIII (December 1969); H. Edward Ransford, "Blue Collar Anger: Reactions to Students and Black Protest," *American Sociological Review*, XXVII (June 1972); and Marshall Frady, *Wallace* (Cleveland, 1970).

The appeal of black nationalism in the 1960s is explained in Thomas L. Blair, *Retreat to the Ghetto* (New York, 1977), and Patricia W. Romero, ed., *In Black America 1968: The Year of Awakening* (Washington, 1969). The man who both symbolized and exploited that appeal is the subject of Archie Epps, *Malcolm X and the American Negro Revolution* (London, 1969), and Peter Goldman, *The Death and Life of*

Malcolm X (New York, 1974). Stokely Carmichael and Charles V. Hamilton, *Black Power* (New York, 1967) remains the classic formulation. Urban riots, which radicals viewed as colonial revolts and conservatives saw as senseless rampages, are examined in Joe R. Feagin and Harlan Hahn, *Ghetto Revolts: The Politics of Violence in American Cities* (New York, 1973); Robert M. Fogelson, *Violence as Protest: A Study of Riots and Ghettos* (Garden City, N.Y., David Boesel and Peter H. Rossi, eds., *Cities Under Siege: An Anatomy of the Ghetto Riots, 1964–1968* (New York, 1971); and Nathan Caplan, "The New Ghetto Man: A Review of Recent Empirical Studies," *Journal of Social Issues,* XXVI (Winter 1970). For the effect of the Vietnam military experience on black attitudes, see Wallace Terry II, "Bringing the War Home," *The Black Scholar,* II (November 1970).

Many of the best studies of the new ethnicity are by writers affiliated with the ethnic revival. They include Michael Novak, *The Rise of the Unmeltable Ethnics* (New York, 1973); Richard Gambino, *Blood of My Blood* (New York, 1974); Richard Krickus, *Pursuing the American Dream: White Ethnics and the New Populism* (New York, 1976); Paul Wrobel, "Becoming a Polish American: A Personal Point of View," in Joseph Ryan, ed., *White Ethnics: Their Life in Working Class America* (Englewood Cliffs, N.J., 1973); Michael Wenk, S. M. Tomasi, and Geno Baroni, eds., *Pieces of a Dream: The Ethnic Worker's Crisis with America* (New York, 1972); and Andrew M. Greeley, "The Rediscovery of Ethnicity," *Antioch Review* (Fall 1971). Peter Binzen, *Whitetown, U.S.A.* (New York, 1970) studies ethnic neighborhoods and the public schools in eight large cities, and William Kornblum, *Blue Collar Community* (Chicago, 1974) focuses on Slavic steel workers in South Chicago. For the political implications of the new ethnicity, see Perry L. Weed, *The White Ethnic Movement and Ethnic Politics* (New York, 1973), and Andrew M. Greeley, "Political Attitudes Among American White Ethnics," *Public Opinion Quarterly,* XXXVI (Summer 1972). A more critical appraisal of the ethnic revival is offered in Nathan Glazer, *Affirmative Discrimination* (New York, 1975), and all-out assaults are leveled in Orlando Patterson, *Ethnic Chauvinism: The*

Reactionary Impulse (New York, 1977), and Howard F. Stein and Robert J. Hill, "The Limits of Ethnicity," *American Scholar*, XLVI (Spring 1977).

A Segmented Society

Many officials responsible for the Watergate break-in and cover-up, and some who uncovered the conspiracy, have published their memoirs. A partial list of authors includes Richard Nixon, Charles Colson, H. R. Haldeman, Jeb Magruder, John Dean, Leon Jaworski, and John Sirica. Journalists have provided more useful accounts. See especially J. Anthony Lukas, *Nightmare: The Underside of the Nixon Years* (New York, 1976); Theodore H. White, *Breach of Faith: The Fall of Richard Nixon* (New York, 1975); and Jonathan Schell, *The Time of Illusion* (New York, 1975). Jimmy Carter's views are presented in his campaign autobiography, *Why Not the Best?* (New York, 1976). His political background is discussed in James Wooten, *Dasher* (New York, 1978), and his election in Jules Witcover, *Marathon: The Pursuit of the Presidency, 1972–1976* (New York, 1977).

Several specialized studies cast light on the persistence of class differences in the late 1970s. Particularly helpful are John A. Brittain, *The Inheritance of Economic Status* (Washington, 1977); Evelyn M. Kitagawa and Philip M. Hauser, *Differential Mortality in the United States: A Study in Socioeconomic Epidemiology* (Cambridge, 1973); Robert M. Hauser and David L. Featherman, *The Process of Stratification: Trends and Analyses* (New York, 1977); and Richard F. Curtis and Elton F. Jackson, *Inequality in American Communities* (New York, 1977). The Department of Commerce study *Social Indicators, 1976* (Washington, 1977) is of crucial importance, as are the appraisals of that volume in "America in the Seventies: Some Social Indicators," *Annals of the American Academy of Political and Social Science*, CDXXXV (January 1978). Different perspectives on social inequality are provided in Robert L. Heilbroner, "Middle-Class Myths, Middle-Class Realities," *Atlantic Monthly*, CCXXXVIII (October 1976); Robert J. Lampman, "Growth, Prosperity and Inequality since 1947," *Wilson Quarterly*, I (Autumn

1977); and Paul Blumberg, "Another Day, Another $3,000: Executive Salaries in America," *Dissent*, CVII (Spring 1978). For studies of feminism and the Equal Rights Amendment, consult Leslie B. Tanner, ed., *Voices from Women's Liberation* (New York, 1970); Jo Freeman, *The Politics of Women's Liberation* (New York, 1975); Catherine Stimpson, ed., *Women and the "Equal Rights" Amendment: Senate Hearings* (New York, 1972); and Gayle Graham Yates, *What Women Want: The Ideas of the Movement* (New York, 1975).

The best analysis of affirmative action is Allan P. Sindler, *Bakke, DeFunis, and Minority Admissions: The Quest for Equal Opportunity* (New York, 1978), which concludes that divisions on the Supreme Court reflect "the nation's conflict and uncertainty about how to reconcile the racial claims of historic justice with the social imperative of racial neutrality." Other studies of the constitutional issues include Ralph A. Rossum, "Ameliorative Racial Preference and the Fourteenth Amendment: Some Constitutional Problems," *Journal of Politics*, XXXVIII (May 1976); Richard A. Posner, "The DeFunis Case and the Constitutionality of Preferential Treatment of Racial Minorities," *The Supreme Court Review: 1977* (Chicago, 1978); and J. Harvie Wilkinson III, *From Brown to Bakke: The Supreme Court and School Integration, 1954–1978* (New York, 1979). The controversy over whether black gains have been real or illusory can be followed in Ben J. Wattenberg and Richard M. Scammon, "Black Progress and Liberal Rhetoric," *Commentary*, LV (April 1973), which criticizes the "institutional gloom" of liberals, and in Joel Dreyfuss, "'Black Progress' Myth and Ghetto Reality," *Progressive*, XLI (November 1977), which criticizes Wattenberg and Scammon for their "adroit statistical manipulation." The question is pursued in greater detail in Sar A. Levitan *et al.*, *Still a Dream: The Changing Status of Blacks since 1960* (Cambridge, 1975); Dorothy K. Newman *et al.*, *Protest, Politics, and Prosperity: Black Americans and White Institutions, 1940–1975* (New York, 1978); William Julius Wilson, *The Declining Significance of Race: Blacks and Changing American Institutions* (Chicago, 1978); Reynolds Farley, "Trends in Racial Inequalities:

Have the Gains of the 1960s Disappeared in the 1970s?" *American Sociological Review,* XLII (April 1977); Martin Kilson, "From Civil Rights to Party Politics: The Black Political Transition," *Current History,* LXVII (November 1974); and Elliot Zashin, "The Progress of Black Americans in Civil Rights: The Past Two Decades Assessed," *Daedalus,* CVII (Winter 1978).

General assessments of ethnicity in the 1970s include Thomas Sowell, "Ethnicity in a Changing America," *Daedalus,* CVII (Winter 1978); William L. Yancey *et al.,* "Emergent Ethnicity: A Review and Reformulation," *American Sociological Review,* XLI (June 1976); and Andrew M. Greeley, *Ethnicity in the United States* (New York, 1974). In "Immigration Policy–Who Gets In and Why?" *Public Interest,* XXXVIII (Winter 1975) Elliott Abrams and Franklin S. Abrams evaluate the impact of the 1965 Immigration Reform Act. For the changing status of Asian Americans, see Victor G. and Brett de Bary Nee, *Longtime Californ': A Documentary Study of an American Chinatown* (New York, 1973); Darrell Martin Montero, "The Japanese American Community: A Study of Generational Changes in Ethnic Affiliation" (Ph.D. dissertation, UCLA, 1975); and all the articles in *Journal of Social Issues,* XXIX (April–June 1973), but expecially Harry H. L. Kitano and Stanley Sue, "The Model Minorities." On Spanish-speaking Americans, consult Bureau of the Census, Current Population Reports, *Persons of Spanish Origin in the United States: March 1977* (Washington, 1977). The political awareness of ethnic groups is stressed in Milton L. Barron, "Recent Developments in Minority and Race Relations," *Annals of the American Academy of Political and Social Science* (July 1975). For a comprehensive study of illegal aliens, see Domestic Council Committee on Illegal Aliens, *Preliminary Report* (Washington, 1976), supplemented by articles in the Washington *Post* (February 2–3, 1975), and the New York *Times* (December 29–31, 1974; March 18–19, 1979). The political controversy over illegal aliens is documented in the October 1977 issue of *Congressional Digest.*

Index

Abington v. *Schempp* (1963), 171
Acheson, Dean, 98, 108, 125, 217
Affirmative action, 240–42, 267, 271–72, 274, 277
Affluent Society, The (Galbraith), 193
AFL-CIO, 269
Agnew, Spiro T., 223, 253
Alexander v. *Holmes County Board of Education* (1969), 238
Aliens: *see* Illegal aliens; Immigrants and aliens
All in the Family (television show), 225
Alsop, Joseph, 256
American Freedom and Catholic Power (Blanshard), 167
American Independent party, 221
American Medical Association, 23, 107
American Sociological Review, 102
Amsterdam News, 70
Anti-Semitism: *see* Jews
Appalachia, 194–95, 197–98, 200
Appalachian Spring (Copland), 53
Arabic-speaking Americans, 36
Architectural Forum, 131
Armed forces: aliens in, 57; blacks in, 76–77, 111–14, 229, 236; discrimination in, 33–34, 76–77, 111; image of American soldier, 50–51, 53; migrations in order to enter, 54–55; Qualification Test; Selective Service System, 111–12, 229: *see also* Korean War; Vietnam war; World War II
Armenian Americans, 35
Armies of the Night, The (Mailer), 220
Arvey, Jacob, 138
Asian Americans, 24, 31, 206, 271, 282–83, 291: *see also* Chinese Americans; Japanese Americans
Automobiles, 15, 129–30, 135, 142, 251

Baker v. *Carr* (1962), 178
Bakke, Allan P., 271; *Bakke* case (1978), 271–74, 291
Bankhead, William B., 32
Baptists, 165, 171–72
Baumgartner, Carl Wilhelm, 58–59
Bell, Daniel, 220
Bell for Adano, A (Hersey), 50–51
Bendetsen, Karl R., 80–81
Bentley, Elizabeth, 94–95, 116

Berkeley Barb, 226
Beyond the Melting Pot (Glazer and Moynihan), 203
Biddle, Francis, 59–60, 78
Bigart, Homer, 194
Bill of Rights: *see* Constitution, U.S.
Birmingham (Ala.), 157, 182, 188, 278–79
Birth control, 165, 169
Bittelman, Alexander, 117
Black, Hugo L., 84, 120
Black Muslims, 232
Black Power, 208, 232–34, 236
Blackmun, Harry A., 238, 273–74
Blacks, 7, 9; and affirmative action, 240–42, 271–72, 274, 277; in armed forces, 76–77, 111–14, 229, 236; and *Bakke* case, 271–74; and bus integration, 74, 153, 157–59, 187; and Carter, 259–60; during Cold War, 108–15; and communism, 109–10, 112, 115; disfranchisement of, 27; employment of, 24, 29, 33, 114–15, 237, 240, 275–76; growing militancy of, 72, 222; March on Washington, proposed (1941), 33–34, 111; March on Washington (1963), 182, 189; nationalism of, 231–37; in the North, 28–30, 239, 275, 278–79; poverty of (1970s), 275–76; race riots, 77–78, 192, 234–37; repatriation to Africa, 231–32; and restaurant integration, 181–182, 186; and school desegregation, 153–63, 182, 189, 190, 238–40, 279; in the South, 25–28, 239, 278–81; in the suburbs, 150–63, 242, 278; and Vietnam war, 227, 231, 235–36; voting rights of, 27, 29, 31, 44, 108, 159–60, 178, 191–92, 280–81: *see also* Civil rights; Segregation
Blanshard, Paul, 167
Bloom-Van Nuys bill (1941), 43
Bloomer Girl (musical), 52
Brave Men (Pyle), 50
Bridges, Harry, 118–19
Browder, Earl R., 44
Brown, Harry, 51
Brown, Oliver, 153
Brown v. *Board of Education* (1954), 153–54, 156–57, 159, 273
Brownell, Herbert, Jr., 159
Bryson, Joseph R., 109
Buddhists, 283, 285
Budenz Louis, 94–95, 116
Bund, German-American, 41, 44, 58
Bundy, McGeorge, 209–10, 212, 274
Burger, Warren E., 238, 241, 255
Buses, segregation on, 74, 153, 157–59, 187
Busing, to achieve integration, 238–40
Butterfield, Alexander P., 254
Byrnes, James F., 33, 61

Calomiris, Angela, 94–95
Capitalism, 102–104
Carlson v. *Landon* (1952), 120
Carmichael, Stokely, 232–33

Carter, Jimmy: and illegal aliens, 289–90; 1976 presidential election, 252, 258–60
Caste, 24
Castillo, Leonel J., 287, 291
Casto, Don M., 135
Catch-22 (Heller), 176
Catholic War Veterans, 126
Catholics: and aid to parochial schools, 107, 165–67, 169–71; during civil-rights movement, 185–86; as immigrants, 283; and Kennedy, 169–72; and McCarthyism, 126; and prayer in public schools, 171–72; and presidential elections, 164–69, 248, 259–60; in the suburbs, 144, 146–50
Caudill, Harry, 193, 198
Cayton, Horace, 30
Censorship, 165, 169
Census Bureau, U.S., 17, 128, 150, 243–44, 283, 285
Center for the Study of American Pluralism, 245
Center for Urban Ethnic Affairs, 245
Central Intelligence Agency, 219, 256–57
Chambers, Whittaker, 94–95
Chancellor, John, 216
Chaplin, Charles, 118–19
Cheever, John, 136–37
Chiang Kai-shek, 99
Chiang, Madame, 81
Chicago (Ill.), 48–49, 73, 138, 186; blacks in, 29–30, 73, 77, 108, 151; illegal aliens in, 288; immigrants in, 36, 248; population decline of, 129
Chicanos: *see* Mexican Americans
China: communist victory in, 97–98; Korean War, 99–100; 1960s, 175; and U.S. war in Vietnam, 209–210; during World War II, 81: *see also* Cold War; Communism
Chinese Americans, 81–82, 121, 145, 282–85
Chinese Exclusion Act (1882), 81
Chisholm, Shirley, 268
Christian Front, 41
CIO, 66, 105–106
Civil disobedience, 182–84, 188, 232
Civil liberties, of aliens, 44–45
Civil rights: 31–34, 77, 107–115, 153–63, 164, 181–93, 231–43, 279; *see also* Blacks; Segregation
Civil Rights Act (1957), 153, 160
Civil Rights Act (1964), 190–191, 240, 267, 269, 273
Civil Rights Commission, 109, 160
Civil service, 187, 237
Civil Service Commission, 192
Civilian Defense, Office of, 46
Clark, Jim, 191
Clark, Joseph, 240
Clark, Kenneth, 154–55, 232
Clark, Tom C., 116–17
Class, 7–9, 15; during Cold War, 101–108; late 1930s, 16–24; late 1970s, 260–70; during reform period, 193–202; in the suburbs, 139–144; during Vietnam war,

Class (*cont.*)
220–31; during World War II, 61–69
Cleveland (Ohio): blacks in, 108; immigrants in, 35; 1950s, 138; 1970s, 263; population decline of, 128
Clifford, Clark, 90, 215, 217
Cogley, John, 166, 172
Cold War, 86–126; and class, 101–108; and communism, 86–101, 105–106; and ethnicity, 115–26; 1960s, 175–176; and race, 108–15; as unifying force, 208; and World War II, 86
Colleges and universities: affirmative-action programs in, 241; desegregation of, 154, 182, 189; 1930s, 20–21, 23, 25; 1970s, 265, 277; and Vietnam war, 222, 226, 229
Colonialism, 111
Commerce Department, U.S., 260
Communism: anticommunist hysteria, 91–99, 107, 120; and blacks, 109–10, 112, 115; and Cold war, 86–101; and fascism, 42–44, 56, 86–88, 91; Henry Wallace accused of, 90–91; among immigrants and aliens, 41–45, 57–58, 115–16; in labor unions, 105–106; 1960s, 176; in Southeast Asia, 209–10; in the U.S., 92–96, 105–15, 116–18, 127: *see also* China; Soviet Union
Communist Political Association, 92–93
Community Action Program, 199–201
Commuting, 130, 134, 137
Concentration camps, 41, 85, 99
Congress, U.S.: and aliens, 43–44, 115, 122–23; antilynching bill, 32–33; busing issue, 239; civil-rights legislation, 108, 111, 173, 184, 187, 189–91; and employment quotas, 240; housing legislation, 21, 107; and Jewish refugees, 41–42; during Kennedy presidency, 169, 171, 187; and Korean War, 100, 119; legislative reform (1960s), 179–81; medical care legislation, 22–23, 107, 200; minimum-wage legislation, 21–22, 275; 1930s, 21–23, 31; poverty programs, 33, 173, 193, 197–202; quotas for immigrants, 122–23, 145–46, 203–206; reapportionment, 178; salary limitations, 62; and segregation rulings, 155, 159–60; Truman Doctrine, 88–89; voting reform legislation, 108; and Vietnam war, 214, 219
Congress of Racial Equality, 110, 183–84, 232, 235
Connor, Eugene "Bull," 182
Constitution, U.S., 237–38, 255; Bill of Rights, 166–67, 170, 178, 257, 271–72; Fourteenth Amendment, 155–56, 177, 191
Copland, Aaron, 53
Corwin, Norman, 53
Coughlin, Charles E., 40–41
Council of Economic Advisers, 174, 197–98

Crack in the Picture Window, The (Keats), 135–36
Crime, 27–28, 30, 222, 244–45
Croatian Americans, 248
Cronkite, Walter, 217
Cuban Americans, 282, 286
Czechoslovakian Americans, 35–36, 38–39, 121

Dallas (Texas): Baptists in, 165; blacks in, 279; shopping centers in, 134–35
Danish Americans, 34, 39–40
Daughters of the American Revolution, 204
Dean, John W., III, 256–58
Defense: civilian, 46–48, 54, 131; contracts, 33–34; national, 18, 22, 54, 73: *see also* Armed forces
Defense Department, U.S., 125, 208–209, 213, 215, 219
DeFunis, Marco, 271
Democratic National Committee, 252
Democratic party: antilynching bill, 32–33; busing issue, 239; civil-rights movement, 159–60, 189–90; and ethnic vote, 60, 249; and labor, 66–67; and McCarthyism, 126; minimum wage, 21, 275; poverty programs, 197, 201, 223; presidential elections, 39–40, 66–67, 108–10, 138–39, 168–169, 178–79, 221–22, 249, 258–60; Southern members, 21–22, 27, 31–33, 111, 187, 190, 195; and suburbanization, 138–39; subversives in federal government, 91; voting rights, 191; white primary, 27: *see also* Congress, U.S.; Republican party
Denationalization Act (1944), 84
Dennis, Eugene, 93
Destination: Tokyo (film), 52
Detroit (Mich.): blacks in, 29, 73, 77–78, 234–35, 242; immigrants in, 36; 1943 race riot, 77–78; population decline of, 128; shopping centers in, 134; during World War II, 73, 77–78
Dewey, Thomas E., 66–67, 108
DeWitt, John, 79–81
Discrimination: *see* Blacks; Civil rights; Segregation
Dirksen, Everett M., 190, 201
Displaced persons, 122–23, 145–46: *see also* Immigrants and aliens; Refugees
District of Columbia: blacks in, 25, 279; 1941, proposed march by blacks, 33–34, 111; 1963 march by blacks, 182, 189; 1967 antiwar demonstration, 220; segregation in, 153, 155
Dixiecrats, 109–10
Dixon, Frank, 71
Dole, Robert J., 249
Dominican Americans, 282
Douglas, William O., 171–72
Draft: *see* Selective Service System
Drake, St. Clair, 30
Drucker, Peter, 104

Eastland, James O., 204, 280
Ebony (magazine), 279
Economic Opportunity, Office of, 199, 201–202

Economic Opportunity Act (1964), 199–200
Education: aid to parochial schools, 107, 165–67, 169–171, 199; busing to achieve integration, 238–40; desegregation of schools, 153–63, 182, 190, 238–40, 279; Elementary and Secondary Education Act (1965), 199; and ethnicity, 246–47; National Defense Education Act (1961), 171; 1930s, 20–21, 23, 25, 30; 1970s, 265, 277, 284, 291; prayer in public schools, 171–72; suburban schools, 143–44; value of, stressed by blacks, 25, 30, 151
Education, U.S. Office of, 246
Egyptian Americans, 282–83
Eisenhower, Dwight D., 138–139, 173; civil-rights policy, 159–61
Eisler, Gerhart, 117
Elementary and Secondary Education Act (1965), 199
Ellsberg, Daniel, 219, 253
Employment: affirmative-action programs for, 240–241, 267; of blacks, 24, 29, 33, 114–15, 237, 240, 275–276; discrimination in hiring, 114–15, 267; federal loyalty program, 91–92; of immigrants in 1930s, 38; during Korean War, 114–115; 1960s, 173, 1970s, 263; and Office of Economic Opportunity, 199–202; shift to Sun Belt, 275; in the suburbs, 134, 141–42, 151; of women, 63, 267; during World War II, 63–64: *see also* Labor force; Unemployment
Engel v. *Vitale* (1962), 171
English Americans, 243–44
Equal Employment Opportunity Commission, 237, 267
Equal Pay Act (1972), 267
Equal Rights Amendment, 266–70, 291
Ervin, Sam, 205–206, 252, 254, 256
Escobedo v. *Illinois* (1964), 177
Ethnic Heritage Studies Act (1972), 246
Ethnicity, 7–9, 15; during Cold War, 115–26; late 1930s, 34–45; late 1970s, 281–92; during reform period, 202–207; in the suburbs, 144–47, 149–50; during Vietnam war, 243–49; during World War II, 54–61, 78–85
Everson v. *Board of Education* (1947), 170

Fair Deal, 107–108: *see also* Truman, Harry S
Fair Employment Practices Committee, 34, 75–76, 108–109, 114–15
Farm Security Administration, 33
Farmer, James, 182
Farms: *see* Rural areas
Fascism: and communism, 42–44, 56, 86–88, 91; among immigrants and aliens, 39–45, 56, 58–59; and racism, 70, 85: *see also* Germany; World War II

Faubus, Orville, 161
Federal Bureau of Investigation, 42, 93–96, 219, 256–57
Federal Communications Commission, 55
Federal Contract Compliance, Office of, 237, 240, 267
Federal Housing Administration, 131–32, 163
Federal Public Housing Administration, 68
Federal Statistical Policy and Standards, Office of, 260
Feminists: *see* Equal Rights Amendment; Women
Ferlinghetti, Lawrence, 186
Festival of Nations (1942), 54
Filipino Americans, 271, 282–83
Finnish Americans, 35–36, 56
Ford, Gerald R., 252, 258–59
Ford Foundation, 230–31
Fourteenth Amendment: *see* Constitution, U.S.
Frankfurter, Felix, 58–59, 176–78
Freedom rides, 182, 187
Freeman, Jo, 268
French Americans, 244, 283
French Canadians, 35, 37, 40

Galbraith, John Kenneth, 193
Gans, Herbert, 140–41, 143, 150
Geneen, Harold S., 262
German Americans, 34–37, 39–41, 44, 57–60, 79–80, 121, 145, 150, 168, 243–44, 246, 282–83
Germany, 205, 207; attitude of blacks toward, 69–71; 1939 pact with Soviet Union, 42, 88–89; World War II, 39, 41–43, 45, 47, 51, 56, 59, 85, 87, 89
Ghetto riots, 192, 234–37
Gideon v. *Wainwright* (1963), 177
Giovanni, Nikki, 236
Glazer, Nathan, 203, 242
God and Man in Washington (Blanshard), 167
Goldberg, Arthur J., 176, 191
Goldwater, Barry, 178–79, 223
Gordon, Richard, 136
Gossett, Ed, 122
Government Contract Compliance Committee, 114
Great Society, 181, 202, 211, 237: *see also* Johnson, Lyndon B.
Greek Americans, 34, 36, 38, 56, 145, 282–83
Green v. *County School Board of New Kent County* (1968), 238
Griggs v. *Duke Power Company* (1971), 240–41

Haldeman, H. R., 254, 256
Hammerstein, Oscar, II, 52
Hard hats, 223–24
Harlan, John Marshall, 177
Harrington, Michael, 193, 196, 198
Health, Education and Welfare Department, U.S., 198
Health care: *see* Medical care
Heller, Joseph, 176
Henderson, Leon, 63
Herberg, Will, 146–48, 150
Here Is Your War (Pyle), 50
Hersey, John, 50–51

Hersh, Seymour, 218
Hippies, 223–24
Hirabayashi v. *United States* (1943), 84
Hiss, Alger, 94, 125
Hitler, Adolf, 41, 56, 70, 85, 87, 89, 91, 97, 99, 112
Holy Name Societies, 126
Homosexuals, 124, 223
Hong Kong, 284
House of Representatives: *see* Congress, U.S.
Housing, 19–22, 24, 29, 68, 73, 107, 129, 131–35, 142–143, 151–53, 162–63, 237, 241–42, 265, 284, 291; affirmative-action programs for, 241; discrimination in, 151–53, 162–63, 187, 237; subsidies for, 241–42: *see also* Suburbs; Urban areas
Housing Act (1937), 21
Housing Act (1965), 199–200
Housing Authority, U.S., 21
Housing and Urban Development Act (1968), 241
Housing and Urban Development Department, U.S., 237, 242
Howe, Irving, 227
Humphrey, Hubert H., 221–222

Illegal aliens, 286–92
Immigrants and aliens: 34–45, 47, 54–57, 59, 61, 79–80, 115–19, 122–26, 145–146, 202–207, 281–84, 286–292; quotas for, 122–23, 145–46, 203–206, 281: *see also* Refugees
Immigration Reform Act (1965), 202–207, 246, 281–282, 286
Immigration and Naturalization Service, U.S., 117, 146, 287–89
Immigration and Naturalization Subcommittee, Senate, 116
Incomes, 18–21, 261–66, 291; and poverty line, 202, 261–262; in the suburbs, 141–142, 151; during World War II, 61–63, 74–75
Indian Americans, 282
Indians: *see* Native Americans
Integration: *see* Blacks; Civil rights; Segregation
Intelligence tests, use of, 240–41
Intermarriage, 146, 279–80, 285
Internal Revenue Service, 253
Internal Security Act (1950), 119–20
Interstate Commerce Commission, 187
Interstate Highway Act (1956), 130–31
Interventionists, 39–42, 46
Irish Americans, 34, 37–40, 126, 144, 150, 168, 203, 243–44, 246, 249, 259–60, 282
Irony of American History, The (Niebuhr), 104
Isolationists, 39–42, 46, 91
Issei, 79–80, 82–83
Italian Americans, 34–40, 57, 59–60, 79–80, 126, 144–145, 203, 243–46, 249, 259–260, 282

Japan: attitude of blacks toward, 69–72; World War II, 46–47, 51–52, 79, 81, 83
Japanese-American Citizens League, 83
Japanese Americans, 31, 36, 145, 285; during World War II, 72, 79–85
Jencks, Christopher, 239–40
Jews, 36–42, 203, 283; and anti-Semitism, 40–42, 47, 125; during civil-rights movement, 184–86; and McCarthyism, 125; and presidential elections, 166, 168–69, 259–60; and Nixon, 249; as refugees (1930s), 41–42, 122; in the suburbs, 144–49; during World War II, 47, 85
Jim Crow, 25, 70, 74, 85, 108, 111, 157: *see also* Blacks; Segregation
Jobs: *see* Employment; Labor force
John XXIII, Pope, 172
Johnson, Lyndon B.: antipoverty program, 193, 198–202; civil-rights program, 159–60, 190–92; and congressional reform, 179–81; Great Society, 181, 202, 211, 237; immigration policy, 204–207; 1964 presidential election, 178–79; and race riots, 237; and reform, 164, 173, 181; tax cuts proposed by, 174; and Vietnam war, 201, 207, 208–18, 237–38; voting rights program, 182, 191–92
Jordan, June, 233–34
Judiciary Committee, House, 204, 252, 254–55
Judiciary Committee, Senate, 204, 206
Justice Department, U.S., 44, 59, 78, 92, 109, 116–20, 123–24, 159–60, 187, 190, 252–53

Katzenbach, Nicholas deB., 214
Keats, John, 135–36
Kennan, George F., 209
Kennedy, John F.: antipoverty program, 193, 197–98; and Catholics, 164–72; civil-rights program, 186–191; immigration policy, 203–204; New Frontier, 164, 187, 202; 1960 presidential election, 164–69; and parochial school aid, 165–67, 169–71; and prayer in public schools, 171–72; and reform, 173, 180; tax cuts proposed by, 174
Kennedy, Robert F., 187, 205
Kent State University killings (1970), 223–24
Keynes, John Maynard, 174–75
King, Martin Luther, Jr., 157–58, 182–83, 188, 234
Korean Americans, 282–83
Korean War, 99–101, 114–15, 119
Korematsu v. *United States* (1944), 84
Kuhn, Fritz, 41, 44

Labor Department, U.S., 43, 174, 198, 201, 240
Labor force, 173, 263; blacks in, 24, 29, 33, 114–15, 237, 240, 275–76; migrations in,

Labor force (*cont.*) 54–55, 67–68, 72–74, 78; in the suburbs, 134, 141–42, 151; women in, 63, 267–69; during World War II, 63–65, 67, 72–75: *see also* Employment; Unemployment
Landis, James M., 46
LeMay, Curtis E., 221
Lenin, Nikolai, 93–94
Levitt, William, 127, 132–34, 162–63
Levittowners, The (Gans), 140, 150
Levittowns, 129–30, 133–34, 140–43, 145, 162–63
Lewis, Oscar, 196
Lithuanian Americans, 34
Little Rock (Ark.), 153, 160–161
Loan, Nguyen Ngoc, 216–17
Lonely Crowd, The (Riesman), 104
Los Angeles (Calif.), 73, 139, 168; blacks in, 73, 108, 192, 234; illegal aliens in, 288–289; immigrants in, 36: *see also* Watts riot
Loyalty program, federal, 91–92, 111
Loyalty Review Board, 92
Lynchings, 32–33, 108
Lynd, Robert S. and Helen M., 16

MacArthur, Douglas, 100, 124
McCarran, Pat, 116–17
McCarran-Walter Act (1952), 123, 205
McCarthy, Joseph R., 116, 124–26
McCollum v. *Board of Education* (1948), 170
Macdonald, Dwight, 90–91, 194
McGovern, George, 248–49, 270
McNamara, Robert S., 209–210, 213
Mafia, the, 244–45
Magruder, Jeb Stuart, 222–23
Mailer, Norman, 220
Making of the President, 1960, The (White), 180
Malcolm X, 232–33
Man's Most Dangerous Myth: The Fallacy of Race (Montagu), 70
Mansfield, Mike, 213
Mao Tse-tung, 98–99, 175
Mapp v. *Ohio* (1961), 177
Marcuse, Herbert, 225
Marshall, George C., 77, 125
Marshall, Thurgood, 273–74
Marshall Plan, 90, 106
Marx, Karl, 93–94, 103–104
Medical care, 19–20, 22–25, 107, 200, 264, 291
Meredith, James H., 182
Methodists, 165
Mexican Americans, 21–22, 24, 30–31, 36, 168, 244, 246, 271, 282–83, 286
Midwest: immigrants in, 35; suburbs in, 147–48
Migrations: of blacks, 72–74, 78; of ethnic groups, 67–68; to the suburbs, 127–39, 145; during World War II, 54–55, 72–74, 78
Mills, Wilbur D., 214
Minimum wage, 21–22, 66, 275
Ministerial Association of Greater Houston, 165–66
Miranda v. *Arizona* (1966), 177

Mitchell, John N., 252–53, 257
Montagu, Ashley, 70
Montgomery (Ala.): bus boycott (1950s), 153, 157–158; civil-rights protests (1960s), 182, 187–88, 191
Moral permissiveness, 222
Morgenthau, Henry, Jr., 21, 48–49
Moses, Robert, 231, 243
Moslems, 232, 283
Moynihan, Daniel Patrick, 174–75, 203
Mumford, Lewis, 42–43
Murphy, Frank, 44, 58–59, 84
Murray, John Courtney, 166–167
My Lai massacre (1968), 218–219
My Son John (film), 96
Myers, William, Jr., 162
Myrdal, Gunnar, 27–28, 71, 194

Nation, The (magazine), 42
National Association for the Advancement of Colored People, 109–10, 154–56, 183, 280–81
National Coalition for Cultural Pluralism, 245
National Council of Churches, 185
National defense: *see* Armed forces; Defense
National Defense Education Act (1961), 171
National Guard, 161, 191, 234
National Health Survey (1940), 19–20
National Labor Relations Board, 106
National Office for Decent Literature, 169
National origin, 8, 123, 204, 243–44, 281
National Republican Heritage Groups Council, 248
National Security Council, 99
Nationalism, black, 231–37
Native Americans, 24, 31, 246–47, 271
Naturalized citizens, 57–61, 118
Nazis, 39, 41–42, 51, 70, 87, 91: *see also* Fascism; Germany
Negroes: *see* Blacks
New Deal, 22, 31, 33, 173: *see also* Roosevelt, Franklin D.
"New ethnicity," 208, 244–47
New Frontier, 164, 187, 202: *see also* Kennedy, John F.
New Left, 225–27, 230
New York (N.Y.): antiwar demonstrations in, 223–24; blacks in, 29, 77, 192, 234; Catholics in, 170–71; illegal aliens in, 287–88; immigrants in, 35–38, 203; 1950s, 138; population decline of, 128; poverty in, 196; Puerto Ricans in, 196
Newark (N.J.): blacks in, 235; immigrants in, 35
Niebuhr, Reinhold, 104–105
Night Comes to the Cumberlands (Caudill), 193–94
1984 (Orwell), 96–97, 99
Nisei, 79–80, 82–84
Nixon, Richard: and blacks, 237–40, 242; and busing issue, 239; economic pro-

Nixon, Richard (*cont.*) gram, 223; and ethnic groups, 248–50; and Jews, 249; presidential elections, 168, 221–22, 248–49, 257; resigns presidency, 255; and Vietnam war, 208–209, 217–18, 223, 230–31; Watergate scandal, 249–50, 252–59; and women's rights, 270

North: blacks in, 28–30, 239, 275, 278–79; immigrants in, 35; integration in, 162–163; whites in, 29–30, 239, 262

Norwegian Americans, 34–35, 37, 39–40, 121

Novak, Michael, 245–46

Nuclear armaments, 90, 97–98, 125

OEO: *see* Economic Opportunity, Office of

"Okies," 67

Oklahoma (musical), 52

Operation Breakthrough (1969), 242

Organization Man, The (Whyte), 136

Orshansky, Mollie, 200

Orwell, George, 96–97, 99

Other America, The (Harrington), 193

Out of Bondage (Bentley), 94

Pakistani Americans, 283

Pentagon Papers (Ellsberg), 219

Perkins, Frances, 43

Philadelphia (Pa.): blacks in, 75, 77; illegal aliens in, 287; population decline of, 128

"Philadelphia Plan," 240

Philbrick, Herbert, 94–95

Phillips, Kevin, 223

Plessy v. *Ferguson* (1896), 153–54, 156

Pluralist theory of American society, 103–105, 115, 121, 139, 166, 245–46

"Policy" racket, 30

Polish Americans, 34, 36, 38–40, 56, 126, 168, 243–245, 260, 282

Political action committees, 66–67, 245

Poll taxes, 27, 108, 112

Portuguese Americans, 38

Poverty, 193–202, 261–62, 275–76

Powell, Lewis, 272–73

Presidency, 254–55: *see also* individual Presidents

"Prestige stratification," 16

Progressive party, 88–89

Protestant-Catholic-Jew (Herberg), 146

Protestants: during civil-rights movement, 185–86; and McCarthyism, 126; and 1960 presidential election, 165–66, 168–69; and prayer in public schools, 172

Protocols of the Elders of Zion (Coughlin), 40

Public Health Service, U.S., 20, 23

Puerto Ricans, 173, 196, 246, 286

Pyle, Ernie, 50

Quotas: in fair employment practices, 240; for immigrants, 122–23, 145–146, 203–206, 281

Race, 7–9, 15; during Cold War, 101, 108–15; late 1930s, 24–34; late 1970s, 270–81; during reform period, 181–93; in the suburbs, 150–63; during Vietnam war, 231–243; during World War II, 69–85
Race riots: 77–78, 192, 234–237
Randolph, A. Philip, 33–34, 111–14
Rankin, John E., 109
Rationing, 64–65
Reapportionment, legislative, 178
Reconstruction period, 156
"Red fascism," 87–88, 90–91, 96, 98
Red Masquerade (Calomiris), 94
Red Scare (post–World War I), 115
Redlining, 132
Reform period (1960s), 164–207; and class, 193–202; and ethnicity, 202–207; and race, 181–93; and religion, 164–72
Refugee Relief Act (1953), 145
Refugees: as displaced persons, 122–23, 145–46; from Eastern Europe, 121–22; Jewish, 41–42, 122: *see also* Immigrants and aliens
Regionalism, 15, 21, 24, 251
Religion, 8, 30; and civil-rights movement, 184–85, 233; and 1960 presidential election, 164–69; and parochial school aid, 107, 165–67, 169–71; and prayer in public schools, 171–72; in the suburbs, 147–50: *see also* Catholics; Jews; Protestants
Relocation centers, 82–84
Republican party: busing issue, 239; civil-rights movement, 159–60, 189–90; comeback in 1938, 22; and communist victory in China, 98; economic program (1960s), 223; and ethnic vote, 248–49; and McCarthyism, 126; poverty programs, 201; presidential elections, 39–40, 66–67, 108, 138–39, 168–69, 178–179, 221–22, 248–49, 258–59; and Soviet development of atomic bomb, 98; stigma of Watergate, 252; and suburbanization, 138–39; subversives in federal government, 91–92; Vietnam war, 222; voting rights, 191: *see also* Congress, U.S.; Democratic party
Retired people: Medicare and Medicaid, 200; opposition to Vietnam war, 227; during World War II, 63, 66
Riesman, David, 104–105, 135, 140
Robeson, Paul, 112–13
Robinson, Jackie, 113
Rodgers, Richard, 52
Romney, George, 242–43
Roosevelt, Franklin D., 40, 46–47, 66–67, 107, 258; civil-rights program, 31–34, 77, 111; and German Americans, 60; and Japanese Americans, 79, 81;

Roosevelt, Franklin D. (*cont.*)
and Jewish refugees, 42; national medical care program, 22–24; New Deal, 22, 31, 33, 173; Polish aspirations, 57; prewar attitudes toward communism and fascism, 42–45
Rosenberg, Julius and Ethel, 125
Rumanian Americans, 34, 56
Rural areas, 17, 19, 23, 33, 138
Rusk, Dean, 209–10
Russia: *see* Soviet Union
Russian Americans, 34, 36, 243
Russo-German pact (1939), 42, 88–89

St. Louis (Mo.): blacks in, 151; population decline of, 128
San Francisco (Calif.), 73, 139; blacks in, 73; Chinese Americans in, 283–84; immigrants in, 36; Japanese Americans in, 285
Scammon, Richard M., 222
Schell, Jonathan, 218, 258
Schlesinger, Arthur, Jr., 173
Schneiderman, William, 57–59
Schools: *see* Colleges and universities; Education
Scott, Hugh, 255
Scottish Americans, 244
Scottsboro boys, 32
Scrap drives, 48–49
Segregation, 25–27, 108–109; in armed forces, 33–34, 76–77, 111–14; in buses, 74, 187; in housing, 151–53, 162–63; in interstate transportation, 108, 112, 187; in restaurants, 181–82, 186, 190; in schools, 153–163, 182, 189, 190, 238–40, 279; during World War II, 70–71, 74–76: *see also* Blacks; Civil rights
Selective Service System: creation of, 111–12; during Vietnam war, 229
Selma (Ala.), 182, 191–92, 279
Senate: *see* Congress, U.S.
Serbian Americans, 248
"Shape of National Politics to Come, The" (Schlesinger), 173
Sharecroppers, 19
Shelley v. *Kraemer* (1948), 109
Shriver, R. Sargent, 198
Shuttlesworth v. *Birmingham Board of Education* (1958), 157
Sikhs, 283
"Silent majority," 208, 222–223
Sirica, John J., 252, 255
Slovak Americans, 245
Smith Act (1940), 43–44, 92–93
Social class: *see* Class
Social Class in America (Warner), 102
Social Indicators, 1976, 260–261, 263–66
Social mobility, 103, 263, 277–278
Social Security Administration, 66, 107, 200, 261
Social status, 8, 16, 19, 65, 142, 247, 285
Sorenson, Theodore, 189

South: blacks in, 25–28, 239, 278–81; immigrants in, 35; living conditions in, 19, 262; population increase in, 128; whites in, 25–28, 239: *see also* Civil rights; Segregation
Southern Christian Leadership Conference, 183–84
Soviet Union: as classless society, 102–103; and Cold War, 86–91, 94–95, 97–100, 106, 112, 122, 175–76; and Cuban missile crisis (1962), 175; development of atomic bomb, 97–98; domination of Eastern Europe, 87, 90, 111, 121–123, 145; and Korean War, 99–100; 1939 pact with Germany, 42, 88–89; during World War II, 45, 56–58: *see also* Cold War; Communism
Spanish-speaking Americans, 36, 120, 206, 243, 283, 285–286: *see also* Mexican Americans; Puerto Ricans
Spingarn, Stephen, 107
Split-Level Trap, The (Gordon), 136
Stalin, Joseph, 87, 89–92, 97–99, 106
State Department, U.S., 43, 89, 94, 98, 112, 124–25, 209, 214
States Rights Democratic party, 109–10
Stimson, Henry L., 80
Stone, Harlan Fiske, 84
Student Nonviolent Coordinating Committee, 183–84, 231–32, 235
Students for a Democratic Society, 226
Suburbs, 17, 127–39, 140, 163; class in, 139–44; ethnicity in, 144–47, 149–50; race in, 150–63, 242, 278; reapportionment of, 178; religion in, 147–50
"Suburban Sadness, The" (Riesman), 135
Supreme Court: affirmative-action programs, 240–42, 271–72, 274; aid to parochial schools, 170; aliens, 44, 117–18, 120; blacks on juries, 28; bus integration, 158; busing to achieve integration, 238–240; and Civil Rights Act (1964), 190–91; employer's use of intelligence tests, 240–41; housing legislation, 242; illegal aliens, 289; and Internal Security Act (1950), 120; naturalized citizens, 57–59, 61; prayer in public schools, 171–72; railroad brotherhoods, 76; reforms of 1960s, 176–78, 185–86, 190–91, 237; relocation of Japanese Americans, 84; restaurant integration, 186; restrictive housing covenants, 109; school desegregation, 153–59, 163; and Smith Act (1940), 93; White House tapes, 255; white primary, 27
Swann v. *Charlotte-Mecklenburg Board of Education* (1971), 238–39
Swedish Americans, 34–35, 38, 40

Taft-Hartley Act (1947), 106
Taiwanese Americans, 282
Taxation: in the suburbs, 152; tax cuts (1960s), 174; during Vietnam war, 214; during World War II, 61–63
Television, 94, 168, 264; and civil-rights movement, 184, 189; and Vietnam war coverage, 215–18, 225
Thai Americans, 282
Thurmond, J. Strom, 110, 270, 280
Treasury Department, U.S., 21, 48
Trinidadian Americans, 282
Truman, Harry S: and aliens, 115, 119, 122; and anticommunist hysteria, 91–92, 99, 107; and blacks, 108–109, 111–14; CIO support of, 106; Fair Deal, 107–108; and Korean War, 100; 1948 presidential election, 108, 110, 113–14; and Soviet development of atomic bomb, 97–98; and Wallace, Henry, 90–91
Truman Doctrine, 88–89
Turkish Americans, 283

Un-American Activities Committee, House, 94–96, 113
Unemployment, 18–19, 21–22, 29, 33, 173, 202, 266, 275–76: *see also* Employment; Labor force
Unions, 29, 33–34, 66–67, 74–76, 79, 105–106; blacks in, 29, 33–34, 240; communist-led, 105–106, 118; and Vietnam war, 223–24, 226
Universities: *see* Colleges and universities
University of California at Davis, 271–74
Urban areas, 17–19, 127–31, 138, 150–51, 178, 286
USA: The Permanent Revolution, 105, 115, 121

Veterans Administration, 129–32
Vida, La (Lewis), 196
Vietcong, 213, 215–16, 227–228
Vietnam war, 207, 208–50; and blacks, 227, 231, 235–236; casualties, 230; and class, 220–31; course of war, 208–20, 250; effect on antipoverty programs, 201, 211; and ethnic groups, 247; and ethnicity, 243–49; last American troops leave, 250; opposition to, 217, 219–20, 222, 227–28, 231, 247; and race, 231–43
Voting and voting rights, 27, 29, 31, 44, 108, 159–60, 178, 191–92, 280–81
Voting Rights Act (1965), 182, 191–92

Wages: *see* Incomes; Minimum wage
Wagner, Robert F., 21–23
Wagner-Rogers bill (1939), 41–42
Walk in the Sun, A (Brown), 51
Wallace, George C., 182, 221–22, 230, 237
Wallace, Henry A., 88–91, 106, 119

Wapshot Chronicle, The (Cheever), 136–37
War Department, U.S., 76–77, 79–80
War Labor Board, 74
War on Poverty, 199–200
War Relocation Authority, 82
Warner, W. Lloyd, 15–16, 102–103
Warren, Earl, 156, 159, 176–177
Washington, D.C.: *see* District of Columbia
Watergate scandal, 249–50, 252–59
Wattenberg, Ben, 222
Watts riot (1964), 192–93
We Hold These Truths (Corwin), 53
We Hold These Truths (Murray), 166
Weathermen, 226
Welfare programs of 1930s, 18–20, 33
Welsh Americans, 244
West: immigrants in, 31, 35; population increase in, 128
Westmoreland, William C., 215
White, Theodore H., 180
Whites: backlash, 237–38; busing opposition, 239; 1930s, 24–29; in the North, 29; race riots, 77–78; in the South, 25–28; in the suburbs, 150–63, 278: *see also* Segregation
Whyte, William H., 136, 139
Wicker, Tom, 210
Wiley, Alexander, 122
Willkie, Wendell, 39–40
Wilson, William Julius, 275, 277
Women: Equal Rights Amendment, 266–70; federal legislation concerning, 267–69; groups, 204; in labor force during World War II, 63; opposition to Vietnam war, 227
Women: A Journal of Liberation, 268
Wong Yang Sung, 117
World War II, 46–85; and the Cold War, 86; ethnic loyalties at outbreak, 39–45; initial American viewpoint, 47, 50, 53; as unifying force, 46–54, 105, 208

Zoning laws, 152–53
Zorach v. *Clauson* (1952), 170